1

It's Hard to Hug a Fat Person

Dedication

If you feel hopeless, I want you to know there is hope
If you are in the dark and the dank, there is light
If you feel unloved and unlovable, I love you.

IT'S HARD TO HUG A FAT PERSON

A Memoir
by Charity Dasenbrock

Foreword
by Carola Bernstein

Imagine walking down the aisle of an airplane looking for a place to sit, trying not to notice the averted eyes or the look of dread when you near an empty seat. Imagine the embarrassment of having to ask the flight attendant for an extender for your seatbelt, saying the words out loud while the person sitting next to you looks on with barely contained disgust. This is a common scenario in the life of a fat person.

I never gave any thought to what it must be like to navigate the world as an obese human being. I always thought that life was hard enough from my perspective as a white, slightly neurotic, aging female—until I met Charity.

We met in a writing group called The Opening, taught by Andy Couturier, a wonderful teacher who provides a safe place for people to find their voice. It was the first class and we were introducing ourselves. When it was Charity's turn, she sat beaming—a white-haired, jolly, female Buddha—in the chair that barely contained her and announced that she had just returned from her "great adventure." I did a double take, wondering how someone that heavy could possibly have an adventure. This was the beginning of my awareness of my own deeply-ingrained prejudice towards fat people. During the months and years that followed, Charity, through her writing and her friendship became my teacher. She introduced me to another world; she humbled me and reminded me that we are all connected and so much the same.

This is an important book. It takes you into the lives of the invisible and makes you realize that everyone has a story to tell. Charity is gone but she left us with this book, a story that she was determined to finish and to share with the world. I loved her.

Early afternoon, Tuesday, January 2017, at home in Capitola, California

It could have gone so many ways. But there was no twisty, turny, painful experience today. No sigh, no pursed lips. No, "Okay, let's get you on the scale." Earlier, as I sat in the waiting room filling out the new patient forms, I took a deep breath and filled in the line asking my weight. Many times I have lied. On some forms, I simply refused to put anything. When asked, I would respond either that I didn't know and didn't want to know, or that it wasn't pertinent to why I was there. This time I was as honest as I could be, not having a scale and not wanting to get on one.

Weight: <u>270 lbs</u>

Height: <u>5'3"</u>

Has your weight fluctuated this last year? <u>yes, a few pounds up, a few   pounds down</u>

Are you comfortable with your weight? <u>honestly, some of the time yes, and some days no but I have damaged myself in the past losing weight, trying to lose weight. I'm working on loving "what is" and care taking myself as best as I can. I want you to know that I am much more than my number on the scale.</u>

"Why have you come today?" was her first question.

"I've had a few colds lately and so feel my immune system needs some help. Plus, I have been off my thyroid medicine for a while and need to get that all straightened out," I replied.

In our consultation, her only remark about my weight was that if I wanted to discuss it with her, I was welcome to do so at any time. I am generally in good health and she could see that from the whole of the form.

Non-judgmentally, my new doctor simply asked me as part of her extensive study of my habits to describe a "normal" day of eating. Calmly, I told her the "good" and the "bad," including eggs and vegetables for breakfast, lentil soup for lunch, some fruit for snacks, and a take-out dinner of chicken tacos, chips and salsa, guacamole, and two glasses of wine. When I mentioned tacos, she said, "Mmm, I love tacos too." Following this comment, we shared information about our favorite taquerias in town.

So different from my early life experiences with the medical profession. I hadn't started walking yet at the age of 18 months. My parents were worried, so they checked with the family doctor. He told my mother that she should stop breastfeeding me because I was getting too chubby. Perhaps this was the reason for my not walking, he suggested. Boom. She took me off her breast, put me on watered formula that was full of sugar and unnecessary ingredients—my first diet. I did start walking soon after, so I'm sure that both she and the doctor gave the credit to the diet. I'm giving them the "credit" for starting me on a lifelong road of dieting and overeating, losing weight and gaining weight.

One of those painful medical experiences happened in San Francisco in 1974. I can still hear the words and can recall some of the faces. I definitely remember my anger and shame. I was working towards a Master's degree in Special Education at the time. After class one afternoon, running for the bus to go home. I tripped on a crack and fell. My ankle! I swore I broke it. I couldn't get up. No one helped me—not a single one of my fellow students at the bus stop, some of whom just stared, and others of whom laughed. That damn bus driver poked his head out and asked me, "You comin' or what?" Did he ask someone to help me when I said that I was trying? No. Someone yelled out the window, "Hurry up, Fatso!" So, all the people on the bus watched me crawl—yes, crawl—to the bus and up the stairs. No one would put my fare in the box for me. Eventually, I pulled myself up, paid, and hopped to a seat, hanging on for dear life to the backs of the seats and my pride. Not a single passenger got up. I thought, "This *is* San Francisco, right?" But those flower children were long gone, those days of love were over in the Outer Mission District.

I got to my stop and somehow got off the bus. I had to crawl two blocks home. Oh God, so painful. I could go a little way, then had to just lie there and rest a while, then crawl some more. A few cars went by, but if anyone saw me, they probably thought I was drunk! Thank God I had on jeans and a jacket, but still my knees and my hands ended up being scraped raw in places. I felt as if those size 20 jeans were both a curse and a blessing. My XXL body may have given me some padding when I fell, but neither my skin nor my nerve endings were any tougher than those of some-one half my size.

Steve saw me from the window of our house. Thank God he was home, since he came running out and got me in his car. He was the only one in our very crowded Socialist Worker Party house who had one. He took me to the Emergency Room at San Francisco General Hospital—ugly, dilapidated, full of desperate people.

Since I had no insurance, the paperwork seemed endless. Steve kept me entertained with stories about his celebrity crushes. "Maybe we will see Michael Douglas here filming *The Streets of San Francisco*. You know his name on the show is Steve. Coinci-dence? I don't think so." Thank you, Steve, for making me laugh while we waited.

Hours went by before I finally saw the doctor. In agony, and with my ankle the size of an elephant's, I was astonished to hear him say the following: "If only you were not so fat, you would not have fallen down while running to get the bus."

"What the fuck did you say?" I replied. "What kind of shit is that? Are you a real doctor?"

He glared at me. "Young lady, clean up your mouth or you will be escorted out of this hospital." Me, who really hardly ever swore. I still don't do it that often. That day I made up for it.

Finally, I got to X-ray. Steve was not allowed in there with me, but I had company—a line of five or six scruffy men in orange suits *chained together*! Yep, it was prisoner day in the X-ray department. Just them with their tattoos and bad teeth and little me in my torn jeans and cute pink blouse. One of them was kind of cute with long curly hair and very well-developed muscles in his arms. He gave me a flirty kind of wink. I didn't know whether to be scared or flattered.

Eventually, I did see the asshole doctor again, and he told me that my ankle was sprained. His main recommendation was to lose some weight. Sadly, I was in too much pain to think of any sort of comeback. I ended up with a prescription for crutches and some lame drugs, not even the good ones. "Steve, get me the hell out of here," I begged.

On the way home, I was quiet, unable to let go of my feelings of shame, embarrassment, and anger. I just wanted to go home, though I'm not sure if by "home" I meant my crowded house in the Outer Mission or my family's place back East in Baltimore where my parents had recently moved. I didn't know what to do except cry and take my drugs. Was this how my life would go? Would the answer to every problem be to lose some weight?

Today, I can relax a bit now having a doctor for whom this is not the case. I look forward to not being afraid or ashamed to be in the doctor's office. I look forward to having an ally in my journey forward.

The next day, after my morning outdoor Bootcamp exercise class
Good Goddesses, that was a challenge. I wish I had some water. I didn't meet my goal of *not* complaining, that's for sure. Ha, I didn't even make it ten minutes. I feel as if I owe my class-mates an apology.

Okay, what I do know is this. I gotta keep going to bootcamp. Meeting twice a week for almost ten years now, the other women and I talk about this frequently. We are all close to the same age. I am the oldest, at age 66, and I have the grayest hair. I'm the only one who still keeps it long. We all help each other keep coming. We all love being outside. Some days we are at the beach, some days at various parks around town. What will we do when that day comes that the class ends and we have to take a class in a gym? I am not at all old yet; but, once I really start slowing down, I'm not sure there will be speeding up again. This makes me think of Mama. She had her share of issues, but she was physically still quite strong when she died, except for the cancer. Her heart was strong. I can still picture the look on her doctor's face as she kept checking Mom's heart those last hours. That heart kept on beating strongly, even as everything else was slowing.

It's because of all that swimming. Mama was not much of a role model for mothering, but for moving every day, she sure was. I should do a blog post about our exercise history. That will wake up some memories. But, it is one of those things in my life that has healed over time. Calisthenics. How old was I? Twelve? Air Force exercises, right? So ironic, the anti-military Quaker mother teaching her daughter a bootcamp-style workout. And look at me now, dedicated to my bootcamp. Definitely a different kind of approach from Mom's. Oh God, there was the tennis, too. In her efforts to force me to move more, she decided I should take up tennis. It was not a good idea for her to be my teacher. We both hated every moment. Hot and humid Ohio in the summertime on a freshly asphalted court at the high school. Lots of her yelling and me crying.

"Damn it, Charity! You're not paying attention."

"I can't see the ball, Mom! Don't yell at me."

"Don't just stand there. You've got to run."

"I can't!"

She had abusive plans and strategies, though now I can realize her intentions were good. It's taken many, many years for me to even somewhat forgive her and to realize that it was *not* normal to be treated that way. Again, like the cookies and dessert, I didn't know anything else, and apparently, neither did she.

Now I'm home from bootcamp, thank God. I'm so hungry. I wasn't hungry waking up today, so I didn't eat enough before class. What to have?

Let's do this right this morning. Listen. Feel my body. What do I need? This is what I write about in my blog and on my Facebook page. It's a chance to stop and focus, listen to my body. What do I want? Think about those cookies from the other day. Think about that non-gluten-free sandwich yesterday. Breathe. Remember the bellyache and the need for a nap. Breathe. Keep that blood flowing.

Okay. How about some eggs and vegetables? With butter. Yay for having vegetables already cooked in the fridge ready to go. So colorful—grated carrots and beets, and I think those are beet greens and onions. I can smell the garlic. I wish I had some avocado. I'll just heat up the vegetables and cook everything together. I feel worthy, blessed, honored to have a beautiful meal.

I treasure this yellow bowl I will eat from. It cheers me up, and it was a gift from my sister-in-law. These green napkins are my favorite, and for now, the tablecloth is still clean. Another part of what I write about for people who don't feel good about eating is making the meal pretty and using the "good" dishes. I can sit and relax with my meal, with nowhere else to go right now. This tastes so good. Thank you, Mother Earth.

I guess I got stirred up with those Mama memories. It's amazing to me how powerful memories are—the difficult ones and the happier ones. Mom and I did make plenty of both. It's because of her that I am in that bootcamp class, and, because of her, I actually enjoyed cooking my breakfast today. The two of us had such fun in this kitchen the last time she came out here five years ago, just a year before she died. Tools and tasks, along with a nearby glass of wine helped open her up. Mama chopped vegetables, set the table, and insisted on doing the dishes. There was such an overabundance of stuff we just never could talk about, but as with so many families, it seemed easier in the kitchen. So odd, that the greatest challenge we had was around food and eating, and yet, one of the things that brought us together was food and cooking. It did not bring us happily together until late in her life, however. Earlier cooking adventures were marred by whatever diet I was on at the time and whether I was gaining or losing weight.

Someone asked me the other day why I called her "Mama." Growing up she was first Mommy, and then Mom. The shift happened when we made the switch from writing each other letters to mostly using the phone—I'm guessing I was in my 40's then. I would answer the phone, and she would say, "Hi, it's your old mama." Every time. So, as a joke, since she really didn't like it, I started calling her "Mama," and then it just became a term of endearment.

I wonder when it was that I was able to start letting go of my anger towards her. Definitely not in my 20's or in the 30's when I was delving into therapy and spiritual development. At some point, the tide did begin to turn. I do recall listening to my mom when her dad died. I remember hearing how angry she still was at him. I said to myself that I didn't want to carry such feelings about family members my whole life, which became part of the impetus to go to therapy and work on my own issues. I understand her more now, and some days there is forgiveness and compassion. I still deal daily with consequences of her decisions and our more painful interactions. My self-esteem wobbles and dips down pretty low. While I don't binge eat anymore, I still struggle with our history of her restricting and denying me food, and me going the other direction. I regret that my childhood wasn't healthier and blame my mother while digging up some anger at her for that.

From my writing notebook
Appetite

Making friends or is it acquaintances with appetite
Can we talk?

Who are you?
enemy companion lover

Appetite
got a tight grip, do you?
Don't go down without a fight.

satiation
creation
alienation
abomination
emancipation
constipation
that train is leaving the station
get on board

oh, what a good appetite she has
but don't say that if she's fat.

Fat people don't get to have appetites unless they're minute and very under control.

You're eating that?

What about if he's too thin? then what? Here, have some more. You gotta bulk up,   dude.

don't sit in a restaurant and enjoy yourself!
eat undercover at home in the dark
see what's in the back of the freezer, doesn't matter how old it is, eat it anyway
That's the kind of appetite fat people have, am I right?

Four of us sitting in a restaurant
I'm the fattest
(of course)
one is on a diet
the other two there to have a good time
let's eat all the things
let's laugh and be loud and enjoy ourselves
let's have food orgasms
What? you're not embarrassed to have people at the next table see you enjoy?
Share your bites with friends
Oh God, you have to try this

The dieter sits quietly, sipping her water, eating her plain meal.
Inside, both proud and feeling left out

This is how freedom feels and tastes
I can eat out loud

in the light.
I have pity for the dieter
and some anger
when she projects herself on me.
I'd rather eat a salad than be fat, she says, looking at me.

What is it about seeing fat people eating that is hard for some?
They are scared. They are scared they will lose control, will find pleasure, will   abandon guilt
What if they eat every bite of their dessert? What if they can't stop once they start   eating and enjoying?
What if they start to look like me?
What does that mean?
They might start to have a twinkle in their eye? Will they wear red or purple or stripes instead of black? What if what you see in the mirror is relaxed, peaceful, beautiful? Maybe they accidentally snort wine out their nose laughing at a friend's joke? They might find out that food is actually entertainment and a social activity, not just nutrition.

Pants with elastic waists are not the end of the earth.

Do I have an appetite or does it have me?
Can I decide on my own what I will eat and when and how much?
Can I fill my plate if I'm hungry?
Can I just eat a few bites without you thinking thank God she is finally back on her diet?
You forgot to say please, take two giant steps backward.
Please, Mother, may I?

How about I worry about what I eat and you worry about yourself?
or better yet, let's not worry.
Let's fill our plates and bodies
with love
and joy.

Let's all have big appetites for life.
Hey, you want a bite of this?
It's really delicious.

4 am, the next morning
    Tina! Off, hurry, get off of me. I gotta get up. I gotta go pee.
Damn it. Come on.
Really, Tina? Am I going to pee my pajamas because of you? Here
it comes. Gross. What a mess. And I didn't get to finish my dream.
I hate when that happens. It fits that I didn't finish this one, though,
since it's another one of those "late to somewhere, I get lost, I
don't have what I need" dreams. Odd mix of people in this one.
Friends from high school that I don't think I've dreamed about
before. Patty from exercise class. Why were these people there?
I'm ridiculously late going somewhere. I'm running and running.
Actually, it felt good to run. I wish I could run like that. Years ago,
I tried to run, back when my knees were okay. It wasn't exactly
running though, more like a very slow jog. It takes a lot of work to
move a body which weighs around 250 pounds. What I didn't
realize would be so uncomfortable while running is my breasts and
my belly taking a beating, bouncing up and down! Now they are
even saggier than when I last tried to jog; now I weigh more, now
my joints are older. I know fat people who run and love it, but I
can't manage. And, in truth, I no longer want to.
    Tina, I wonder if you wish you could still run and jump too.
Jeez, two old creaky women in this house, you 16-years-old and
puking on the floor, me 66-years-old and peeing my pants.
    When I was a little girl and woke in the night wetting my
pants, I think I got comfort from my dolls. I wonder how often that
actually happened and for how many years. I do remember Mom
scolding me. I did have some tests done at some point but I don't
think anything came of them. I also remember being embarrassed
and not wanting my brothers to know. One older and one younger,
they could easily gang up on me and give me a bad time. Of
course, they would find out. Wet sheets, having to take a shower,
my room stinking when I wet the bed and didn't tell Mama. That

never worked. I was never able to talk with her about it. When I tried, she would push aside any worries I shared about it and say either that I slept too hard and didn't wake up in time or that I was lazy.

I'll strip the bed, wash the sheets in the morning, and love that little girl who was so ashamed.

Evening

A powerful day today, packed with emotions and introspection. Reflecting on Mama, missing her even with all the negatives.

Most of the difficulties we had were centered around my weight. Shopping for clothes was a biggie, whether that was for school clothes as a young girl or when she would gift me with a shopping trip as an adult to find clothes for a trip we were taking together. Once, with one of the many therapists I have seen, I came to the conclusion that if Mom focused on my weight, then she didn't have to feel her feelings about herself. Such poor self-esteem she had, thinking of herself as unlovable, unattractive, not smart enough. It took me many hours of work with that therapist to come to that kind point of view about her, that's for sure. There are threads of stories never to be remembered. There are difficult feelings that probably will always remain.

My parents moved from small rural Celina, Ohio to the big East Coast city of Baltimore, Maryland when my brothers and I were all in college. My dad had the opportunity to leave his hated job at the farm machinery company to start a brand new career as a fundraiser for the American Friends Service Committee. I saw this as a great opportunity for my mom also—perhaps she could take the chance to go back to school which she often talked about or find an interesting and fulfilling job, something she never felt she had as a stay at home wife and mom. After many mostly one-sided conversations with her about it, I realized she just didn't feel capable of making that much change. "I can't go back to school. I'm too old. I'm not smart enough." She was 50 and had gone to

Vassar College. My young 20-year-old feminist self was so frustrated with her.

Enough reflecting on that. I am determined to get these clothes off the floor and into drawers and the closet. I need to buy some clothes soon. Now, that was a part of growing up that was fraught with a full array of emotions. These days, there are lots of comfortable colorful clothes available to plus sized women. What a silly euphemism—"plus sized"— and almost everyone has a different idea about where that size starts. This pink shirt has to go, too many stains. When I was young, Mom hated pink. I loved it and had to fight for pink in my life. She never gave into my desire to paint my bedroom pink, though I have a picture in my head of bedspreads with pink on them. I have only ever met a few other women in my whole life who did not have a pink room as little girls. I recall mine being a kind of aqua color. I can see and hear myself there, playing with my dolls.

Summer, 1958, Ohio

"It's so hot out today. I hope Mom doesn't make me go outside. I don't like it when she takes her cross pills and needs her nap time. We all have to go out until she says we can come back in. Sometimes, she locks the door and then I have to pee outside. My brothers like that part. I want to stay here and play with you, so we have to be very quiet. Let's pretend it's not hot and we can have cookies and tea in my old pink tea set. Mom let me use this scarf to make the table look pretty. I love yellow, but I wish it was pink. I wish my whole room was pink. But Mom hates pink. When I grow up I'm going to have a pink house!

"Here's a place for you, Ginny. I like your new purple dress. You look fancy in your ribbons. I just wrapped them around you and didn't sew them yet, just used safety pins. Mom and I helped at the hospital yesterday handing out flowers, and I got to keep the ribbons. I love it when there are lots of purple ones, even though that means someone had a funeral. I've never been to one of those. It's for dead people.

"Betsy Wetsy, did you wet your pants again? That's what you do. Good thing I don't mind. Sometimes I wet my pajamas at night. Mom does mind when I do that. I'm too old, but you are just a little girl. Let's change you. There.

"Raggedy Ann, you have to sit over here in your special chair because you are so big. I washed your apron and Mom helped me iron it. She washed you for me too. You are clean and pretty again. The babies can be over here with me.

"You girls all look so pretty. Not like me. You should see the ugly clothes I got for school. I can't show you because they have to be sewed so they fit better. One dress is way too long! It's a kind of blue, with some ugly flowers on it. None of my friends have to wear clothes like that. No one else in third grade wears ugly grown-up dresses or teenager clothes. There weren't very many clothes that fit me, because, not only am I too fat, I'm too short. There is one pretty pink one. Mom didn't want to buy it because she doesn't like pink. I love pink. She said okay because it was one of the ones that fit me. The lady in the store looked kind of scary. She never smiled. I didn't like her. I heard her tell Mom about a diet she was on where she ate a lot of grapefruit and celery. Gross. I'm too fat, Mom says. I have to try harder, Mom says. I do try. I don't want to be fat. I don't want to eat celery. I don't want her to be mad at me. I cried because I couldn't find the dresses I wanted. Mom said bad words and got cross with me, so then I cried some more. And then she cried. We did both feel a little better when we looked at shoes and we each got some new ones. I got school shoes and she bought some fancy high heels. She loves shoes!

"All the long drive home, she looked so mad. She made that weird sound with her teeth. She and my dad talked about my clothes at dinner. She said she was sad for me, but she sure looked mad. I was so embarrassed, why did she do that in front of my brothers?

"'Fatty fatty, two by four, couldn't get through the bathroom door. So she did it on the floor. Licked it up and did some more!' The kids at school say that.

"Last night, before I went to bed, I stole some cookies that Mom made. I tried to save some for our party but I ate them all. They were chocolate chip, my favorite. I'm sorry. All we have are pretend cookies. They won't make us fat and ugly."

Thursday, bedtime in California, 2017

Oh, so good to get in bed. Clean sheets.

Great Spirit, Ancients Ones, I give thanks for this day, this full day. I give thanks for the love in my life. I give thanks for all the abundance. I pray for those who are lonely and lost. I pray for those who are hungry and cold.

I give thanks for my life.

2 pm the next day, at the computer writing a blog post

Sigh, how many damn times have I written about cookies? I wonder if I can ever get to the heart of what the cookie thing is about. Why cookies? I think I need to talk about the Girl Scout cookies, about hiding cookies in my underpants, about all the cookies I've baked for others. I've made myself pretty vulnerable on these pages over the years. Am I in the mood to be that vulnerable today? I think so. It's my mission. Shining the light in those dark, shame-filled places. Saying what other people can't say yet. Being honest. That's what I've decided to do with this phase of my life, right? Okay, start writing.

Who Stole the Cookies from the Cookie Jar?

Any of you remember that "game"? I hated it, as you will see after you read a few more paragraphs.

Cookies. You've read my posts about them before. Whatever kind of language you want to use, they are my nemesis, my gateway drug of choice. They are troublemakers for me! Enticing bites of sweetness, preferably containing chocolate of some sort. One minute: delicious and satisfying; the next minute: a potential train wreck of not even tasting them really, just scarfing them down as if I were still a child hiding in my room with my stash of stolen cookies. Even if I can find pleasure and enjoyment in them, it often is brief.

I did that. Stole cookies. A few years ago, a friend shared her feelings upon hearing me casually tell her about not being allowed to eat cookies growing up. She found it heart-breaking that I thought taking some cookies from the family jar available in the kitchen was stealing. For me it was just a weird kind of normal. I was not allowed to eat cookies. *Maybe* one out of the oven when my mother and I were making them. And yes, this same friend pointed out how bizarre *that* was. That since I made the cookies, I was actually stealing my own cookies! I shocked her in the telling of it, and, in turn, she shocked me by pointing out my disconnection from the whole event. I really hadn't taken it in how cruel and abusive that all was.

My mom and I would bake, making snacks and desserts for the "boys" in the family. Our time together in the kitchen was full of lessons, cooking up some love, telling stories—but we would typically not eat anything we made, my mother choosing not to and me not being allowed to. My dad loved dessert, and it would be on the table several nights a week. My mom usually made some sort of fuss about how she was not having it, consistently and sternly denying herself any kind of "treat." I understood at a very early age from my parents that I was chubby, plump, overweight. They never used the word "fat"—too shameful a word, I guess. Without them actually ever saying it, I always knew it was a great shame for them to have a fat daughter. I felt ugly, like maybe I was a mistake, like something was dreadfully wrong with me. Dessert for me was considered too fattening, so my end-of-meal treat would be some fruit, some diet jello or just watching the others eat their desserts. On those occasions when I did get something sugary, oh was a big deal made of it—"how lucky I was," or some such thing.

I did find ways to eat those sugary items, just not at the table with the rest of the family. I would sneak into the kitchen when my mom was outside or busy upstairs. Heart pounding, hands sweaty, I would oh-so-carefully take the lid off the cookie jar and grab a few. Don't drop the lid! Don't drop the cookies. If I had pockets, in the cookies would go. If not, they went down my pants and got tucked into my underwear. As I crept carefully up the stairs to my bedroom, trying not to make any noise, I had to somehow hold my legs together and hang onto my pants so nothing would fall out. I was so scared that I would get caught and shamed, so it was a relief when I got to my room. Safe. I also became stealthy about how I opened the refrigerator and meticulously scraped off bites of whatever dessert was in there, gobbling them down quickly, all the while holding my breath. I'd wipe away any crumbs and then casually get myself a drink of water as an acceptable reason for being in the kitchen should someone else enter.

When I was a Girl Scout, I was often one of the girls who sold the most cookies, because my mother always bought enough boxes to supply the male members of her family for the year. When Mom was in town or out working in her garden on the other side of the house, I could slip out to the garage, quickly get a box out of our freezer there, put it under my shirt or again down my pants (Brrr!

Frozen!), and run back to my room. The challenge was always not to be seen or heard by anyone. Some days, I ate the whole box all at once, eating them quickly one right after the other. Other days, I was able to stash them under my bed and eke them out over a period of time. I never got enjoyment out of those cookies, I could never really savor the sweetness beyond the first moment. Then there was the rush to the bathroom to brush my teeth, hoping no one would smell the toothpaste and figure out what I was doing. The fear of being found out and punished was powerful. There would be severe scoldings and shaming lectures about the awfulness of lifetime fatness. The disappointment. The embarrassment. Needless to say, there were also the difficulties of getting the empty package out to the garbage can and burying it deeply enough so no one would notice it.

I did frequently get caught. Hello. My favorite Girl Scout cookies were either the peanut butter ones or the chocolate mint ones, both of which left quite the aroma on my breath and in my room, especially if the box was stashed under my bed (which it usually was). Just recently, one of my brothers surprised me by sharing that he, too, stole cookies from the freezer. He would open the bottom of the box and take out a few, then put the box carefully back in the same position. He told me that both brothers also did this with ice cream from the house freezer. Same thing, open the bottom and eat. I gathered they experienced a great deal of glee when Dad took out the container for his almost-nightly ice cream and his spoon would go right through to the empty space. The difference here is that they didn't get shamed for what they did.

I stole food for years. I'm not sure how old I was when I started— probably as soon as I was big enough and could figure out how to reach the cookie jar at the very back of the kitchen counter. Even when I came home to visit as an adult, when I stayed up later than my parents, I would find myself quietly searching for something in the cupboards that they wouldn't notice missing. Once in a while, I brought my own cookies in my suitcase, Still, there was furtive eating and an element of fear of getting caught.

Mom's greatest fear for me was not for my safety or my happiness. Her biggest fear for me was that I would be fat. Growing up, being fat was a fate worse than death. Well, we managed that one, didn't we Mom? I became that nightmare when I did indeed become obese in my 20's. It was a kind of revenge which was sweet until it wasn't. Friends have pointed out to me that when the whole withholding dessert and cookies thing was going on, I was not that fat. I was a chubby kid who got fatter as the years went by. When I graduated from high school, I wore a simple white cotton sleeveless sheath dress, size 18, that I made for myself. Large, yes—but not as grossly obese as my mother had led me to believe.

I don't really have any memories of times as a child when my mother was relaxed about me and food, my weight, my body. Or about herself and those issues also. She definitely brought her own childhood problems into motherhood. I can imagine the shame and horror she felt when our family doctor suggested to her that the reason why I was not walking at 18 months was because I was too fat! I look at those photos of baby me through young adulthood with shock and amazement. I was chubby, yes. Obese, no!

I've been eating too many cookies lately. It's hard to tell you this, but, we need to bring this conversation out of the shadows and into the light. How many cookies is too many? My current benchmark is when I stop enjoying them, that is too many. For quite a few years now, I have been eating cookies that, in terms of ingredients, are about as healthy as you can get. I make them myself or buy them from a bakery or a healthy store. I don't waste my money and time on low-quality cookies anymore. Sometimes I can find great pleasure in relaxing and eating one or two. Sometimes, I find myself eating too many. Last week, I bought a bag and ate about a dozen cookies in one afternoon. Back in the day, that and more was the norm.

Do cookies taste good when I eat a lot of them? The first few do, then not so much. Do they feel good in my belly? If I am calm and feeling good, they do. If I am scarfing them down one after the other, the answer is "no." I can get heartburn and/or acid reflux. My belly bloats and I feel uncomfortable. Sometimes eating the cookies is a "fuck you" sort of moment, but the person who is getting f'd up and over is me, not anyone else. So why do I continue? I know bits and pieces of the why—they have to do with rebellion or comforting and numbing myself. I can—and do—punish myself for feeling good, confident, happy, and full of zest for life. I know about killing those good feelings with shame and sinking down into familiar depression, anxiety, and low self-esteem.

The nutritional facts about sugar are clear. I've studied eating psychology and learned about finding, acknowledging, and celebrating the sweetness in my life. I understand the importance of transparency, of honesty, of sharing, of community. And yet...I can find myself once again being held back by longing to belong, to feel I matter and there is a place for me at the table of life. It's like being stuck in my room with an empty box of cookies, not knowing how or when I can get it to the garbage can and on with my life.

So, here this goes, out into the ether. I'm shining the light on my shame, on my feeling like a fraud. If you overeat or binge, don't feel alone. If you have shame about eating or about your body, don't feel alone. I'm telling you about my experience so that I don't feel so alone. Sometimes that little thought is enough to move mountains.

Friday morning, chatting with my 15-year-old cat
Thanks for snuggling with me all night, Tina, for sticking with me and all my tossing and turning. My TMJ is sure acting up this morning. It's definitely an emotional response. Memories. Eating something forbidden. Hiding food. Chewing so fast.

From my writing journal
It sneaks up from behind
or inside
or from below
icy fingers of dread
of inevitability
the fog rolls in
not like little cat feet
but like mind stopping heart stopping breath stopping darkness

the unceasing need to swallow the scream
the non-negotiable march towards the dark
grabbing my ankles and pulling me down
suffocating
terrifying
and at the same time I'm numb
I'm protected
Life becomes backwards and inside out
the dark protecting me from the light
from the good and the love
the horror becomes my safety net
Numbness gives me one more day of life.

Later that morning
My bingeing was not limited to cookies or any particular kind of food. I've decided the common element among the foods was a high percentage of fat. That could have been pizza or

Mexican food. Something deep fried. It might have been sweet, like a whole large container of ice cream. Potato chips. Doughnuts. Some days, I might have a giant steak and an equally large bag of M&M's. During the Thanksgiving season, when pumpkin pie is on sale, you can still find me buying myself a pie. Back in the day, I would buy several and eat them all, a whole pie at a time. When I moved from my last house eighteen years ago, I found several plastic pie cases (empty) tucked in my bottom desk drawer.

Bingeing never really had much to do with being hungry, though it involved consuming huge amounts of food. Friends without histories of bingeing are amazed asnd aghast. They ask how could I physically eat so much. I don't know. I know sometimes I would also be amazed and aghast and wouldn't even feel that full. Now, when I eat too much, I suffer later from acid reflux, from a belly ache, from a sort of hangover the next day. It could be that I did have those consequences then but was able to ignore them, being so out-of-touch with my body.

When I was actively bingeing, I never thought of the "why." Now, I recognize fear or grief or shame at the base, but it always quickly escalated into being about punishment. Unnamable emotions made manifest into something more manageable. When I was young, I became a "bad girl." "You are a bad girl!" I'd say, parroting words I had heard from my mother if she found me eating something she had not given me. As I grew older, I developed thoughts of not deserving to feel good, to enjoy food, or have much of any kind of pleasure. The deeply engrained notion of my being disgusting reared its ugly head often. "This is what disgusting unlovable people do" —fulfilling the expectation of always being unlovable.

I still have some of that sneaking and hiding food energy. So bizarre. I've lived by myself for 40 years, with a few long-term guests here and there. But mostly, I eat alone, with no one looking at or caring about what food I have. Sometimes, when I buy cookies or chips, I will put them in a desk drawer or a different cupboard from the rest of the food. Is this so that no one finds it? Or perhaps it's a remnant from dieting days. Maybe I'll forget where I put the package and won't be able to eat it all right away.

Those strategies are classic for a reason, but I see an element of shame underlying them. I don't want anyone to know I still eat those foods or am tempted to eat all of them.

God, shame is such an ongoing theme running through all of my life. Being shamed by family members for my weight, shamed at school by teachers and classmates. Shamed by doctors.

And then there's the shame caused by the sexual abuse from my grandfather. As a girl, I repressed the experiences and held the memories secret even from myself until I was in my 30's. As an adult, I've come to know this abuse is behind a great deal of the shame I felt as a young woman but didn't understand.

Bedtime,1965, Christmas vacation at my maternal grandparents' house

I'm sleepy...but I sure want to finish this new Nancy Drew story. Some of it is silly, the way she is so perfect. It's a little old-fashioned too. I guess I'm a little jealous of her perfectly matched clothes, how athletic she is, her handsome boyfriend, Ned. Her little blue convertible. We probably wouldn't be friends in real life, but I love the stories.

Someone told me that it is actually a man who writes them. I wonder if that is true? It seems strange. Except for the fact that we both have great dads, I am really the opposite of Nancy Drew— another reason it's weird that I like her.

Oh no! Footsteps. He's coming. Oh God, help me. Please, not again. I still hurt so much. I finally got my first real bra and I couldn't wear it today because it rubbed where he pinchcd me so hard. He told me last night that he's been coming in my bedroom since I was a baby. I don't know. I can't remember any time before then. I am so scared. It was the worst thing ever. Maybe it's not him, maybe it's Dad coming to say good night. No, I can smell the cigarettes.

My grandfather appears in the doorway. He's wearing the new blue sweater my mom gave him for Christmas. In his hand is a glass of ice and some kind of drink. He's got kind of a weird smile

on his face and his eyes are big behind his thick eyeglasses. I
carefully put my left hand under my pillow.

"No! This time I say no. Don't come in. Don't tell me to be
quiet, I don't care who hears. I want them to hear. No! You will
not kiss me. Please, don't hurt me again. You are disgusting and
evil. You stink and I hate you. It's not right."

He comes into the room anyway, puts his glass on the table
by the bed, and gets really close. I can smell his breath. Alcohol.
His arm reaches out to touch my new Christmas nightgown but I
scoot back just fast enough. His face is bright red. He tells me I am
a fat, ugly girl. Oh, I feel dizzy, but I reach under my pillow and
pull out the knife I stole from the kitchen earlier that day. I am so
scared but it feels really good in my hand even though it's getting
really sweaty. I'm trying not to cry, but I can't help it. Can I do
this? I can hardly talk but I somehow make myself.

"I have a knife, look! I said don't come in. Get out! Yeah, I
got it from the kitchen. I will use it. I will tell. I know you told me
not to. I know you told me you would hurt Dad. That's not gonna
happen. I'm a teenager now, I can hurt you."

He just laughs. It sounds creepy. He doesn't say anything for
a while. He moves away from my bed and picks his glass back up. I
hear the ice cubes as he takes a big drink. I feel sweaty, sick, like
I'm going to puke. He looks at me for a long time and says, "No
one loves you. No one ever will. You'll never be anybody." He says
something I can't hear, then walks out and pulls the door closed
behind him.

Oh gosh. I did it! Oh God. I'm laughing and crying. I know
he's wrong. Dad loves me. I know Mom loves me even if we fight
sometimes. Shh. Oh God. I said I would tell but I can't. I just can't.
Shaking. Can't breathe. My heart is pounding and my stomach
hurts. I wonder if Chaney heard him. She's right next door in her
bedroom. I know she loves me. She lets me hang out with her in

the kitchen when I want. I sit on a chair and watch or sometimes I get to help her cook. She gives me chocolate chip cookies, my grandmother's favorite. I love Chaney. I wonder if she will miss the knife. She probably knows about him already, but I can't tell her either. What could she do? I bet she can smell his cigarettes.

I wonder if he will come back. I need some water, and I gotta pee. Is he still in the hallway? I don't think so. Shh. I don't think he will come back tonight.

It was Nancy who helped me, Nancy Drew. Thank you, Nancy. I will always love her. She was smart and brave, and so was I. I figured it out. It's what Nancy would do, except that she would tell her friends and her dad. I can't. Some of my friends say I'm too old to still read those books. But I love them. Maybe they saved my life. Maybe they saved my stupid grandfather's life. I wonder if I really could have stabbed him? It's a pretty big knife. I'm gonna keep it here until we go home. I'm pretty sure Nancy never killed anyone, but she probably could have if she needed to. Thank you, God…. and Nancy.

In the wee hours, back in present-day California

No sleep happening here. Grandfather, that bastard. He died around 40 years ago but still lurks around in my head. And he still manages to get some digs in once in a while. For years, especially when I was in therapy, I would have random body pain and nightmares. Now I mostly hear the words, though I still don't like shutting my bedroom door. "Fat ugly girl." "You'll never amount to anything." Thanks to time and opening more and more to love, they don't have much power.

I held the secret for many years. Secrets take their toll. I never did tell my family, until one day while in my 40's, I decided to tell my older brother. After being in therapy on and off for years, I felt the need to tell someone in the family, but I was not ready to speak with my parents. He was, and still is, the relative with whom I am the closest. Thankfully, he believed me while not quite understanding the whole story—how I had "forgotten" and was I sure the memories were real. I was in that same place, not really understanding the hows and whys of the memories either. It was a heartfelt conversation which deepened our relationship.

If my grandfather had still been alive when I started remembering, I would have confronted him and told my family. And now, most of my friends know. No more secrets. No more shame.

7 am-ish, Saturday, on Facebook Messenger with my dear friend Hannah, who lives up in the mountains with a beautiful garden and chickens. We have been in an ongoing Shamanic study group together for somewhere around twenty years.

Hannah: Good morning.

Charity: Good morning. You're up early. Me too.

H: Yeah, lots to do. Just wanted to check in; was thinking about you last night but was too late to call. I got a little worried about you. You okay?

C: Yeah, sigh. Though, I've had a lot of old painful memories returning and I wet my bed the other night. I had to pee badly, and I couldn't get Tina out of my way fast enough. Thanks for listening to me yesterday. I can't believe that stuff still comes up. Challenges with food and eating. How old are we? And we've still got the same issues? It's enough, already. Oh well, life goes on. How are you?

H: I know. Same shit, different day. I'm okay. I'm so tired of not feeling well. I've got to just suck it up and not have coffee today. That's my goal. I've got a headache coming on already so I might do a diluted thing. Loads to do today. Or I might wait until tomorrow.

C: Coffee is your nemesis! And medicine for your migraines at the same time. That's tough. You'll do the right thing. I'm still trying to relax into the whole "needing to tighten the food reins" thing. That's still the big deal for me. How do I once again clean up my act from a place of love? And not feel so much shame about having fallen off the wagon? I have to say, I hate that expression. What wagon? and sometimes, I just plain jump off the damn thing. I know what to eat and what not to eat, what makes me feel good, what makes me feel sick. I gotta not think about the weight part, just don't eat the damn gluten and sugar! and doesn't that sound loving and kind to myself?

H: LOL

C: LOL, wahhh.

H: One thing at a time.

C: Yep. No cookies for me today. I wish I could say *cookies* are medicine. We can do it. I just have been feeling sort of like a fraud, using my blog to spout off about body positivity and loving your body, then freaking out and eating a lot of cookies. And they weren't even that good.

H: Sorry. I can't really relate to the whole cookies thing, as you know, but I get it about feeling like a fraud. Sometimes I think someone is going to discover I'm full of bullshit or something. Say one thing and do another.

C: Good writing material, I guess. "Grist for the mill," as Ram Das says. Blog post, here I come. Hey, speaking of Ram Das, did you see the picture of him at one of the women's marches? Bundled up in his wheelchair. Reminds me of the other phrase of his I like, "We're all just walking each other home."

H: I did see that. I wished he would have worn a pussy hat! I gotta go. Text me if you want later. I'm off to go paddling.

C: Have fun!

Lucky Hannah, going out on the ocean. Oh, how I love her. I so need our semi-regular phone and Facebook check-ins, our conversations, our friendship of twenty-plus years. We can both be a bit prickly at sometimes, and at other times very nurturing. I think we balance each other pretty well.

Later that morning, getting ready to go to Ecstatic Dance

I feel a little as if I have a hangover. It's all those memories. I take this time to remind myself how those experiences shaped my life, where they've led me—from the pain and powerlessness to compassion and immense strength. My self-esteem has felt the weight of all this my whole life. I still struggle with quieting Grandfather's cruel voice. I still work at proving him wrong. I *am* somebody.

I need to move and get some hugs. Work up a sweat and let go of more of that abuse that seems to still be in my muscle memory. What to wear? Oh, I should wear those red leggings. They'll get me going. I need me some fire. Fire in the belly. Red shirt? Why not? Burn up that dance floor. Watch out. Better put the fire department on speed dial!

See you later, Tina.

At the dance

I just got here, and I'm comparing already…me to my old self, me to the beautiful skinny women. It's hard to get my mind to stop, hard to just be in my body. Quit it, Charity.

I'm a fat island surrounded by tall willowy women and handsome men with defined muscles. Perfect people. Of course, this is not the whole story. I see other women tugging at their clothing to keep it in the right place, other women whose breasts bounce when they move. Women and men with bellies that stick out. But I am the fattest one here today. I see no one else that I consider fat. I should be used to it by now, but it's embarrassing. I feel my cheeks flush and my breath catch. Am I really the only one? I hope I can work through those emotions and keep coming. I don't totally feel as if I belong here.

I like to dance, so, on one hand, it doesn't bother me. That's why I'm here, and that's why we are all here. On the other hand, it bothers me that I still notice it and keep track. I imagine people looking at my stomach hanging down ("Really? She wears leggings?") or being grossed out by my size.

I wonder if anyone else is thinking about their size and whether or not they fit here. I know I am not the only one with body image challenges. I know the DJ personally, and once, he and I had a healing conversation about men and body image. This handsome man who loves to wear androgynous colorful clothes admitted to having worked hard on loving his natural thinness, to accept the word "skinny" as I have worked to accept the word "fat." He said, "I used to be teased a lot about being so thin, got called names because of my big nose. High school young men can be pretty cruel in the locker room. It wasn't until I got really comfortable dancing that I was able to accept and appreciate my long legs and all that they could do for me."

I treasure those times when I forget to think about my size. I should just get over it and let this old fat woman shine, feel good, feel what needs to be felt. What happened to that fire? Think red leggings. Sssss. Sizzle. Sizzle the schizzle out of those leggings, girl! This kind of dancing is really about being inwardly focused, so I should close my eyes. Take some deep breaths. Listen. Listen to what *my* body is telling me. Can I open my ears and my heart and really hear my body's voice? I am strong. I am full of the power of love. I've learned to dig deep for it. I've learned to ask for it embrace it, embrace myself.

Two hours later

Oh god, that was fun! It felt like letting go but it was really letting *in*, deep in my body. I've got hips, and I'm not afraid to use them. I joined a few of those skinny girls. A friend danced over and whispered in my ear, "You are rockin' the red, girl!" We were sweating buckets. We were all on fire. A few other people looked as if they wanted to remind us of the rules, of which "No talking" is one. But others smiled at us and all our giggling. Good thing laughter is so contagious. I don't think anyone has really ever figured out why that is. Wouldn't it have been great if all the dancers in that room had started laughing with us?

I remember reading an article about a village, I think it was in Japan, where the children in one classroom started laughing and couldn't stop. Soon, it spread to the whole school. So, they closed school for the day and sent the kids home, but then all the families started laughing. I forget how long it took for it to stop.

I'm going home. My job here is done.

From my writing notebook

Enough already, Life is too short to take it all seriously!

Cookies
I ain't no rookie
That's a bet not taken by any bookie.

Chocolate's the best
but don't eat the rest
I just need to digest.

So serious
I am curious
That's better than being furious.

What about peanut butter?
the crumbs will sputter
as my heart goes a flutter.

I want something sweet
don't give me buckwheat
the heat comes in on the downbeat.

Last but not least
lemon is a beast
Bring on the love feast.

Sunday morning, phone call from Hannah
    Charity: Hey girl.
    Hannah: Hey, how are you? Things settling down?
    C: Yes, thank God, but I still got a lot going on inside my head! Noisy in there. Lots of chatter. I need to transfer some of my focus back out into the world. It's exhausting. You?
    H: God, tired too. I've been working too much. You've got too much going on in your head, I have too much going on in my life. Lots of work projects to do, which is good. Labels, magazine layouts. There's always something to repair—the chicken coop, the toilets. Garden to tend to. We so often are such interesting mirrors for each other. Opposite ends of issues.

C: That is true. I do think we often provide each other with balance. Like a teeter-totter, finding that sweet spot where the whole thing is level.

H: That can get a bit boring though.

C: Yeah. God, I hated teeter-totters growing up. I was pretty chubby and weighed more than my friends, so I'd have to scoot forward, and they'd have to scoot all the way back. Then someone would get off, and the other would come crashing down.

H: I can't really remember if I spent much time on them. I liked to climb the jungle gym—now that's a terrible name—and go across the monkey bars. Who named these things anyway? Teeter-totter, monkey bars, jungle gym? That jungle gym thing has a tinge of something not quite right. How'd we get on this topic?

C: Us balancing each other out.

H: Oh yeah. You want to go out to eat tonight?

C: That would be fun. We are on the same side of the teeter-totter on this issue! We could eat red meat together. I could use a steak. I'm about to grow feathers and *bawk* like a chicken.

H: Yeah, I'm up to my ears in eggs. Good thing I digest them well. I've been eating a lot of them.

C: Oh, I'd love to have some.

H: Okay, great. I'm doing something right. My chickens are happy anyway. So is my garden. I'm also up to my ears in kale. Fortunately, I really like eggs and kale.

C: I saw a thing on Facebook that was a recipe for something called "Boyfriend Steak." A big juicy steak with butter sauce. Just what we love. How sexist and offensive is that name though? Too fattening, too manly, for us delicate women to eat, I guess. And how sad is it that so many women won't eat a steak while they watch their men chow down on one, wishing that's what they were eating? So, let's go be each others' "boyfriends." We'll eat the steak *and* the vegetables. And I can tell you my idea I have about going on a big road trip.

H: Okay, I'm curious. It's a date. I'll see you later.

I really relish red meat. Sometimes it seems crazy to me that I used to be a vegetarian. I believe raising meat sustainably is possible. I'm so lucky to live in Santa Cruz, California, where consciousness is high, where ranchers and farmers are doing the right thing, where there are farmers' markets.

I've been thinking about going on a long road trip around the country later this year. Getting in my car and visiting friends. That will be an interesting and difficult part of it if I go. I'm starting to talk with my friends on the East Coast and deciding if it's doable to take a few months, just get in my car and go. Most of the people I would see love to cook, enjoy healthy food. Among many other ideas, it would be fascinating to see how many farmers' markets I could find.

Eating well, eating ethically. Some places it's not so easy. And of course, I find it really fascinating that there are plenty of people who don't really care where their food comes from. They just don't want it to be expensive. And they don't care about the ethics.

I always try to be ethical not just in food practices but all the aspects of my life. I work at avoiding people whose ethics are not in line with mine but that is not always easy.

In this "senior" phase of my life, this post menopausal phase, I find it easier to surround myself with and yes, attract, people who are ethical and have integrity. People who are kind, who are honest. Life has taught me plenty—sometimes painfully, sometimes dangerously—about discernment, about being able to judge a person's character.

As a senior in high school, I decided to attend a women's college and was accepted to all to which I had applied. I spent my first year at Mills College in Oakland, California. Being at an all-female school was not what I had hoped, but I loved being in the Bay Area. With my parents' reluctant permission, I spent the summer sharing a sublet apartment in San Francisco with two friends. We were all looking forward to finally having some "grown-up" sort of freedom. I'm not sure we really met those goals. I never found a full-time job. I cobbled some work together and, with some pitching in from my roommates, I was able to pay my share of the bills. We made some friends who were willing to supply us with the cheap red wine we learned to enjoy. Living in the big city was exciting but eventually proved to be more than I was ready for.

Summer 1970, San Francisco, the morning after

What the hell was that? How could I have been so stupid— thinking all romantically, that it would be magical and wonderful? I was so scared and didn't know what to do. I want to throw up. I've got a headache and my whole body is sore. I'm so embarrassed. I'm an idiot. What do I do?

I answered the phone one day and was immediately enchanted with the caller's sexy voice and French accent. He was calling the woman we are subletting the apartment from. When he invited me over, all I could think was, "Here's my chance to meet a sexy guy and maybe have sex" —to not be the only one of my group who is not doing it. It didn't even occur to me that it might not be safe. I said, "*Oui*, come pick me up." I should have just hung up the phone. No, I had to go. Stupid! I put on my favorite blue jeans and my beautiful Mexican embroidered blouse. His car—that should have clued me in. Dark blue, real wood inside—very expensive, very fast. We went all the way to Marin County. I had no idea where we were going. I was still in the excitement and potential romance. When he brought me to an amazing house, I thought, "This guy has money." That only made me more excited. A glass of wine. Damn, why did he have to be so good-looking? Soft milk chocolate-colored skin, sexy blue silk shirt. He rolled me a big fat joint. Then, out came the cocaine. I didn't even really know for sure that's what it was until he teased me about not wanting any. Thank God, I didn't do it. Then he kissed me, which led to more kissing. His lips were soft, and it felt good at first. He slipped his hands inside my shirt. We took off our clothes. His hands moved more roughly, and I got scared. Where was the romance now? I asked him to stop. When he slapped me, I knew I was really in trouble. I tried to fight. I did try. I did my best to kick him and shove him off of me. He was way too strong for me. He just laughed at me and called me a silly American. He said such ugly things, calling me a bitch, a whore, and other words in French I didn't understand. He shoved his penis in my mouth, causing me to gag and want to vomit. I could hardly breathe. Later, he shoved his hands between my legs and forced his penis in. Oh Lord, it hurt. I cried and screamed. But all he did was tell me to shut up. *Ferme ta guele!*

Then the doorbell rang. What? He got up, answered the door naked and brought some guy into the room. "Don't pay any attention to her," he said. "She's just the whore." Then he opened his closet. It was full of bricks of pot. A light dimly went on in my brain, and I suddenly got why he had all this luxury. Money and bricks exchanged hands, and the guy left. This French drug dealer refused to take me home, even after I begged him. I didn't even know where I was. Somehow I got through the night, staying as close to the edge of the bed as I could. As the sun came up, he got out of bed and seemed completely disgusted. I got dressed. I never want to wear those clothes again. He pulled me out to the car and, without saying much, drove me quickly across the Golden Gate bridge and home.

My roommates were excited to see me, wondering how it was. I could not tell them what really happened and made up some lies instead. Pleading a hangover, which made them grin, I went to my room. I sobbed and fell into a restless sleep.

Present-day Santa Cruz, Monday afternoon, reading email

Here's a line: "Art creates hope and healing." I think seeing beauty creates hope and healing. Making art creates hope and healing. Seeing other people making art is inspirational and allows hope. Note to self! Make the time for writing, that darn knitting project, playing the piano. All the things. Even those silly, fun coloring books. And gardening! A garden creates hope, growth, future, possibilities—so important in these dark days. Dark days of winter, dark days of politics. Dark nights of the soul. This seems like a choice way to describe some of what our country is going through now: America's dark night of the soul. A night which will continue for a long time. There is always hope. Hang on to that. It's not over until it's over.

Later, listening to music

Gladys Knight and the Pips. I forgot how crazy I was about them. I still wish I could sing like Gladys and dance like a Pip. I'm fascinated by all those old school backup dancers, but the Pips were the best I think. The Temptations? The Jackson 5? I still say the Pips. Better to sing like Aretha *and* dance like a Pip! Maybe in my next lifetime. Dance like Tina. Sing like Etta James. "Tell Mama all about it." Top it all off with a little Lady Gaga. Damn those Facebook people body shaming her because she has a little belly fat. Good Lord, you want to see belly fat? Aretha and I could show them some belly fat. Probably the Pips that are still around have got some belly fat too.

From my writing notebook

(words on baby onesies for sale online)

"pretty eyes and chunky thighs"
"hunky and chunky"

oh aren't you the cutest baby?
such chubby cheeks
look at those thighs
the dimples

oh my precious chunky monkey, I just want to squish you
poke you, kiss you, tickle you, pinch you
love you to death

What is your mama feeding you? so big and so handsome
Give me some sugar
Sweet baby cheeks
turn into worried looks and concern
What *is* your mama feeding you?

chubby babies are cute
until they aren't

When does that happen?

18 months and not walking, the Dr. suggests
it might be because you weigh too much
Mama stops breast feeding
watered-down formula
the first of many diets
Is it when you are two and your grandfather starts putting his
hands in you?
When?

Maybe when you are 6 and want to go to ballet school but are
told
you are too fat
When no one wants to play on the teeter-totter with you because
you are bigger than they are

Oh darling, you have such a pretty face.
You could be a pretty girl
if only you'd lose some weight.
Don't you think you'd be happier if
you were thinner?

Hard-boiled egg diet
Metracal
tiny piece of cheese and an apple
school lunch
no dessert
no ice cream when the family stops at Dairy Queen

Did you know that by age 8
most girls not only know about dieting
 but want to lose weight,
have tried some sort of method?

dieting

starving
fasting

anorexia
bulimia
bingeing
purging

not so chubby now
not so pretty now
hating herself
disgusting himself

I don't want to go to school today, Mom.
Can I please stay home?

Tuesday morning, email exchange with Tom, a.k.a., "Mr. Flannel," a newish friend/companion/not-a-boyfriend, whom I've met at our marimba school. He recently expressed interest in spending time together. I don't call him Mr. Flannel to his face, but since he frequently wears flannel shirts, I have given him this nickname when I talk about him with my friends. He lives in a cabin in the woods, has been single his whole life, and has a deep melodious voice and a sweet smile, as well as a very full head of white hair.

Yay, an email from Mr. Flannel! He's so very old fashioned; he writes emails like letters. I miss getting letters. There's a sweetness to them. Respect. Politeness is underrated these days, I think. Like that conversation he and I had last week about sex. He was polite and respectful. He needed to let me know he absolutely isn't interested in having sex—with me or anyone. He did it in a thoughtful way. And, in truth, I have some mixed feelings. A few times, I have wished there was the possibility of being more than friends, but there just isn't that kind of passionate chemistry.

Neither of us feels it. And I *am* seeing the plus side of being friends with him—"friends with no benefits," as someone said when I told her. I do feel sort of sorry for him, though, shutting the door on that part of his life. I guess he shut it quite a few years ago. He's only 67. I need to remember that that's about him, not me. It's not *me* he's not interested in, and his lack of interest is not about my attractiveness. I don't know why he has those feelings; he hasn't opened up about that. Obviously, he likes me. I like him. I told him I would appreciate it if we could be a little more affectionate. He looks like a big cuddly bear, but he doesn't like to cuddle. He has stepped up a little since I told him. Ironically, he does give good hugs.

From: Tom
To: Charity
Subject: movie

Dear Charity,

Thank you so much for your recent note. I am sorry it has taken me a few days to reply.

I was thinking about your movie idea. I'm not sure what you would like to see. I don't actually go to the movies that often but would be willing to give it a try. Perhaps a comedy? Something light to take our minds off of world events? I look forward to your suggestions.

Yours Truly,
Tom

From: Charity
To: Tom
Subject: movie

Tom,

No need to apologize. I am one of those people who look at emails every day, which I know is not your style. I do appreciate how polite and considerate you are, thank you.

How about the newest *Star Wars*? It's not a comedy but is that something you might like? Something light would be good too. I could use some laughing. I'll take a look again and see if anything catches my eye.

How about Sunday?

Charity

From: Tom
To: Charity
Subject: movie

Dear Charity,

Something has come up and I may have to work on Sunday. Unfortunately, I won't know until Saturday so you may not want to wait until then to make plans. What do you think?

By the way, I regret to tell you I have no interest whatsoever in *Star Wars*. And I agree, I don't think it's a comedy. Haha!

Tom

That evening

Huh, I thought he'd be into *Star Wars*. Oh well. Obviously, I'm not that into it either, otherwise I would have gone to see it already. It still cracks me up how formal he is. Old fashioned and polite. And, it cracks me up that I respond in the same way. It's a bit like being around someone with an accent. It gets easy to pick that up and sound German or Canadian.

Bummer about his working. If we don't get together, I'll be disappointed. I'm wanting to be clear with him about my emotions, which so far hasn't been too difficult. I'm not sure why I thought it would be. I am adept at expressing my feelings. I'm delighted to have found out that, while it is difficult for him to express his feelings, he can listen and hear mine. This is healing for me to be with a man who can listen. And probably good to remember that it's not my job to "fix" him or turn him into someone he is not. I'll just meet him where he is.

Okay, it feels important to keep communication honest and open. He might have shut his door but I didn't shut mine. The more comfortable I get hanging out with Tom, the more there's room for being comfortable with someone else, someone in addition to him. I told him that when we talked about not having sex or a romance. I said I would stay open to other possibilities.

For now, I'm enjoying the conversations, the dates that aren't really dates. We're finding out things about each other—books we like, places we've been. We've shared a few childhood stories; there's not lots in common there. The whole making-a-new-friend process is fascinating. What we find important to know about another person says a lot. I want details. I want to know about his past, his hopes and dreams. He likes to live in the present and begrudgingly tells me so when I ask about living in San Francisco in the 70's. We were both there around the same time, which is kind of fun. We are most comfortable talking about music, I guess. We have marimba in common. That's how we met, passing each other as his class let out and mine came in. I watched him for a long time, thinking he was attractive and wanting to chat with him but being too shy. One day he heard me talking about a concert I had been to and came up and asked me if I'd like to go with him sometime. I calmly (on the outside) said, "Yes," and gave him my contact info, looking to all the world as if I did such a thing all the time, when, in fact, it had been many years since a man had expressed any kind of interest.

Someone to share with, someone to listen to me—I'm gonna soak it in. I appreciate the interest and attention. Finally. Turning up the volume on the self-esteem dial.

Thursday, 3 am, lying in bed, listening to the rain
Ahhh, I hear rain thrumming! It must be coming down hard if I can hear it. One of the sad things about being hard of hearing is that I don't often hear the rain falling. It's such a soothing sound—

a universal one. I know most of the Californians who are awake tonight and listening are grateful. This land is thirsty. Tomorrow will be fresh and clean. The air will smell good. Petrichor. I just learned that word. The smell of the earth after rain, a result of some sort of chemical oils that get released. My body relaxes, my skin feels nourished even though I'm not actually out getting wet.

Later that morning, reading Facebook
     "It does take courage to be comfortable in one's own skin," says my friend Kathleen. Indeed. Am I everyday? No. Am I today? Yes.

From my writing notebook
You can call me fat
I don't mind.
Queen told us all what Fat Bottomed girls do

Chubby
Plus size
Curvy
but oops sometimes the curves are a little wide
Thick

She was a big-boned gal

Daddy called me pleasingly plump
His little butterball

Baby got back
and front
and all around

Fun to dance to in a song
maybe embarrassing in real life

Cass Elliot
soft dresses, big voice

Of course she died young, they said, look at how fat she was.

Aretha got fat
people worried

Queen Latifah dared to call herself a queen
white people didn't quite know what to do.

Some women get bigger to feel more powerful
to be visible
oops, society has those backwards
taking away power/voice/visibility from fat women

Go ahead and call me fat
See if I care
I make the world go round.

Early bedtime
    Ahh, bed feels good. So tired.

    Great Spirit, Grandmothers and Grandfathers, thank you for my life. Thank you for this beautiful, powerful day. I am grateful for your teachings. Thank you for helping me stand tall and be proud of who I am.

    I'm thinking about prayer, about how important it is to me. I prayed as a child, though, as a Quaker family, we prayed silently. Before dinner, we'd hold hands around the table and say our own prayers. Dad would squeeze someone's hand when he thought we were all finished, and then we'd send that squeeze around. Now, in my Shamanic traditions that I practice, I pray a lot. I gather with my friends and pray together out loud. I make pilgrimages to places around the world and pray. I pray just about every night and morning. I'm gratified by having that thread all the way through my life.

Poor Mom. While she was happy to come to the weekly prayer circle my spiritual community has in order to satisfy her curiosity when she came out to visit, she was so uncomfortable with our out loud and sometimes exuberant prayers.

Next day, mid-morning, at the coffeehouse, on the computer

Whoohoo! Black tea. Caffeine. Here we go. I'm in the mood. I'm ready for some of that caffeine jazz, ready to get my brain buzzing. Almond milk, honey. So satisfying. This tastes just right. Hopefully this won't make me too caffeine crazy. It's tricky finding that feel good balance.

Today is one of those days that I need to be around people. I'm not really lonely, but I don't want to be alone. Get some buzz from caffeine, get some buzz from the busy atmosphere. This coffee shop is a good balance of quiet and productivity, creativity and relaxation. I need to dive deep today, process some things through writing, get this blog post done, and, at the same time, feel part of the world.

It was cathartic to write about Mama today. It felt really powerful to end the post with the ice cream story. I still find it amazing that she went so many years without allowing herself chocolate or ice cream. And, it still makes me sad for her.

Dad was her opposite in many ways. He took great pleasure in eating, in relaxing. He worked hard and rewarded himself. I had the privilege and family duty of spending some time with him in the weeks before he passed away. He had a rapidly manifesting form of dementia. It became too time-consuming and difficult for my mom to take care of him, so he was moved into a special care unit at the retirement facility where they lived in Pennsylvania. After he was settled, Mama took herself on a Mediterranean cruise, a much needed vacation. She was an inveterate traveler and had been staying home with Dad far too long. She went with the care unit staff's blessings, as well as her children's. As fate would have it, after she left, Dad fell. The unit could not stop his bleeding and needed family permission to take him to the emergency room. My parents had set up complicated instructions, wanting no extraordinary measures in their elder care. Did this emergency room trip qualify? My older brother, who was their executor and had power of attorney, decided no, that this did not count as an "extraordinary measure." He decided that their instructions did not mean they should bleed to death. The EMTs who responded to the care unit's call were able to stop the bleeding, and no hospital trip was needed. A week later, the unit informed us that they thought he had pneumonia and should go to the hospital. Again, they needed family approval. After some debate, my brother told the facility that we wanted him to go to the hospital. At this point, I volunteered to go be with him for a week or so. We also decided not to tell Mom, not to get her off her ship and bring her home. He was in the hospital for a few days. It turned out Dad did not have pneumonia, but I think the shock of falling and getting sick made his dementia develop more quickly. For most of that week, he did not know who I was. It was a painful time to be sure.

He returned to the memory care unit, I returned to California, and a few days later, Mom returned as well. Dad went into a coma right before her return. I came back to Pennsylvania, and Mom and I had a stressful evening together worrying about Dad. Around midnight, she got a call to come to his room, which was now in the medical care unit. He was near death. She did not understand, being jet lagged and worried, but when they called again a few minutes later, she understood. The process of her coming downstairs to the guest room, waking me up, and waiting while I got dressed lost us precious minutes. We hurried to his room but were too late. He had already died. We each had our few minutes with him, then began the "what-do-we-do-now?" process. For several years, I felt terribly guilty about being so slow, thinking that it was my fault that Mom didn't get to say a final goodbye to him.

Her death was dramatically different. Mom, after some weeks of treatment and of being in severe pain and being completely overwhelmed by cancer and the loss of her bladder, decided to stop eating and drinking. Her doctor, with some regret, agreed to Mom's wishes. I was still there helping, so Mom told me and I listened while she called my brothers to come for one last visit. Our family was together for her last week. We all took turns sitting with her, keeping vigil, and we were able to be there with her for her final breaths. So painful and so powerful. She was tough to the end. Five days after her last bites and sips, her heart stopped and we said our farewells.

My Mama Never Loved Her Body

I have been in an outdoor exercise class for about ten years. Now, we are a small hearty band of over 55-year-olds, with the exception of our wonderful fearless instructor. Our needs have changed over the years. For me, now, the work is about keeping the strength I have. I'd be happy to have some more endurance and stamina. And I need to keep moving my creaky joints, staying flexible and being as energetic as I can. Plus, it's great being out-side!

My mother was athletic as a girl and young woman, and she played field hockey, lacrosse, and tennis in high school and college. While at Vassar, she earned the nickname "Ex," which stood for exercise. Her family and friends from those days called her that her whole life.

My brothers and I grew up around this passion she had, but to her very great regret, none of us shared it. We lived on a lake, and I did enjoy swimming in the summer and ice skating in the winter. These activities were fun. But, PE classes or any sort of "extra-curricular" sports, no way. As I got older and chubbier, her efforts to get me moving increased. I got my revenge one summer at age thirteen, when her plans for me to exercise more and lose weight backfired in that *she* developed muscle and got a little buffed up doing the Air Force calisthenics routines we did together. I think she had to buy some new blouses. I'm pretty sure I hated almost every minute of it, and I didn't lose any weight.

Now I know this was abuse. This falls along the same lines as my recent post about stealing cookies. I knew I hated the way she treated me (and I hated her in those moments), but it was my life. I was just a lazy fat kid who was a great disappointment to her mother. One of the outstanding examples of this was when she decided I needed to learn to play tennis. Did I want to play tennis? No. Did she even ask me? I don't think so. Was it any kind of fun? *No.* Not for either of us. There we were, sweating up a storm, crying up a storm, yelling up a storm. Not only was I not able to easily run around the court, I had (and still have) challenges with depth perception. Instead of starting out slowly, teaching me how to hit the ball, doing something to make it fun, etc., she would hit it far enough away from me that I would have to run to get to it, see where the ball was, and figure out how to hit it back to her. Not a lot of built-in success. Fortunately, it didn't take long for her to give up on me and tennis. She continued her love of the sport for many years.

As I said earlier, I love to swim. She took advantage of this, and we enrolled in Lifesaving Certification together, me in the Junior class and she in the Senior. I did all right but suffered under her constant scrutiny and the competitiveness that made her need to be the best in the group, even though—or especially—because she was at least 20 years older than her fellow students.

I don't mean to make this all a rant against my mother. I loved her dearly and miss her terribly at times since her death almost seven years ago. We had other activities and interests in common—knitting, our love of mystery/detective stories, traveling, and cooking. I'm happy to have had plenty of healing around all of our issues. (Obviously, there is still a bit of an angry edge!) Thankfully, while she was still alive, I was able to move from a place of anger to having compassion for her.

After growing older and dealing with my own problems through therapy and all the other avenues I pursued, I see Mama in a different light. Her parents gave most of their attention to her brother, their son. Their household was not one filled with affection. She, like me, had all her material needs met and lived a privileged life. What she lacked was love and respect from her family. Her self-esteem was almost non-existent. She was smart, attractive, very friendly, and giving, and yet, she thought she was fat and ugly and stupid. Mom pushed herself constantly. She felt she was never good enough at anything. Mom didn't swim because she loved it (though she really did). She always swam as if someone was chasing her. So competitive with herself, but so angry and afraid.

She proudly weighed the same at 89 as she did in her 40's. She weighed herself daily and would eat even more sparsely than usual if the scale dared to creep up even a few ounces. Some would say this is a valuable habit. In her case, it was not. She didn't do this out of love or wanting to do something that would make her feel good. It came from shame and anger. She found no pleasure in eating. As fiercely and often as she exercised, she didn't love it. I wasn't witness to a lot of her joy.

I'll end this with a truly healing story for both Mama and me. She had been in a lot of pain, and right around her 89th birthday, she was diagnosed with bladder cancer. She had surgery to remove her bladder but was unable to cope with the day-to-day practicalities of having an ostomy bag. The cancer had already spread to her spine and some places in her abdomen. Her strength left quickly, and she moved into the nursing care section of the retirement community where she lived. As her appetite waned, her doctors gave her permission to have whatever she wanted. Amazingly enough, what did she want but chocolate ice cream! My whole life, I thought my mom didn't like chocolate or ice cream. Turns out, it was her iron will and discipline that never let her have any until the end. Those last few weeks, she would eat a few bites of some sort of lunch and have a bowl of chocolate frozen yogurt. In the evening, the few bites of dinner began with her beloved gin and tonic. Sometimes George, her gentleman friend, brought himself a glass of wine and had cocktail time with her. Her small dinner ended with a bowl of chocolate ice cream (sometimes even two scoops) with nuts and marshmallows , even though her appetite wasn't much. One evening, as I was sitting with her while she ate, she asked me if I wanted the staff to bring me some. Not since I was a little girl had she offered me ice cream! I hardly ever eat ice cream, and, food snob that I am, I really didn't want that sort of ice cream. I'm also lactose intolerant. But, this was an amazing moment, and my mom and I quietly enjoyed our chocolate ice cream together on our trays in her small room. When she first was in the nursing care wing of her retirement community, she got out of bed, put on her bathrobe, and ate at a small table. By this evening, she stayed in her hospital bed using the swing aside tray, and I sat next to her. I had to step out and cry a few tears before coming back to kiss her goodnight. I am so glad this is one of our final moments together. Soon after, she made the decision to end her life by stopping eating and drinking. Her doctors and our family gave her our support, although her choice saddened us. She enjoyed one last bowl of ice cream and declared herself ready. There is interesting irony and something very moving that chocolate ice cream was the last thing she ate.

From my writing notebook
Dad

Desperate in his hospital bed
struggling to remove his diaper
I have to go to the toilet
I have to go to the toilet
Dad, I say quietly,
You can't get up

You have to stay in bed
Just go in your diaper, it's okay
Just go.

He looks at me with horror in his eyes.
I try not to mirror that back to him.
The nurse wants to restrain him
I stroke his arm and hold his hand.

I love you, Dad.
It's okay, just go.

Later that day, he did go
He is gone,
wandering deep into his world of dementia
and hallucination.
As I enter his room,
he is again frantic
this time as a captain of a British naval war ship
facing certain disaster
trying to save his ship and his men
fighting an unseen battle on the sea
fighting an unseen battle in his brain

Did I come to sign up?
Was I there to join the battle?
He asks me with tears in his eyes

This
This from my father, the pacifist
the World War II Conscientious Objector
who faced derision and hatred for years.
spat upon for his decision
called traitor
Instead, he chose a lifetime of speaking for peace.

Now, fighting for his life on a 19th century British war vessel

a beautiful well-made ship, he said,
Look at her wood and her sails, now tattered.
I have to save my men and my ship.

the man who loved to sail
the man who hated war

He didn't know who I was.
was I ready to sign up?
The war was raging
He needed more sailors

I slipped out into the hallway
tears running down my cheeks
What should I do?

Dad
my sweet dad

As I returned
I saluted him and said
Yes, Sir. Where do I sign?

He was able to leave the hospital
after battling the sea and those unseen enemies
He never was the same after that

My Dad
my rock
my source of endless love

I see us dancing
my toddler feet on his as he guides me around the living room
I see us dancing
to some 70's rock and roll
at my brother's wedding in Oregon, go Dad

I hear him speaking his truth at Quaker meeting
I hear him arguing with my brothers
I hear him struggling to learn to use the computer

There he is
yet again buying more tools to fix something at my house
swallowing his frustration at me not being more like him
I see his twinkling eyes and wry smile
as he tries to elicit groans from me with his latest puns

I see him holding hands with my mom
both as young parents off to the New Year's Eve dance at the Elk's Club
and as elders shuffling down the hall to bed

my Dad
Kissing the top of his head, I say goodbye for the last time.

Praying before falling asleep

Ancient Ones, I give thanks for my life today. I give thanks for the life my parents gave me. I pray for their spirits. I give thanks for the memories and the healing of our relationships.

Thursday morning

It's so great to have a house cleaner again. Cleaning is not something I enjoy. I love it when the place is clean, but I can't seem to keep up a routine. House cleaning is a skill that is learned, that needs to be taught. I did not learn it growing up. The house was clean, but my mom didn't really want to do it. She didn't learn it growing up in a wealthy family who always had someone else do the cleaning and cooking. My mom loved to cook. House cleaning, not so much. So, we always had a housecleaner—once a week, or maybe less often than that; I'm not sure. My mom just had other activities she preferred doing. We could afford help, so there it was. Hmm, yet another way I am like Mama, both in housecleaning skills and having money to make my life easy. I've finally declared myself retired from personal chef work after not having any clients for a very long time. Family money has paved the way for a comfortable rest of my life.

Being a girl in the 1950's, there were many lessons—even if they were never called that—on how to be a good wife and home-maker. Mama did teach me how to cook, sew, and iron. I loved to iron, especially Dad's stuff. I started out on his handkerchiefs which he used every day, white cotton ones, ironed and folded so they fit nicely in his jacket pocket, and I eventually worked my way up to his work shirts. Crisp, button-down collars —tedious to iron, but not when my heart was full of love for my Papa. Now, my ironing board is loaded down with all kinds of stuff, and I am not even sure if my iron even works anymore. Cleaning out Mom's apartment after she died, I found a few of Dad's hankies that she apparently had kept to use, so I kept and used them too. They've worn out and are gone now.

It's probably time to deal with my deeper issues around cleaning and cluttering. I've done a great deal of work since the old days, but I'm still not where I'd like to be. Cleaning seems to be all so connected with self-esteem, with self-love, with stories I carry about myself. I deserve to live surrounded by peace, by beauty. I deserve to feel good in my home.

It was embarrassing today to have Chrissy clean my fridge. She discovered a few scary-looking things and too many jars with dribs and drabs of ancient condiments. Again, I can feel like a fraud. I can talk up a strong nutrition story, and I'm all about being transparent and open. I do acknowledge the connection between rotten food in the refrigerator and inadequate self-care. It's time to see if it goes the other way—if having a clean fridge leads to more care about and for the self. Right now, the fridge is sparkling, clean-smelling, ready for some fresh vegetables and other food which gives me pleasure. The floors are really clean too, and the bathroom is all sparkly and fresh. I wish I had a window in there. I so wish I could redo the whole thing. It's too small, and I hate that bathtub, the tile. It's hard to lovingly take care of something that gives you no pleasure! And, that connects right back to my own self-care. If I'm not loving myself, I'm not going to do the care, and vice versa. The more I amp up tending to myself, letting myself feel pleasure, the more pleasure I feel.

For now, it's clean. Home maintenance. Self-care. It's all connected. I just get tired of caring for both the house and myself but who else is going to do it? Obviously, it doesn't work to ignore either one. Well, on to the next thing. Get some greens from the garden. I do love them, but I could use some new ideas for how to prepare them. I think I will pick as many as I can, steam them, and have them ready to eat, ready to create into exciting things. Sounds like some teaching from the greens there, too. Getting ready to become exciting, not knowing when that moment will come. One minute quietly growing, the next minute getting chopped up and added to a sizzling pan of excitement. Becoming something delicious, a nutritional powerhouse. I'm not only ready, I'm becoming a delicious powerhouse of a woman. Biding my time waiting for the perfect moment. No, not waiting for it, but *making* a perfect moment. And with my own definition of perfect.

The next morning, 3am

That was a complicated dream. I'm often amazed at how quickly dreams can be forgotten. It's fading already. In "real life," when I lived in Oregon, I used to go to the sweat lodge often, most often at one particular one in Portland. The leader was a big Native American man with long gray braids and a quiet demeanor. I remember that he liked being called an Indian—he didn't hold to things being too politically correct. Tom was there. Tom from the Oregon days, the first Tom. That was one of our first "dates"— going to a sweat lodge. I later found out that he brought dozens of women to the sweats at that place in Portland. In the dream, I could hear the chanting, smell the sage. Ha, thinking about the politically correct—once someone spat and it landed on the hot rocks in the middle of the lodge. Tom, who did have Native blood, somehow scraped it off with a towel which miraculously did not catch fire, all while making some disparaging comment about the person who had spit. There was a moment's silence, then the leader of the sweat landed a great big wad of spit on the fire and began to sing.

Made me laugh. In the dream, there was none of that drama, just prayers and singing.

How odd that Tom was there tonight in my dream. And now there is a new Tom in my life.

Saturday morning, walking at the beach

This morning's dream about Tom has me thinking—looking back and recalling some of our times together. Times that run the gamut from excitement and longing to frustration, disappointment, and anger. I'm finding myself reminiscing about Aurora, his daughter, the girl who became the daughter of my heart, and focusing now on when I went back to Oregon for Tom's funeral. Whoa, feelings galore! Regret. Anger. Worry. I needed to go to face some of those feelings. I needed to go to see Aurora, hold her and be with her.

It was difficult, hearing all that grief and praise for Tom. Maybe he did change in the last few years of his life. With a fair amount of distance now, I wonder how I got caught in his snare. There he is sometimes in my memories—so handsome, with his brown skin, his long warrior hair—both the poet and the con man.

I had hoped he would fall in love with me. Now, I thank God that didn't happen. He got pneumonia and then got diagnosed with HIV. I wonder how long he had it before the diagnosis.

Did he know? Did he suspect? How many women did he lie to? How many? He lied to me on that one day that we had plans to have sex. Boy, that sounds cold, which it was. I soon realized he thought of it as a "mercy fuck," that he was doing me a one-time favor. It's sad to say, but on that day, I was willing to participate.

"Yes," he said, "I get tested regularly, yes, I am clean."

I had known him for a few months at that point. Even though I'd seen him juggle several women who didn't know about each other, even after he asked me to watch Aurora while he went on a date, even when I realized he was counting on Aurora to keep his secrets, I wanted to be with him. So naive. So, he decided to let me have my turn. He came to my massage office one afternoon when I had no appointments. I turned the sign to "Closed" and locked the door. I had worn my best black underwear that day and made sure I smelled like roses and sandalwood. We took off our clothes and laid down on a blanket I had spread on the floor. He kissed me a few times. We touched and tasted each other, then he lost interest and got up to get dressed. As I looked at him, wondering what in hell was going on, he said, "This was a bad idea. I'll see you outside on the steps." I put my clothes back on and rushed to the bathroom. I did not want him to hear me cry. I splashed my face with cold water in an attempt to stop the tears and the embarrassment, then I met him outside where we sat on the steps. He gave me a soulful look with those beautiful eyes, then he dropped the giant nuclear bomb. "You are too fat. I will never be in love with you because you are fat." There it was. One of my biggest fears, one of the things that fat people get told. He will never love me because I am too fat. "And neither will anyone else," he added. That hit smack dab in the middle of the target on my heart. What? When later I learned of the HIV, I decided there had been some form of divine intervention and that my life had been saved by our putting our clothes back on. Years later, thirteen since I met him, at his funeral, I could still hear his voice saying those words. Even now, I occasionally—okay, more that occasionally—still believe him. No one will ever fall in love with me because I am too fat. So far, he has been right. Damn him. If I believed in hell, this is where I know I would find him now.

The hard part of the funeral was seeing Aurora—his daughter, the daughter of my heart. I tried to reach out to her. She was in shock and seemingly didn't want comfort from me. I can understand it, but it still hurt. She had been living with a new family for some time at that point, and they had gathered tightly around her. Again, I can understand and was happy she had that love and support, but I was full of regret about our relationship fading.

I can still see her, too, when I first met them after placing a personals ad in the Portland weekly paper. I was looking for a man with strong spiritual beliefs. Her dad brought her along on our first meet-up, which was at a playground. She was four years-old, so sassy and smart, with those big eyes,. As soon as I met her, I knew she was special. Right away, I saw something in her, felt something in my heart and was willingly captured by this charming girl.

I grew to love her so deeply, and she became the daughter of my heart.

It became clear even before the "trying to have sex" event at the massage office that Tom and I were not destined to be a thing. I continued to love Aurora and spent as much time with her as I could. When she was young, I would go to their house and watch Disney Princess movies over and over and over. She loves to sing, has a striking voice, and, of course, knew all the words to all the songs. Soon, I did too, and we would both sing along. We would also watch her video of her mom, the only part of her she has left. When I met Aurora, she was separated from her mother and they were not allowed to see each other. About a year later, her mother died of a drug overdose. Aurora also knew every word her mother said on that video and would join in speaking along with her. For years, every time I came over, she would get out the video and we would solemnly watch it together. Sometimes, when she came to my house, she brought it with her. I hope she still has it.

Over the years, I delighted in taking her clothes shopping. We had packfuls of fun together, and it helped me heal a bit from the anger and trauma of my childhood clothes shopping with my mother. Her dad wouldn't always be happy with our choices and sometimes flew into a rage, demanding that I take them back. Aurora could usually talk him out of that.

She traveled with me. We tackled homework together. We toured museums and art shows. I sent her to summer camp. I attended her school performances and loved being at Family Day. I knew some of her friends, and she knew some of mine. It was a lovely relationship until her dad got sick. Then, what was left of her family circled around her, and it got more difficult to see her. I had been thinking of moving to California to be with some friends, and after it became more complicated to be with Aurora, I didn't have any strong reasons to stay in Oregon. After the move, I tried to stay in touch, but here we are today. So distant. I'm heartbroken. She didn't even hug me when I said goodbye. I know she was deep in grief. I get that. Maybe time will change this. I hope as she grows older, she thinks of me with love and happiness for all that we had. When my friends talk about how much I did for her, I always come back with how much she has given me. It feels as if I won't see her again, but I will reach out and see.

I had confusion about Tom for many years because he left me this dual legacy—one of deep love for his daughter and subsequent regrets about not seeing her, and another of deep anger towards him, part of which got turned towards myself. It took me some hard work to forgive myself for my hopes and wishes about him.

Saturday afternoon, phone call with Mr. Flannel

Tom: Good afternoon, Charity.

Charity: Hi, Tom

T: I find I am not needed for the work project on Sunday, just my regular few hours. I know it is rather late notice, but I don't think I want to go to the movies. I'm wondering if you'd like to have some supper instead.

C: I'm glad you don't have to go in. I know you don't work a lot of hours, but it's nice for you to have a day off. Supper sounds good to me. We can go to the movies another day. Where shall we eat?

T: I quite enjoyed that restaurant we went to last time, how about you? Would you like to go there?

C: Sure. I seem to remember we both enjoyed our meals.

T: That we did. Shall I come pick you up at 6?

C: Great, thanks. Though, if it's easier, we could meet there.

T: No, I'll come get you.

C: You know, this is an interesting thing about our friendship, letting you do things for me. When I was younger, being a feminist meant doing everything myself, being tough and independent. I never wanted men to help me. "I can do it myself, thank you." Now, I don't want to be so tough. I know I am independent, and I know when I need help and when I don't. It's not really about help, is it? It's about care and respect.

T: I see what you are saying. I was brought up to do those things, and I always have, but I don't feel obligated. It has nothing to do with thinking you can't do something.

C: I know. I get that and appreciate it.

T: I enjoy it.

C: Sorry to cut you off but I need to go. I'll see you tomorrow. I'm looking forward to it.

T: As am I. Have a good day.

Sunday, after dinner and tea with Tom

That was nice. The food was okay. Not really a ringing endorsement! Tom's an interesting guy. He just doesn't really care about food that much. I know a few people like that, and it seems so odd to me.

Tom doesn't like me to praise or compliment him. Tonight, after he told me about his family and their difficulties, I commended him for the hard work he has done on himself. When I saw him shudder a bit, scrunch up his nose, and purse his lips, I knew he was rejecting my offering. He then followed with a change of subject, turning it back to me. It's kind of like pulling teeth. As for me, maybe I'm too open and share more than he can handle. Neither one of us has been married or had a long-term relationship, so we haven't had much practice in this getting to know each other and sharing stuff.

Sometimes I can push the compliments away also. I will take them in to a point, but then I start thinking, "Please don't give me all this attention!" There are times I like to shine in the spotlight, but overall, I don't want to be made the focus of the conversation. I hope I don't get that odd expression on my face the way he does. Humility is one thing, and low self-esteem is another; sometimes they are easily mixed up. I haven't entirely decided which applies to Tom. Or to myself at times, for that matter. Relationship really is a fascinating mirror.

I dig having someone to talk with though, even though there are awkward or difficult moments. From time to time, I do get lonely. The conversation doesn't have to be deep and important. I hope we have time to grow our friendship into something strong and long-lived, not romantic, but close and based on love and kindness.

Sometimes I think the part about accepting his "care" of me, his respect and politeness, is the key to why we are spending time

It's Hard to Hug a Fat Person   60

together. I'm over the "don't do it for me because I can do it for myself" stuff. Okay, maybe not over it entirely. I'm still working the actual asking for help. I appreciate his helping me in the car and the way he walks on the street side of the sidewalk. Who knew I had that in me?

Thinking of the two Toms stirs up emotions that I like to keep dormant. I don't like looking back at my whole life and seeing what I *didn't* have, when the focal points become the lack of a loving relationship, a romance, a husband.

Do I still even have room for romance? Sometimes I wonder. Sometimes I'm just plain not interested, and sometimes I just give up. It's easy for some people to say, "There is someone out there for you." Or, "Keep working on yourself and he will come." Or, "Being friends with Tom is pushing away an opportunity for someone else to come in." All that makes me feel that not being in a relationship is all *my* fault, that *I'm* doing something wrong, or that I *am* something wrong. Just saying that brings tears and that old ache in my heart. Okay, that's an old, old story that, thank the Goddesses, is being re-written. I'm so not in the mood to start feeling sorry for myself, or to think about this more tonight. We had a good time, I've had a really good day.

Tina, come snuggle with me. Let's get cozy. Thank you for being nice to Tom. He's not a pet person, but he was okay with you. How can someone *not* be a pet person? My heart broke a little when Tom told me that he's never had a pet. I feel badly for people who've not experienced that love, both the receiving and the giving. We learn a lot about affection and devotion from our pets that we really can't learn from anyone else. I've never *not* had a pet, except for in college. Well, there was that time, sophomore year, when I found a cat. I got busted by the dorm security people for having her in my room, and I had to figure out what to do. During spring break, I snuck that cat home on the plane. If I had hidden her in my dorm room for a few weeks, surely I could get her on the plane, right?

The silly cat pokes her head out of my bag just as we are boarding. The flight attendants notice, of course. After petting her, they inform me this is not allowed. Oh really? I have a cat in my purse? I guess I did know that. They actually did let me on the plane with her, in spite of the rules. That was way back in the day. Flying was so different then. There weren't as many seats on the plane. Had they done away with smoking sections by the time I was in college? What a joke! You could be in the non-smoking section, and the people right behind you were in the smoking section. There was no security, no fuss. Bags were smaller and everything fit. But, in general, pets in purses were still not encouraged. When my parents picked me up at the airport, I had to explain to them why I was showing up at their house with a cat in my purse that they were going to have to take care of for me. I knew they would do it.

Monday morning 8 am, Facebook Messenger

Charity: Hi, honey. Good morning.

Hannah: Hey, good morning to you too. How was dinner with Tom yesterday?

C: We had a nice time. Not spectacular, but nice. Nice was okay. Thanks for asking. I hope soon you'll get to meet him. He's into Shakespeare, goes to a monthly read-aloud group, so we talked about that. Not that I know a lot, but my expensive liberal arts education helped me hold my own. My mom would have been proud.

He doesn't seem inclined yet to invite me to his house. "Extremely messy," he says—messier than mine. That, in a weird way, made me feel proud, recognizing I am pretty comfortable having people over. There have been many years when I wasn't— plenty of shame and depression. His comment takes the pressure off of me. No need to get obsessive about cleaning before he comes over. What's new with you?

H: Nothing new. I've just been working a lot. Some interesting jobs right now. I'm learning and doing some new things on the computer, challenging my brain some. Finally making some money.

C: Great. You needed that. I've been a little worried about you and your money flow, that whole scene.

H: Yeah, I've been worried too. These are challenging times for graphic design. I feel like my creative juices are flowing again, finally. When the work dries up, so does the creativity sometimes.

C: Yay! I agree with you. I could use some help getting mine going a little more strongly. I read something in an email recently about needing to go to the creativity gym. Needing to keep those muscles—the creativity muscles, the artistic muscles—exercised and flexible. Keeping them fed and worked. It does sort of seem that the less you use that creative impulse or drive, the harder it is to get back, just like with the actual muscles of the body.

H: Man, that's true. True about a lot, I think. Makes me want to ponder other gyms I could go to, other "muscles" I could work out.

C: Such as?

H: Hmm, the tolerance gym? Haha. Not really funny though. Lots of people need to work on those muscles. It might be pretty crowded in there. How about the patience gym? That might be too much work. I'm not sure that is a skill or a muscle that can be developed. You have it or you don't. Is that true of tolerance too? Can it be learned?

C: That patience gym would be pretty crowded too. We'd get to practice our patience waiting to get in! I recently learned that in Japanese, those words are the same—tolerance and patience—meaning something like "putting up with." Isn't that interesting? I do think tolerance and patience can be learned. I've seen folks for example who grew up being told that gay people are wrong, for example. Later in life, they meet and make friends with someone gay and do a complete 180.

H: Okay, true. I guess my feelings about that are colored by the daily horrors of our political world where tolerance seems to be disappearing rapidly. I don't have hope for some of those folks, or for He-whose-name-shall-not-be-mentioned.

C: Oy, let's not go down that road today.

H: How about you? Have any great gym ideas?

C: I wanna go to the love gym. LOL.

H: God, not me.

C: Ha, I know that. I meant the open-heart kind of love gym. Going to the love gym, get on the love train. Remember that song? "Love Train"? The O'Jays?

H: Sort of, not my kind of music. From the 70's, right? I was more into rock.

C: It might have been the 60's. Well, I'm off. Just wanted to check in and wish you a good day, make sure you know how important you are to me. Thanks. I love you.

H: You are important to me too, and I love you too.

My day gets off to a great start when it begins with a chat with Hannah. We truly are each other's solid support system. I think we've known each other for twenty years. Sisters on the Shamanic path, as we say. She is right here for me and I am there for her, and will be into the future. There, here—same thing. Lucky. Important. Blessed.

Okay, now I gotta put on some music. Me and that old soul music, Motown, old school R&B. Love Train. "Soul Train"! I loved that show—me, a little fat midwestern white girl trying out those moves. But, I was born in Detroit, so that there must be Motown in my blood. Here's a little Smokey Robinson. Ahh, *the way you do the things you do*…Let's dance, Tina.

Got Momentum?

It's been a little more than a year since I completed a year-long artist immersion program here in Santa Cruz called "Momentum." It required a considerable commitment of time and energy, and it pushed me forward, turned me upside down, and shook me up. I came out of it with a great love of writing, confidence, and a new spirit of adventure. I stepped into creativity and found my inner Artist.

Since then, I have been writing poetry. I have taken some gorgeous photos. I am taking piano lessons from one of my friends in the Momentum group. I have remembered how important it is to take time to make art, to make it fun, and embrace the process.

We ended the year with a public performance of our various projects. During the year, I finished up and almost completed the publishing process of a book, invigorated this blog, and remembered my love of dancing.

Here is the talk I gave on that closing night:

So, here I stand to tell you about my book, *Though The Fire, Cooking Our Way Into a New Relationship With Food.*

I want to start by telling you about a conversation I had in the last few weeks with a well-meaning, long-time friend. I was catching her up on some things that have been going on for me. A (different) close friend and I were not getting along, and this had put me in a challenging emotional place, feeling *way* too many emotions. Shockingly to me, I reverted to my old habits of eating my emotions and gained some weight. I have been upset about this and experiencing a lot of shame around the fact that I *still* have this way of coping. She commented, "You'd better get your shit together because the book is coming out. You need to stand up in front of people, look good, and sound good if you want to be taken seriously."

I knew that, to her, this meant I'd better lose some of that weight. I thought about her comment, knowing that she meant it in a loving way. I'm about to turn 65, and this is not the first time I have heard thoughts like these. I have logged a lifetime of those conversations, many of which have been with myself! Who am I to stand here and talk about eating and food? Well, I happen to think that I, saggy belly, shit not together, am exactly the person to talk about it.

We human beings are still an experiment. It doesn't take someone perfect to help someone else. I know what it is like to hate my body and my life. I know what it is like to eat a whole bag of cookies. I know what it is like to have people be disgusted by me, AND I know what it's like to push people away because I feel that I am disgusting. I know what it's like not to fit in, both literally and figuratively.

In this program, we heard and talked often about shining the light on darkness, about playing in the light. After my year in Momentum, this is what my writing is about. It is about shining that light in those dark places, those scary places inside me, inside us. Shame can't live in the light. Ignorance and intolerance don't live in the light. Love lives in the light, and in honesty. Acceptance lives in the light.

So, while I soon will have a book, and I have videos and writings to show for my year in Momentum, what I've just told you might just be the most powerful thing I am taking with me. I am a writer and a storyteller. I am becoming a Crone and I have much to offer you. I'm not perfect. I don't want to be perfect. I am growing and blossoming, playing in the light and telling my story. My work is to help myself and to support others on the same road."

Later that morning

Mmm, I'm hungry. In the mood for what? I've got some sweet cravings this morning. Crackers, butter, and jam. No protein in that mix, but right now, I don't care. That's what I want. Now I sound like a little kid. "I want what I want." The teenager then chimes in and says, "Fuck you, I'm having it." Either have it and enjoy it or don't have it. I'm going to have it—put it on a nice plate, take my time, enjoy every bite. Maybe have some almond butter too. I've got high-quality gluten-free crackers, organic pasture butter, homemade jam. Not a thing wrong with any of that. Something to drink. Breathing and relaxing. The sun is out. It's warm enough to eat outside.

From my writing notebook

Here comes Appetite again
What to do?
It's too early to go to bed, too late to eat
Just thinking that makes me hungry
No
but…
What do I want?
Sweet? Salty?
Am I just thirsty?
I don't really need any food.
Need/Want
Lots of therapy trying to figure those two things out

Food is not a dirty word.
Everyone eats

"Ah yes, but do you have to eat so much? say the Critics.
You eat enough for several people sometimes
 It's rather disgusting
You don't seem to know when it's enough

and really, you should eat less"

Appetite answers,
  "oh no
  More is better
  Too much is even better
  I'm the boss of you
  I'm the king of this hill!
  Just try to get me off my throne
  Come on, what you got?"

I got nothing today
I'm so tired and kind of sad
I need peace and quiet

  Appetite says,
  "I think you need cookies
  They will pep you up
  Just for today, don't worry about the ingredients.
  Cookies will fill you up, make you happy
  Forget about your troubles
  Come on, you know you want them
  Chocolate"

No, thank you

  "Thatta girl, say the Critics
  We know we are right
  and are glad you see the light.
  It's about time you listened to us.
  Uh oh, wait, what are you doing?
  Stop!"

  "But, cookies, says the Inner Child
  Cookies, all for me.
  I want them.
  My favorite.

Don't say no."

"Right on, says Appetite
You're such a pretty girl
too bad about the fat but you can worry about that later" part.

The Critics applaud the comment about the fat but the Child cries at their tone of voice.

"Fuck, yeah! Says Rebel Chick
Remember when you used to get stoned and eat cookies all night?
That was awesome".

The Critics aren't quite sure they like the language but applaud the sentiment.

What? what happened?
I don't want these cookies.
Stop!
I said no.

Inner Child reaches out her hands
"Please?
I'll be a good girl tomorrow"

Appetite chuckles about the being good tomorrow.

Damn it, go away
I said I didn't want any
Why don't you believe me?

The Critics chime in again with "Bravo!"
The Child says, "I want them!"
The Critics tell her, "Go to bed."

Rebel Chick groans. "Come on old lady, let's party!"

I wish you would all go away and leave me alone

"Nope, these are yours
take them or leave them
(as if you could)
Sure you will have remorse
and yes, heartburn
There will be crying
Do I know my girl or what?
So...
Are you in or out?"

In! says the Kid
Out! say the Critics
In! says Rebel Chick
In! says Appetite with a big grin
and a flash, bang, boom
I'm left bereft with an empty bag and some crumbs
all alone and quiet again

From a friend's Facebook page

"Unleash your grace upon this world and make no apologies for who you are...Become enamored with your intensity. Fall in love with your determination. Look into yourself, look into your-self, wherever you turn." -Matt Kahn

What a beautiful quote! This takes me back to the other day on Facebook, that conversation about not having to defend my feelings about myself. No defending, no apologizing. Cool. Where is my intensity? Inner intensity and the intensity of thoughts and emotions abound in me. But only occasionally do they work their way outward. That's something I'm trying to learn from Hannah. There is a place of balance somewhere between the two of us, between my being too laid back and her being so busy. Not that busy and intense are the same thing. Hannah's ability to stay focused on the task at hand and get shit done is powerful.

I'm scared of being intense. I'm scared of falling in love with my determination. Better to fly under the radar and anticipate failure. Although, really—is that better? After all these years, I am remembering that failure is what was expected of me as a child from my parents and grandparents. I can hear my mother introducing her three children: "This is our older son, our artist. This is our younger son, and he's our little genius. And this is Charity, our sweet little girl."

In high school, I knew I would not amount to much. My teacher, Agnes, at boarding school, let me know frequently that I was not living up to my potential, but she never offered any help or support in getting there. A sweet girl with few talents. I certainly know now that I have many talents and skills, and I truly value my sweetness. But, still sometimes, there are those days when I feel myself shrink and just become one big apology.

"Unapologetically unleashing my grace." Unapologetically! I have spent a great deal of my life believing I had nothing to unleash and much to apologize for. Nothing that could come roaring out, nothing that would make a difference.

9 pm, bedtime

Come on Tina. I'm so tired, come with me. Please. Of course not, when I need you, see how you are. Cats. Phooey on you.

Ahh, a good day. I did well today.

Great Spirit, thank you with all of my heart for my life. I am blessed and lucky. So grateful for all I have. I had an interesting day, full of grace and love.

Friday morning

I'm thinking about food, thinking about nourishment and nutrition. Thinking about the upcoming Ayurvedic cleanse I decided to do. Food is more than just the sum of its nutrients. It's nourishment, and it's meant to make us feel good. Humans are the only animals who actually get pleasure from food. Yet, look at how many of us deny ourselves that pleasure. It's only been in recent years—truthfully since my mom died—that I have considered the idea seeking pleasure in my everyday life through eating.

From changing up my diet with Ayurveda, writing that blog post, and talking with my Ayurveda practitioner Talya, I've come to realize that I need more nourishment from my food. Ayurveda is so complex. I'm trying not to view it as yet another "diet." Nourishment is, at its core, not just nutrition. Nourishment from warm foods, both in temperature and spice. Nourishment from easy digestion. I've somehow moved away from cooking a bit, so now is a good time to return to all the additional preparations of soaking grains and nuts, longer cooking times, and using multiple layers of spices. That will bring nourishment, some joy and pleasure, and creativity into my life.

I could actually pull out some cookbooks from my very large collection. Time to cull a few again, I think. The last time I tried, I was not so successful. I think I was willing to let go of one. Ha! It felt so satisfying to recycle all those paper copies of recipes I had for my personal chef business, since I didn't need them anymore. I don't miss the hard work of that job, but I do miss the creative side of it. I got such satisfaction from figuring out the menus, finding recipes, working with my people on what they wanted, and helping them fill out my questionnaire that included questions about their food preferences, their history with food, and if they had any sort of health goals related to my cooking for them. I had that job for about 8 years. It was fizzling out just about the same time as my body's joints were telling me it was getting too hard to schlep all that stuff around and stand at the stove for so many hours.

I remember those sweet potato patties I used to make for the people up on the big hill. I've forgotten their names, but boy, did they have a great kitchen and a fabulous view of the ocean. I cooked in their guest house kitchen. Truly wealthy people, vegetarians, lots of children, several of whom I cooked for a few times. Those patties, "Krishna cakes," are delicious, nourishing, and Ayurveda-friendly. Sunflower seeds, coconut, ginger, jalapeño, cumin, coriander, cinnamon, nutmeg, miso, coconut flour, red onion, coconut oil. Okay, I'd better go shopping. I'll get those ingredients. Tina says don't forget cat food. As if.

That evening, on Facebook

A post from the Curvy Confidence Coach:

"YOU'RE NOT BROKEN...AS MUCH AS IT MIGHT FEEL LIKE IT SOMETIMES. Maybe when you think you're broken and you feel like you're on a never-ending track of trying to "fix yourself," consider instead that you're actually BRAVE for being willing to peel back the layers of what isn't really you and do the work of discovering your most authentic self...You can be enough as you are, and still be working towards another possibility of who you might be. You are allowed to be both a masterpiece and a work in progress at the same time."

Those last two lines are the important part! I wish I had written that. I can be enough as I am. I am enough as I am. I can be a masterpiece *and* a work in progress at the same time. I am able and allowed to love myself and work towards change at the same time.

Yes! Go! Do! Love! I'm channeling my inner cheerleader. I need her. Thankfully, I don't think I ever felt left out because I wasn't a cheerleader. I was always sort of disrespectful towards those girls, thinking them shallow. They were too pretty. Much of the time, I liked being different, being an outsider. Other times, depending on my age or my interests at the time, I wanted to be one of them. It did at times get confusing. I was in a Girl Scout troop for seven years with mostly the same girls, so we went through lots of changes together. In seventh grade, some of the more popular girls—cheerleaders, at the top of the social ladder—formed a club. The "I Hate BethAnn Curry" club, it was called. How cruel and awful is that? Well, BethAnn and I shared the bottom of that social ladder in our Girl Scout troop—me because of my weight, BethAnn due to her family's economic status. To my amazement, those girls asked me to join their club. Wow. A chance to be in with the in crowd. So, I said "yes." As members, we each had to call her anonymously on the phone and make fun of her, tell her "I hate you." It is to my extreme regret that I did this. As soon as I hung up the phone, I cried and cried. I gave her a note in school the next day and apologized, asking her to eat lunch with me. When the other girls saw me, that was the end of my very brief rise in social status.

My whole life, I've felt broken; I've felt that something was inherently wrong with me. I've felt unfixable. Because of this, I learned to numb myself, to not feel my body at all. I learned to ignore any sort of signals my body was sending me such as problems from overeating, changes in my digestion, or pain. I learned to numb my emotions as well. I don't really know how I learned to push it all away. It must have been difficult and painful. Even now it can be hard to connect the two, and my emotions will manifest somewhere in my body.

I am so grateful that those "broken" feelings are waning. Still, there at the core, they come out to play sometimes, come out of the dank and the dark. That damn dank dark! During my years of focusing my therapy on the sexual abuse, I did a lot of hypnotherapy. I had a very strong image of myself being the worst pile of dog shit imaginable. Rotten, moldy, putrid. Session by session, the pile got smaller and smaller, less vivid, less stinky. There's really just the tiniest of pieces left there. The dark places have gotten smaller and smaller too. When some comment or event triggers me, the shadows grow, the dankness grows, the shit grows. If I have a bad day, the pile says, "Of course you did, you piece of dog shit." If my joints hurt, it says, "Of course they do. You are dog shit, don't forget. Smelly. Disgusting." On and on. It's enough. I am enough. Oh yes, I have things to work on, but I'm not broken.

What's really fascinating is what triggers it most often is not being hurt in some way, but feeling positive, happy, or focused. Wearing a new dress and hearing, "Oh Charity, you look so pretty today!" can do it. Daring to have hope, daring to look forward, daring to dream. "How dare you?" says the pile of shit. "Don't forget me, I'm still here."

I do dare. Every day is a new day, and I get out of bed and do my best. Each day that I can, I shine my brightest light into that dankness and say, "No." I say no to thinking I am disgusting and unworthy of any kind of love or hope or kindness. I say no to the pain of the past. I say yes to being present with my emotions and feeling alive in my body, no matter how I feel about it that day. So, tomorrow I will do that. I will go dancing. I will start my cleanse. I will dare.

Saturday morning, dancing

I'm wearing blue for the ocean, for the depths, for the yin today. I'm feeling more inwardly focused, honoring the depth of my emotions and their wisdom. I'm lying on the floor, stretching. Cold, hard, honey-colored wood. Many feet have danced on this floor. Even though I have all this padding, it hurts to lie here after a while. I feel my spine wanting to stretch. I lie on my back with my arms overhead, making myself as long as I can. I feel my ankles, which are a bit swollen today. Turning them in circles feels like it will get the fluid moving as well as the rest of me. I am happy to be here but feel a little shy. It's a challenge for me to relax in public, to let myself feel safe down here where it's hard for me to get up, but I do, because I am ready to move around in a bigger way. I can't do it in a hurry, nor do I look graceful in the process. I dare myself. Am I afraid right now? No. Feel unsafe? No. Feel vulnerable? Yes. Vulnerable is okay. Those emotions are powerful to work with. Feel. Vulnerable and safe at the same time. There's that masterpiece/work in progress thing again. No one is out to make fun of me or make me nervous. People aren't paying any attention to me at all, for the most part. That's why we are here, to be with ourselves.

Now I'm wandering around the dance floor, walking at first, swaying my hips and arms to the beat. I'm a "better" dancer from my waist down. I'm never quite sure what to do with my arms. Mmm, my hips want to move around, remembering those belly dance classes I took so long ago. Memories of ancient tribal times. Inside, I'm moving like a snake, undulating. Not sure what it looks like on the outside. I close my eyes and don't care.

Afternoon, waiting for meeting with my cleanse leader and group

Today's the first day of the cleanse; so far so good. I've got that first day anxiety/hunger. I don't want this to feel too much like a diet. I'm not about losing weight, though that might happen. It's only a week, and hopefully it will kickstart some basic changes. Memories are emerging of the old diet days, the old starvation/deprivation days—the days of the fad diets. I was there either pushed into them by my mom or sucked into them on my own. Even now, sometimes when I eat a hard-boiled egg, I can remember the times I did the "hard-boiled egg and grapefruit" diet. That was all you ate for the first two meals, then you had a somewhat regular dinner. One of the summers in high school, my mom found Metracal, one of the first commercial liquid diet/meal substitute drinks. I drank a can for breakfast and lunch, then ate some sort of "regular" dinner. I can't remember much, but it smelled and tasted like chemicals. It was disgusting. My mother was thrilled to discover it for me. I imagine I lost a few pounds, which I gained back in the following weeks. In my twenties, on my own, I tried "the drinking man's diet" (not that I needed an excuse to drink alcohol). This one was very high in protein and fat, plus it included a glass of whiskey every night. You were actually "allowed" to eat a bowl of whipped cream! Of course, there also were the sensible diets prescribed by doctors and the big-name programs. I never lost any weight on the crazier ones.

I've lost and gained hundreds of pounds over the years. Sometimes I lost up to 75 pounds, and one time I lost 100. That was one my most recent and last stint at Weight Watchers. I maintained the loss only briefly. Slowly, over the 10 years since, it's almost all been put back on. I don't know for sure what I weigh now. I had a knee replacement in 2012, and they had to weigh me to get the correct dose for anesthesia, but I asked them not to tell me the number. Other than that, I haven't been on a scale since. Back in those intense diet days, I would weigh myself many times a day. Get up and weigh myself. Pee and weigh myself. I ate breakfast, then stepped on the scale. If and when I pooped, I would weigh myself afterwards. Middle of the day, I would weigh myself. I followed this routine day after day. I made myself crazy, and it was not useful.

The memories of punishing myself either with excess food or not enough food have put me on edge. Will I get enough food this week? Did I do something bad to deserve having my food restricted? That comes straight from childhood memories. I find it so incredible that all those voices and feelings are still there. That's why the mantra of coming from a place of love, of self-care, of nourishment is so important. Instead of looking at this process as a punishment, I want to look at changing my eating as a gift to myself. It's all about love and kindness, peace of mind.

It turns out that this cleanse is about all of that. The approach is that of love and kindness. Being adventuresome and trying new things. Our goal is not so much about what we *cannot* do but what can we add to our diet and our daily routines that will help us feel good. I have a booklet of recipes and will be adding in more lentils and some grains, lots of pungent spices such as cardamom, turmeric, and cumin, and using grapefruit and coriander essential oils in my daily body care practices. I'm into it.

Later that evening

What an eventful day. Dancing, meeting my fellow cleansers at the health food store, and starting the cleanse. I feel nourished in my body, heart, and spirit.

Thank you, Gods. Thank you for giving me the courage to look at myself with love and kindness. I'm grateful that I'm not sore. I'm grateful that I have the freedom and the means to get to choose what, how, and when I eat. I'm grateful for being willing to make changes in my life when it's not flowing.

3 am, waking from a dream

Oy! Here it is, 3 in the morning again, and I'm peeing like mad. At least I made it to the bathroom. I need to remember this dream. It's an important one. Here you are, Tina, you woke up too? You're my sweet girl. No dream cats this time, sorry.

I'm in Yellowstone, in the lake. Only, this time, it's warm, or warmish. Oh my God, that water was so cold last year. I yearn to actually be able to swim there, to float around surrounded by those snow-capped mountains and look up at the Big Sky.

Perhaps one day I'll return to Montana, to that place. Anyway, I'm in the lake. I have a fabulous red bathing suit on and the same body I have now. I'm paddling around, wondering if I will encounter fish. I don't. Two bald eagles fly overhead and circle around a few times, doing that circle dance they do with the thermals. I turn over and float, watching them. The ranger comes and orders me out. He tells me that swimming is not allowed. I don't want to believe him. Is this a new Presidential Order? I feel myself getting pissed off and wake up. Damn, I wish I could have continued so I could have had it out with that Ranger or at least gotten more information.

Oh, I could really feel the coolness and freshness of that water. Nourishing, cleansing. Those eagles. I could see them really clearly. That's a wonderful thing about dreams. I didn't need my glasses. Eagles have profound meaning to me and to the Shamanic traditional path I now follow. Grandmother Eagle Goddess. She gives us the breath of life. And eagles have that glorious ability to see great distances. Up above, they see the whole picture. I know I can get stuck in the small things and forget to widen my focus. Ignoring the ranger business, perhaps it's time to just float and take in what's around me.

Sunday morning

Cleanse day two. I'm having my lemon-ghee-cinnamon drink. It's tasty, though I realize cinnamon is not on the list of acceptable foods. Ugh, I don't even want to use that word "acceptable." Too diet-y. Oh well. I've got some soup for when I'm ready. Pushing the liquids, cleansing the kidneys. Moving stagnation, moving the junk.

I get such pleasure from my Sunday morning routine—a *New York Times* crossword puzzle, albeit last week's. Two weeks ago, I finished it! Not gonna happen this week. I'm about a third of the way through, and I am totally stuck. I'm putting it away for now. I might go back to it, or I might not. *That* is a way I differ from Mama. Not being able to stand leaving a puzzle unfinished, she would work and work, swear at it, grit her teeth. Every once in a while, she would call me to ask me about one of the clues she thought I might know. Unlike her, I am willing to toss it if it's not fun. I'm the same with books, television shows, movies. I don't need to know the answers or the ending. For Mom, the crossword wasn't about fun. It was about competing with her own mother who finished it every week in *pen*! Thanks Mama for introducing me to the erasable pen. It looks as if I *can* do it in permanent ink, which is fun to show off on those occasions I take a photo of my results and post them on Facebook.

I admit, I inherited the crossword gene from some pros, and so I occasionally feel pressured by the puzzle. I resisted the lure of the *New York Times* puzzle for years as a rebellion against that gene. But I couldn't hold out! The force is strong. Plus, as I get older, I know I need the exercise for my brain. The puzzles start out easy on Mondays, getting progressively harder as the week goes by, with Saturday being the most difficult. The Sunday puzzle is hard and larger than the others. I pretty much stick to Monday through Wednesday and Sunday. I manage to finish the Sunday puzzle only every few months. But I keep trying.

Crossword puzzles were something Mama and I could do together, a neutral ground, as it were. I'm so glad I can tap into happy memories. During some visits, or when we were traveling, we would take turns filling out the answers that we knew, asking each other for help and passing it back and forth across the breakfast table.

9:30 pm, home from a Ralph Towner concert, getting ready for bed
That was great music! He is so talented—awe-inspiring really. I had a wonderful time with Tom. I like that he is a little more open now, and so am I. During the concert, I asked if it was okay to put my arm around him. He said it was. We had a sweet hug goodnight, with a quick friendly kiss on the lips. Even with his strong beliefs about intimacy, he is a fabulous hugger. Solid and steady, he can hold a hug for a long time.

I'm not as bothered by his facial hair as I thought I would be. Those old abuse memories are not so devastating anymore. Grandfather's painful bristly mustache. Scratchy. Itchy. Rough. Of course, it went places on my little girl's body that no mustache should go. When those memories emerged in my thirties, I amended my list of what I had been looking for in a partner, adding "no facial hair."

Now, here's Tom with a full beard *and* a mustache. Fortunately, he takes consistent care of them, keeping them clean and trimmed. Neither is scratchy or rough. The first time our faces touched, I was astonished, having been afraid of the moment because of those Grandfather memories. I felt the same thing when we first had our goodnight kiss on the cheek, though the moment was so brief there wasn't any time to process it. But later, I was so relieved that it hadn't scared me or grossed me out.

Jen, who rents the back part of my house, and I sat in the sun together today, sharing stories of men in our lives. She asked me about Mr. Flannel, and I told her about last night. The subject of Tom from long ago came up, and it got interesting comparing the two Toms.

That's another way my relationship with *this* Tom is so healing, so welcoming. I'm changing the stories—stories of men with mustaches, stories of men named Tom. The first Tom was twenty-seven years ago. Good God. I thought I was in love. I'm oh-so-glad I have changed my idea of what love and relationship looks and feels like, about what I want and need, what I want it to feel like. What is possible.

I told Jen some of the story of Tom and Aurora, about what a womanizer Tom was, and about how things unfolded between us. It brought a mess of the old emotions and I started to cry. She hugged me and burst out with, "He said what? What an asshole!"

Damn, I believed him. Did it make me lose weight? I think that was part of his goal in telling me, beyond the simply being cruel part – the idea that he thought it would be helpful for me to know what *all* men thought, which he knew because after all he was in a men's group! He had already been telling me I should go to Overeaters Anonymous.

It did my heart good to hear Jen get so angry at First Tom. My life is so different now. The memories of the abuse from my grandfather are not as clear as the more recent events with Tom Number One, but all of those memories have lost some charge. I continue to move on and find my confidence, my pride, and my femininity. I'm showing those old bastards that they didn't ruin me. Grandfather's been dead for a long time, and I'm still here. First Tom is dead, and I'm still here. While no man has fallen in love with me (yet), I no longer believe it to be true that no one will just because I am fat. And, if no one comes along, I know that my life is rich and at times glorious.

And isn't it so interesting that present-day Tom doesn't want to have sex with me either? But in this case, the story is entirely different. It's about *him,* his needs. I got to go to a fabulous concert with a lovely, hairy man who treats me with respect and kindness. Awesome. Just breathe that in for a while, girl. Let in the gratitude, let go of what needs to go.

From my writing notebook
Memories of men

I have held love in my arms.

first kiss
stolen kisses,
I want to kiss you everywhere
love letters
I can't wait to see you again
long ago love

The truth - there isn't much in that treasure chest
but treasures there are
Not all my memories are terrible.
It's the hope chest at the end of the bed
containing the yearnings and fashionings of a young woman.
sweetness for the elder to take out and remember
the tastes and smells of passion.
Hear the whispered words of love
Look at his exquisite face
as I touch those cheeks

Senior Year of high school

my sad-eyed poet, hair hanging
in his eyes
soft lips
Bruce, first to hold me with love
and eagerness of desire
What are these new feelings?
Dare I dream in color?
Boarding school held us within its walls - the occasional explora-
tion outside the boundaries
Lying in the grass, whispering and waiting
Full of hope

Off I went to college while he finished his senior year.
the letters flew back and forth!
Me in California, He in Pennsylvania

We survived a year then went to college in Wisconsin together
At last, free to discover,
to touch - first shyly then fiercely,
 to dive into that deep sea of emotion
and physicality,
 to fly high with our new wings.
Free to dance and sing and laugh

learning about love, learning about sex
not the grandfather, not the rapist
learning to be
body to body, heart to heart, soul to soul
finding the wild,
 the glorious,
tender and sweet
mingled with the heat of wanting so much

But
what happened?
so in love.
it got suffocating

Charity Dasenbrock   81

fear of letting go
fear of holding tight

Afraid of abandonment, I pushed him away.

Cruelly.
My blade was swift
 and merciless.
I was left bereft
wounded by my own hand
I pushed him away so he wouldn't.

Proactive
you might say.
As some women who discover they have a gene for breast cancer
get double mastectomies,

I Cut him out.
I ripped myself away from my first love
We had called each other soulmates
It was excruciating.
How was I to have known it would be so painful?
Deadly
Relentless
I never fully recovered from my own surgery

I saw him in San Francisco once some years later
on the bus
a chance meeting
We were confused.
 Speechless, it threw me off course
No numbers or plans were exchanged.

Therapy in my late twenties
I learned about orgasms
I had never had one

I didn't know I could.
Years later I would uncover reasons, but
would that have changed our time together?
He apparently didn't know that much either as the subject never
came up.

I found his address through school connections.
We weren't that far apart geographically.
I wrote and apologized for my cruelty.
He had moved on he said as he thanked me.
That was that.
It was supposed to make me feel better.
It took many years before it really did.
It took many years before I ever had an orgasm
 and even then, not with a partner.

Fast forward to around 2008
Facebook
Now in my mid 50's.
I get a message from him
Still geographically not so far.
How are you?
What have you been doing?
Would you like to get together?

We wrote back and forth for a while.
We talked on the phone
partly honest with each other,
both holding back something

He had a woman partner but they weren't sexually involved right
then
Her children hated him.
He was lonely.
(so was I)

Did I want to meet him?

We could have lunch by the water in Sausalito.

Memories got stirred up as we stumbled our way
Feelings got stirred up.
My one love
I had had sex with other men
No lovemaking or romance, no hopes and dreams since that boy
becoming a man filled me
Since I fed and filled him.

There had been dream killers and hope devourers.
There had been bad decisions
There had been violence and pain

Soulmate still? Were we ever?

I wondered if we could fall in love again. Could I dare to have
those deep feelings again? I wanted to find out.

The fumbling got a little more serious and some tentative plans
were made
As we continued towards each other
he asked what was I feeling?
He was ready to meet me.
Was I attracted?
Did I want to have sex?
no strings attached, no commitments, he was married.
He was struggling
 with bisexuality and anger.
He was starving
himself.
Flags went up
fiery red, deep blood red
I said no.

No.

Powerful
Necessary
Sad
Disappointment

We never did see each other
 and let go of being Facebook friends.
I once again let go of the hopes and dreams

I still sometimes see him in my mind, his big black glasses and his dark thick curly hair, reading me poetry.
Those beautiful lips.
I can feel that thrill when I found a letter from him in my mailbox.
I see us tangled up in his tiny single dormitory bed, no room for us to move apart, hoping his roommate would stay at the library a little longer.
Caught up in all that hope for the future, dreaming big, having all that energy and passion rolled up in sex and romance, in staying up all night, in wanting a better world, feeling young and carefree.
It was sweet and it was everything I had dreamed about as a girl.

My only love.
Now a memory folded carefully in that chest of hopes and dreams.

2:00 am

Awake! Thinking about Bruce, my boyfriend, his junior year and my senior year in high school. He was a poet and wrote me beautiful letters when I went off to college in California. I was not happy at Mills College, partly because I missed him, so I transferred to Beloit College in Wisconsin, where he had gotten accepted. Sadly, we broke up after being there together for six months or so. I haven't thought about him in a while, so I was surprised that I needed to write that poem. It has sure stirred up memories. Memories of Grandfather. I know it was because of his cruelty that I wasn't able to fall fully into that love with Bruce or anyone else. When I was with Bruce, I didn't know it was possible to find pleasure in sex. It is still hard for me to really let go, physically and emotionally: hard to go deep, let someone love me. I still have yet to have an orgasm with a partner. Well, even more, I haven't ever had a long-term partner as an adult.

These memories piss me off and bring up such grief. Here I am, thinking about how my relationship with Bruce fell apart. I got scared by the depth of it all. In our sweet first love innocence, we thought of each other as soulmates. Our conversations were deep and very emotional. Oh, we were so young. I loved him so much, more than I thought was possible. It frightened me that I could feel that way, that I could be that vulnerable—though I don't think I used that word. His feelings for me were more than I could bear. I just didn't trust that it was real. I felt like I was drowning or suffocating. It was beautiful, and it was awful. I was so cruel to him at the end. I just cut our relationship off in one night, in one horrible conversation. I was not logical. There was not any one thing I could point to that was wrong. Apparently, I just needed to metaphorically slash and cut him off at the balls. I reverted to the only way I knew. Like with Grandfather, when I threatened him with a kitchen knife. While I don't really remember many details of what my Grandfather did during those twelve years of sexual abuse, I do remember great physical pain and such a sense of abandonment, aloneness, and despair. I remember his deep hatred of women and girls. I have vivid images of that last day. I can see him in my mind, hear his voice, feel how scared and brave I was. Twelve years of Grandfather's sexual abuse, from which I disassociated immediately and completely, and which I buried deeply, except for that moment on that day. I felt some of those same emotions after ending the relationship with Bruce, even though I wouldn't actually remember the abuse from my grandfather many years later. Such pain and despair. I felt abandoned, even though I was the one who had done the abandoning.

Oh, I worked hard in therapy for years. Finally, my shitty self-esteem, my chronic depression, my inability to deeply connect with men started to make sense. I had many different therapists who used many different modalities. After being a massage therapist for a few years in my early 30's, I decided to study hypnotherapy to see if it might be useful in my practice. As part of my training, my teacher who was a psychotherapist took me on as a client. One day I said, "Last night I had the weirdest dream about my grandfather. I never did like his mustache, and in this dream, I could see it and it was really big and I was crying."

"Oh honey," the therapist said, "I don't think that was a dream."

As we continued to work over the next few years, she guided me into those dark places of abuse memories, holding my hand when needed, managing a way for me to curl up in her lap when needed. She believed every word I said. One of many who have helped me throughout my life. I thank them all for their service to me. I repressed/suppressed/was oppressed by those memories until my mid 30's. I still wonder why on that evening, reading Nancy Drew in Grosse Pointe, Michigan over Christmas vacation, I didn't dissociate, and I was able to remember Grandfather's abuse and be present. And it brings up all the wonderings about why this shit happens anyway.

I'd done some good spiritual searching by the time memories began to emerge. I deepened my studies and practices of Shaman-ism, praying every day, being grateful, asking for healing. I went to the sweat lodge to purify. I went on vision quest to go beyond my limits. I gained confidence and both outer and inner strength, becoming, I believe, strong enough to finally deal with those memories in a healthier way than I was able to when I was younger. In the early days of therapy, I shared my story—in particular, the details of the incident with the kitchen knife—with my friend Robert. He gave me a look that was full of both compassion and testosterone and said, "Yeah, I've felt that knife danger-ously close to *my* balls a time or two."

"Really?"

"Oh yes. One time was in response to an admittedly kind of smart ass remark I made. You turned quite red and told me to shut up. Your hand was kind of fisted at your side." He added that now some of my reactions to him, to sexual humor, and to some of our mutual friends made more sense. "I believe you," he said "I'm glad you survived to tell me the story."

This conversation, while it both shocked me and made sense at the same time, inspired me to continue the needed inner work to be able to thank the knife and let go of it, put it back in the kitchen drawer, wash my hands, and carry on.

11:00, phone call with Hannah
Charity: Hey, good morning.
Hannah: Good morning to you.
C: What a night I had. Thoughts, dreams, memories. Didn't get much sleep!
H: Dang, I finally had some good sleep. What's up?
C: Well, I've started a cleanse with an Ayurvedic focus. It's already stirring shit up, figuratively and literally. I have been feeling the need to shake things up, to learn some new nutrition ideas, to get a female perspective. Ayurveda seems to balance the masculine and feminine very well and suits that need really well, as it is about nourishment and is very individualized. What's good for you isn't necessarily going to be good for me, and vice versa.

I've had some good realizations lately, even before the cleanse. Some emotions have shifted finally, feeling some healing and letting go. Some of those old layers of pain, abuse, shit dropping away. Shit about the abuse, about my Grandfather, about being raped that summer in San Francisco, about lost love.

H: Oh, I can understand why you didn't sleep so well. I'm sorry but also glad this shit is coming up. Time to let it go, not have it control you so much.

C: Yes, beyond time.

H: Good luck. Tell me more about your cleanse. Like the ones you've done before?

C: This cleanse is all about nourishment, more about adding in rather than taking away. Saying no to some foods, but no real deprivation.

H: Great. Those rigid cleanses can be so difficult and not always necessary. So, what does that mean you are eating?

C: Mostly the same food we talk about all the time, and what I eat when I'm on track. That's a phrase I'd like to eliminate! Ugh. There is no track. More a reset sort of thing than a cleanse. I've been curious about Ayurveda for a long time but not enough to explore it. Apparently, now it's the right place and the right time.

H: Great. Good luck. Back in the day, I knew a lot more about Ayurveda than I do now. I love all those herbs and spices, too. I've been feeling pretty good lately, in a really comfortable easy place with my food these days.

C: That sounds good. I'm once again getting there. It's so easy for me to slip out of it. I am eating some fruit this week but I'm working on losing my sweet tooth and my wine tooth.

H: I've got more than one wine tooth!

C: Well, me too. I got a whole mouthful of teeth with cravings!

H: Better than not having any teeth, I guess. Hey, my worker boys are here to help me out with some stuff. I'd better go. Bye, love you. Keep me posted. I'm here to support you.

C: Thanks. Backatcha. Love you.

Hmm. I'm not sure if it's thinking about and worrying about this cleanse or if it's the Grandfather energy popping its ugly head in lately, but all I want to do is eat. Even with the good Ayurvedic additions, even with loosening up guilt and allowing some of my self-given restrictions to loosen. I won't binge. But there's a big part of me that just wants potato chips and alcohol. Those were staples of my diet for so many years, and they played a huge role in keeping me isolated and safe. This strategy started while learning to live on my own after college, first as a way to help me forget feeling lonely, then as a way to keep bad memories quiet. I never did make any close or long-lasting friends those years in San Francisco. I was depressed and not very confident. A bottle of wine and a big bag of potato chips often was dinner and long into the evening munching. I didn't have a television, but I discovered a local radio station that played old radio shows and that's how I spent many an evening.

Afternoon, resting

I'm feeling a combination of sleepy and wired. More cleansing stuff, maybe. I didn't eat any chips or drink any wine, which I am glad about. I just need to slow down. Close my eyes and slow down my brain, even with all I need to do this afternoon. First things first. How about some music? Without words. I've fed my body really well: now I need to feed my soul, let my body rest. I need to play my piano and practice today too. I wasn't sure how it was going to be having Melanie teach me because she is young and can be loud, but it's been great.

I remember my job interview at the massage school in Portland in the mid 80's, when I was talking about my varied teaching experiences with children and mentally retarded adults. I said, "Teaching is teaching. Working with adults isn't so different from working with children." That idea did not go over well with the school director. It probably wasn't the only reason I did not get the job, but I bet it figured in there somewhere. I ended up at the other massage school in town, and I absolutely loved working there, teaching pathology and getting to create their aromatherapy program. I'm so proud of that. I think I was a good teacher. Some of my preschool training did help me be spontaneous and creative. It is true that once you are a teacher, you are always a teacher. It may be in my future to teach cooking of some sort.

I had two piano teachers during the eight years I took lessons as a child. The only thing I remember about the first one was the teacher sitting behind me, which gave me the creeps. I also remember that he would eat potato chips during our lesson. (Ha, again with potato chips. Perhaps my adult bingeing began with his mentorship—all that crunching in my ear!) After him, I had lessons with Mrs. Cook, Judy's mom, which gave me the time to hang out with Judy, who was into poetry and beatniks. We were both in the seventh grade and became friends. She wore black every day and experimented with wild and garish makeup, which I wasn't allowed to use at that point. I seem to remember her wearing white eyeshadow and gold lipstick. Eventually, I bought my own gold lipstick and wore it at school. There, I also added black tights (the only black I owned since my mom didn't think it was appropriate for girls to wear) to whatever else I was wearing, then took them off before I went home.

When we went to Judy's house after school, she and I made slices of toast and coated them with butter and sugar. They had Wonder Bread and a sugar drawer at their house! We had neither. Our family ate only nutritious bread, and there was never free access to the sugar in the house. After buttering the bread, we would press it into that magic drawer of sugar, eat it quickly, and make some more. Then, we would listen to Bob Dylan or Joan Baez, read poetry, try to write, or do some homework. Usually, Judy would make herself a cup of coffee. I tried to like it, as drinking coffee seemed to go with the whole Beatnik thing.

For the most part, I enjoyed my piano lessons, but Mrs. Cook and I got frustrated with each other. I wanted her help learning Beatles songs, and she was a steadfast believer in teaching only classical music. When it came time for me to go to boarding school at age fifteen, I decided to stop my piano lessons. And now here I am, after a 50-year hiatus, learning a fun mix of classical, New Age, jazz, and popular tunes. I finally get to pick whatever sheet music I want. One of the first pieces we worked on was "Imagine," by John Lennon. Oh, be still, my teenage heart—though George was my favorite.

10pm, praying in bed

Ancient Ones, thank you for my good life. I thank you for helping through all my hard times. I pray for my loved ones who are struggling in their lives with their health, with families, whatever challenges they have. Thank you for teaching my how to pray, for knowing I can reach out to you anytime and anywhere.

Wednesday mid-morning phone call with Hannah

Charity: Hi, how are you? How's your morning?

Hannah: Gah, terrible actually. So frustrated and so over all my problems!

C: Ohh, I'm sorry. What's going on?

H: Oh, I don't even want to talk about it. Same shit, different days.

C: Well, anytime you need to talk about it, let me know. Anything I can do?

H: Yes. Distract me for a few minutes.

C: Perfect! I've got a doozy of a story. A whale of a tale.

H: What's up? Are you okay?

C: Oh yes, but I just had a wild experience. I was verbally accosted at the grocery store by an overly enthusiastic and freaked out middle-aged woman. And "accosted" is just the right word. This woman just marched right up to me in her sequined velour sweat outfit at the checkout counter and started frantically talking and gesturing dramatically. She had seen an "obesity autopsy," as she was calling it, on TV earlier. It apparently inspired her to do some shopping for good food and to be a "minister" to those who were in need of her story. Her cart was full of beautiful carrots, apples, broccoli, and who knows what else. She's telling me loudly how gross the autopsy was. This really fat woman had died of a heart attack, and the report made a big point of showing all the layers of fat. Apparently, her heart was destroyed, all her organs were a big mess. The people doing the surgery apparently were making very disparaging remarks, rude jokes, and letting the viewers know all about all the health risks she had had.

H: Rude and gross. And?

C: She was so horrified by the show that she came running to the store to buy vegetables and good stuff. She's a bit chubby, but not that overweight. Her rant went on and on, until finally I couldn't take it anymore and interrupted to say, "I'm sorry you are so upset, but why are you telling me this? You don't even know me."

She looked at me and said,"Well…," and pointed to my stomach. "Aren't you afraid you are going to die?"

I took a breath. Here was a moment, which way should I go? First, I got really pissed. How disrespectful and invasive! I'm none of her business. Why do people assume so much about others? She saw me, and I'm fat, therefore, I must be terribly ill. I must be desperate to change my body. Or, at least I should be, she thinks. With that, I felt sorry for her. I took it as a teaching moment and told her that we all die eventually, and that every day we have the choice to choose love over fear and over hate. I took a deep breath, channeling some fiery but kind Goddess energy. "I see that you are choosing love by buying food that will make you feel good. and with feeling good about yourself, you can choose love over the fear that those TV people were trying to instigate and perpetuate," I said. I also said that, if she would like, we could sit down and have some tea, and I'd be happy to share some more with her about what I do to get closer to loving myself, no matter what I look like or what society decrees I should look like. I let her know I'd be interested in hearing her story. "I have some tools I could share with you to help with your fear," I said at the end.

That took the wind out of her sails, and she didn't quite know what to say other than that she didn't have the time! With a big grin kept inside and another deep breath, I said, "I hope you will keep making the time to choose love over fear," and wished her a good day.

H: Haha! After that, I am sure she didn't know what to say.

C: She didn't. The cashier and I just looked at each other, not quite knowing whether to laugh or cry or what. I just paid my bill and left. It was hard actually, and it did make me angry. The nerve! I kind of wanted to slap her for her invasiveness. But, I was in a pretty good mood, so I chose to see her in a different light.

H: You are a better woman than I am. I'm not sure what I would have said.

C: I definitely had some things to say to myself after I got in my car. I let loose with that part if me that wanted to slap her and wanted to call her nasty names. How dare she? Then I gave myself some love for not living in that kind of fear so often.

H: You really didn't want to let her have it? I know you don't really like getting angry.

C: I still can't vocalize or articulate my anger so well: you're right. I do hold it in. Part of me wanted to punch her. At least I could express it in the car. I do think it was a conscious decision, not one being led by fear or embarrassment.

I feel sorry for her, really. It could have triggered me more than it did, because just a little before that, I was telling my boot-camp girls about cleansing and looking towards losing some weight. So, the universe plays funny tricks on us sometimes. It was an opportunity to be kind—to myself and to her. To not take someone else's problems in. It was more about her than me. And to continue to love myself no matter what.

H: That gets hard. I'm not feeling so deserving of even my own love right now.

C: Aww, I'm sorry.

H: Thanks.

C: I love you. What are you doing for yourself today? You have any free time?

H: I've got a mountain of work, but I'd really like it if we could get together. I don't know that I need to talk things out, but a change of scenery would be really great. Do you want to go to the Arboretum?

C: Sure, and we could go to that art exhibit also.

H: Great, 3:00?

C: Great, see you soon.

Later that morning, catching up on some cooking

Today's the last day of the cleanse, but I'm going to keep working at it. A week without sugar has been interesting. I feel good but tired, which is something to pay attention to. It feels deep, like a symptom that eating and drinking sugar covers up. True fatigue, not just blood sugar crashing. I'm thinking that releasing some brain fog and other sugar-related stuff is what helped me cope so well with that woman earlier. I actually surprised myself with how calm I appeared and how articulate I was. I really rocked that interaction!

There wasn't a lot of meat on the cleanse. I'm cooking some chicken, and oh my God, it smells so good. Adding some garlic and all the leftover vegetables from the fridge. Hello, homemade chicken and rice soup. So wholesome—better than the can.

Soup is so comforting. What makes a comfort food? I've done a lot of thinking and talking about this, from interviewing prospective personal chef clients to find out what their comfort foods are. Some clients would ask me to make healthier versions of dishes, such as macaroni and cheese, one of the apparently ultimate American comfort foods. Too cheesy for me. Some people think that if the food is healthy, it doesn't classify as comfort food.

Some of my discussions with friends about comfort food have given me some insight into the connection between food that comforts us and overeating. I can't even remember the last time I had macaroni and cheese, but how often do you hear about someone just eating a tiny serving of it? My friends who choose that as their comfort most often eat a large to very large bowl of it while watching some favorite television show.

What I am curious about is the connection between comfort food and overeating or bingeing. I think there is one. I haven't got it all figured out for sure. For me, it all boils down to why am I eating.

My days of food bingeing are over. I know the binges were more about punishing myself in some way, making myself feel sick. I still do overeat. Most of the time, when I overeat, it doesn't really come from a place of seeking solace and I still find myself "needing" to punish and hurt myself. But, there is a difference between overeating and bingeing. I can overeat, and it's not a binge, such as when I have seconds and get too full. Going to a restaurant and eating all everything I order, that can be overeating, but it's not a binge. Eating a whole bag of potato chips or a bag of cookies when I am not even hungry, that *is* a binge. But, then again, once when telling a friend about eating a bag of chips, she just looked at me and said, "You call that a binge?" She was serious. It gave me pause. Here was a very healthy person who occasionally eats a whole bag of chips in one sitting! She doesn't consider herself a binge eater.

So, what is a binge? I can go back to the terrible old days and remember eating a whole pizza, drinking most of a bottle of wine, and adding some chocolate to the mix, followed the next day by enough Chinese take-out food to feed a family of four. Guilt and shame would get me to eat less and/or "better" for a few days or so, then maybe doughnuts would call my name. I'd buy a box of a dozen and eat them all, one by one, washing them down with a pot of coffee. I think those qualify as binges.

When I was a massage therapist in Hillsboro, Oregon, my office was a few blocks away from Taco Time, a not-very-authentic Mexican restaurant. I regularly ordered their deep-fried flour tortilla rolled up with either refried beans or mystery meat inside. What is it about fried food that calls me, still? Mostly I went through the drive-thru on my way home, getting my usual order of one each of the bean and meat tortillas, a Diet Coke, and sometimes fried tortilla chips coated in cinnamon sugar. Some days I doubled the order and to make it look as if I were actually ordering for two, I ordered two drinks, one diet and one regular. I could eat all four of those burritos and often did in the car before I got home.

Someone once at one of my many diet program meetings "confessed" to her belief that "food doesn't count if you eat it in the car." Lots of nervous giggling and shuffling followed that remark.

I would never start the day thinking, "Oh boy, I'd like to have a binge today!" I would wake with the intention of being calm and in control, especially those mornings when my stomach would complain about the previous days input. But, so often, it seemed the shift would be unconscious. Even now, even as my diet has continued to change and eighty percent of the time my food is high-level nutrition with lots of planning and cooking, I can lose the intention of conscious careful eating. At first, things are okay. Then, seemingly before I know it, there I am, in the store, buying whatever I want or some inner voice is demanding and coming home to eat it all. Of course, it's not fully unconscious. I don't black out; I can get myself to the store and back. Sometimes there is a very conscious "fuck you" moment where I decide to eat whatever it is and damn the consequences. How *that* looks for me lately is going out to a restaurant and having a burger, french fries, and a few glasses of wine. Eating all of it. More than enough. Knowing none of that is good for me and my digestion. At some point in the meal, I lose the pleasure, and it's often followed by acid reflux at bedtime and some suffering. Is that a binge? Overeating? Or is that "just" not making a good choice? And does it matter? That restaurant scenario happens fairly regularly—partly because I really do like hamburgers. There's a nice bistro-style eatery ten minutes from my house by car. The hostess recognizes me and is friendly when I come in. Once in a while, I will see someone I know and we may choose to sit together. More often I sit at a table for one where I can watch the action in the kitchen. The meat there is grass-fed and the wine is high quality. Okay, the french fries, not so much. They get coated in flour, so that adds to their digestive nightmare for me, but they just taste good. I usually take my book when I go there, and it can take me an hour or an hour and a half to eat my meal. To me, that is very different from a full-blown binge which is done quickly. Often binges are in secret as well, not in popular restaurants.

Oh boy. How did I get on this? I can feel shame coming on. I'm sending you back, no thanks today. The cleanse is doing its work, I think. Me doing my work. Letting go. That woman this morning. I won't take in her fear. I think reminding myself of how my life used to be is helpful at times.

A few hours later, getting ready for bed

Whoa, what a day. Digging deep is taxing. I need to honor that and give myself permission to rest. Oh yes, and permission to feel proud of what I've done.

Ancient Ones, thank you for my life today—my full, rich, good life, full of so much healing and love. I thank you for my community, my family of friends. Bless them all. I pray that I can help the world change, that people's hearts can be open to those who are different, people who have chosen different paths to follow, that my heart can stay open to loving myself. I pray for more love and kindness in the world.

From my writing notebook

I get told, Charity, you are too nice.
What the fuck does that mean?
Does a nice person even say "fuck?"

I don't believe there is such a thing as too nice, too much kindness.

I am so proud I can be kind
Compassionate
Generous
Loving

Some people grow up never knowing kindness
Never feeling that warmth, that gift
Never feeling as if they had anything to give

I say it over and over.
The world needs more kindness.
The world needs more kind people.

My mom had a whole drawer full of cards.
for birthdays, anniversaries, special occasions,
She sent them just because

She knew the names of the clerks in the stores
and my friends' names and
 was nice to them
She could have a conversation with anyone

How about being kind to yourself?
Now that's a radical thought.

Is it really that we are here, on this planet, to be lonely and afraid?

Saturday morning, after dance
     It was interesting dancing with Steve. "Mr. Big Arms," of the dancing story I wrote last year. He has powerful arms, powerful muscles. I'm so attracted to men's forearms. I'm not talking size here. I am fascinated by the muscles, hair, veins, hands. Mmm. That first dance, last year, I was so enchanted by his attention. I still find seeing his beaming face and outstretched arms wonderful,

but I wish he would tune into me a bit more. Dancing with him is all about what he wants, where he wants to go, his speed. I don't feel as much connection with him as I have felt with other partners here. Mostly I just dance by myself but cherish the partnered moments, when I know deep connection is possible.

Here's another dancing story. A close friend was totally into waltzing and encouraged me to go with her to an ongoing waltz class here in Santa Cruz about ten years ago. I was not so excited about it, but I wanted to check it out. Oh my god, that guy, my first partner of the day. "You must do what I want you to do!" His idea of leading. Really? Ooh, if he knew me, he would not have said that. We were in pairs, changing partners every few minutes. I still don't have a lot of experience with that kind of dancing, although I'd love to be good at it. We had gotten instructions about a form to follow, which most of us didn't quite get. "You must do what I want you to do." Yeah, like that's going to happen. Apparently, that's what he heard when our instructor was teaching us about leading and following. And, in the middle of our dance, he stopped and said that in a pretty loud voice. I don't think so, asshat! Not that I was a good follower, either. The teacher checked in with me about how I was feeling after that and talked a little more to the class about what leading on the dance floor is really about. It should be like gentle suggestions, not orders, he said. For the rest of the class I stayed upset and embarrassed by being the center of attention during that particular dance.

Boy, there was some wild dancing going on today. I got a little envious of how some of those women can move, can be lifted up in the air. Again, out of around 100 people, no one else there was fat. I wonder if any of them might identify as fat, or might think they are? Everyone's idea of what qualifies as being fat is different.

I've been coming to this Saturday morning dance for a little less than a year. It's a couple of hours each week. I'm here two or three times a month. It gets me moving. It gets me with people. I started coming as a part of the year-long artist program I did last year, as both the leaders and many people in the group were dancers. I am getting comfortable moving my body and having this body be seen. I'm working on giving myself permission to take up space. What a big deal that is! When I connect with my body on the dance floor, those old uncomfortable memories become more integrated. That makes me think of Bruce again. We loved dancing together—at informal spontaneous get-togethers listening to music on the weekends and at formal dances in high school. Sometimes even folk dancing after dinner at college. I can honor that girl in me who loves to dance and teach my waltz class partner a thing or two. I will cherish the sweet memories and create new ones. I will develop not only those dancing muscles, but also the muscles of connection, of grace, and creativity. I hope. I hope I stick with the uncomfortableness and the challenges.

Sunday morning

The crossword puzzle is far beyond me today. That is just fine. I have plenty of ways to occupy and enrich myself, starting with some appetizing soup for breakfast.

I feel well. I've actually lost a few pounds, I think. I'm not making the cleanse about that, I can't. Really, I can't make my weight the focus anymore at all. Just noticing. I can't get sucked into the scale. I won't.

Getting my blood sugar stirred up by some chocolate is no big deal compared to some of my ugly eating back in the day. Digging in the trash for leftovers, chopping pieces off something straight out of the freezer. I would buy huge amounts of food at the store, come home and eat enough for a whole family. Piece after piece, bite after bite, there went a whole pie or cake, a whole pizza. Going through a fast food drive through and getting double orders of burgers, fries, etc. and eating it all myself.

I'll have a big cup of ginger tea, sit in the sun, and count my blessings. Think about how I can focus some of my energy outward, do some service, help the neighbors, cook for someone, something.

Next evening, after saying goodnight to Tom

We had another of those awkward sideways, both-of-us-in-the-front-seat-how-do-we-get-to-each-other kinds of hugs. I forgot to undo my seatbelt. I think I kissed him on his ear! We could both laugh about it this time.

Such a better conversation we had at dinner. I've been pretty chatty with him lately, so I worked at drawing him out. It was a little like pulling teeth getting him to share information and feelings, but I did hear about his family and challenges with his sister. We commiserated about the difficulties in ever-changing adult family relationships. I wanted to know more about his spiritual journey, since he has mentioned having several teachers. But I couldn't get any more out of him. Maybe he'll share more later.

Our conversation took me back to the old days of the mid 1970's, to a spiritual study/meditation group I was in, made up of people from my work at Head Start as well as some of their friends in Portland. We met twice a month for several years, on the new moon and the full moon.

I think being part of that circle, for me, was more about fitting in with my friends than it was about actual interest in the explorations—which ranged from meditation and channeling to taking ecstasy and doing past life regressions. We had deep curiosity and a need to find our places in the world. We all were a little lost, some more than others. So willing to explore, diving deep to satisfy our yearnings.

My twenties were rough. Drinking. Sexual experiences were few and far between, and they ran the gamut from mediocre and ugly to painful and dangerous. I felt lost, and I needed help. I knew that, at least, and I was searching.

As I grew older, my search expanded. I was part of a witchy women's group, which was full of singing and drumming, wearing colorful dresses, embracing our femaleness and our bodies, and learning about the Goddesses. I also discovered Native American sweat lodges—praying, singing, sweating out impurities. Some were in city backyards with moldy carpet to sit on. One was out on some friends' property where they raised bison. Some of the ceremonies were quite traditional, and others were co-opted by white people, adding their own made-up ways. Some were so full of wounded people that the pain was palpable and the anger too much to bear. I occasionally went to sweats associated with a recovery clinic. On some nights, I could taste the alcohol in the air as it was sweated out in the lodge. I learned discernment through those experiences. I learned to trust my intuition.

For a few years, I went to a rapidly growing New Age church which gradually turned into a successful venture with a huge following. I loved the singing and the praying, but it just wasn't enough. I still can remember how it felt to take communion there on Easter. Finally, after my childhood longing for ritual.

I grew up a little Quaker girl who wanted to be a Catholic. Our family went to the Presbyterian church in town because there were no other Quakers around, but we also had our own Quaker meetings (which is what Quaker religious observances are called) at home, just the five of us, being quiet, praying silently, thinking good thoughts, and waiting for Spirit to move us to speak, which I don't think ever happened to any of us except for Dad. I believed in God and I liked to pray, but I did get bored. I wanted to be baptized, I wanted Communion, I wanted to go to Confession. I would sometimes go to Catholic mass with one of my best girl-friends, Mary Lynn. That church seemed like such a magical place to me—so ornate and grand. I was mesmerized by the Latin, the chanting, the incense. I even loved the kneeling! It was so different from our quiet Quaker tradition of praying silently. My parents were supportive of my interest in Catholicism to a point. They let me go to mass, and I went to Catholic summer camp with Mary Lynn one year. She stole one of her mom's rosaries and gave it to me so that I could pray with it. The nuns at camp also were supportive of my interest—again, up to a point, because, well, I wasn't Catholic. I did get chastised several times for using my left hand to cross myself. Oops. Mom and Dad drew the line at me going to catechism classes and actually becoming a Catholic. Quakerism doesn't have any such rituals or teachings. There is just God and us and no need for rosaries, catechism, or kneeling, priests or ministers. Their decision led to much pre-teen angst and drama, but it didn't take too long to get over it. I moved to other interests, such as Greek and Roman mythology, followed soon after by Eastern mysticism.

I started learning about body freedom and acceptance in my two women's groups in Oregon. We were women of all ages and sizes. Sometimes we freely did some ritual without our clothes on, and we openly discussed menstruation and let ourselves bleed on the earth. We had glorious feasts and celebrated soberly and with pleasure. One weekend, in my group which met monthly up in the mountains outside of Portland, we participated in a "finding our spirit animal" shamanic journey. We paired up and lay next to each other on the ground. Drumming and chanted ensued. Macy, the woman leading us sang and asked us to go within and vision. We were to look for a teaching, an animal, for our partner. I let the drums and the sage that was burning transport me. I found myself swimming in a river. Upstream with the salmon. My partner journeyed to the jungles of Central America, heard jaguars screaming in the night. It was incredibly powerful for both of us, and even more powerful as we began to learn about those individual animals and what they meant for us in our lives. The group disbanded after about five years. A few years later, I ran into that journey partner. We shared our tattoos that we each had gotten of our spirit animals. I have a beautiful jaguar on my left thigh. For me, she embodies grace and agility which physically I do not, but she reminds me to expand my definition of those qualities. She represents bravery and is an ever-present reminder of how brave I have been in my life and how brave I still can be.

In the sweat lodge were men and women, all modestly clothed but sitting tightly. I met many people from the Native American community. I learned about prayer. I learned about humility and found strength and endurance to face the heat and my limits. I found it both odd and so healing that the seat lodge is where I found safety when all my therapy and retrieving my abuse memories got overwhelming. The ancientness of it all, the sacredness of being in the "womb of our Mother." There is where I learned about the Grandfather we all have, Grandfather Fire who is full of wisdom and love for his children.

All that exploring led me to Shamanism in 1982. With friends, I went to a workshop deep in the woods of Oregon. I knew about shamanism intellectually from college, but this was my first time hearing the chanting, the drumming, and the rattling that is part of the ceremonies. I felt those rhythms and the words that I didn't understand in my bones and in my heart. I got visions from the colors in the art and the images of circles, spirals, the deer, and the eagle. I heard stories about creation and danced my prayers into the Earth in our ceremonies. I'd prayed my whole life, but this was a new but almost innate way to express myself. My yearning to find some meaning in life and my questions began to make sense to me. I just knew deep in my soul that I was home, that this was my path. There's no other explanation of why it resonated so. I just *knew*. I absolutely believe in the power of prayer. I absolutely believe that all life is sacred. The Earth is my Mother. The Fire is my Grandfather. Finally, family. A healing family. Finally, home. Finally, I could hear my Soul say, "Yes, this is it!"

A common thread through my whole journey has been the need for community, that need for connection and love. I appreciate having met so many amazing people. This history gives me stability and strength.

I still sing songs now and then that I learned in my women's group. I still go to the sweat lodge. I have beliefs that are not too far from Quakerism about pacifism, activism, spending time in silence, and finding the sacred and holy in all things.

7-ish, Tuesday morning

I think I dreamed of singing last night—probably a result of remembering the chants of the Catholics, our women's voices raised in joyous song, and the sacred songs of the sweat lodge. I love to sing. Too bad I'm not better at it. Too bad I can't make my living at it. I was in the choir in school and played the piano for the junior choir at the Presbyterian Church. I've considered being in community chorus groups, but I've never done it. I've thought about singing lessons. Aurora and I used to sing together. I can see us in the car belting out some song we both knew at the top of our lungs. Trying, sometimes successfully, to harmonize and sound lovely. On a good day, I can carry a tune and hold my own. But lately, my voice isn't as strong. Ever since that last bout of pneumonia five years ago, my breathing is sometimes labored, and I can't get enough air to sing fully. I'm starting to sound a little raspy—like Grandmother, like Mama. A "whiskey tenor," my mom used to call it. I can hear it coming.

"Charity and the Bodacious Tatas"—that was the name of my imaginary girl group in the 80's, with me as the piano player and lead singer. I still think that would have been a great band name. Back in those days, the tatas were perkier and would have looked fabulous in my leather bustier. If you can imagine a mix of Stevie Nicks, Aretha Franklin and Tina Turner, that would have been me, rocking out on my piano.

I still want to be Aretha Franklin. I adore her and have for 50 years. Talk about tatas! Hers are gorgeous. I'm sorry I never saw her in concert. I love that video of her singing for Carol King and the Obamas at Carol King's medal celebration, where she sang "You Make Me Feel Like a Natural Woman" and dropped that fur coat. Damn, that was a Diva moment if there ever was one.

Wednesday morning

Wednesday is "Senior citizen discount day" at my favorite grocery store. I enjoy shopping with all the other gray-haired folks. Life slows down. We all take a bit more time. It's been a difficult realization that I am now one of *those* people who takes forever to get her ID out or to pay for something. I see this most in the airport and the grocery store, when people behind me have to wait.

This morning, while conversing with one of the workers about cabbage in the produce section (whether we preferred red or green), discussing the benefits of grass-fed beef with the butcher, and wondering out loud about all the different choices of toilet paper, I found myself chuckling, seeing my mama in me—chatting everyone up and being friendly. One of the things I loved and admired about my mom was how she could find something to discuss with anyone.

In the checkout line, I got in a conversation about persimmons with the woman in front of me, distracting her to the point that she forgot to ask for her discount. The young checker took care of it anyway. Then, I discussed coconut water with the dreadlocked young woman wearing an exquisitely embroidered blouse behind me, finding out which brand she likes best. So then, *I* forgot to ask for *my* discount! Again, the checker was sweet and patient, though the coconut water woman in the beautiful blouse got a little impatient. The bagger was an adorable young man with an elaborate hairdo of many lengths and colors who kept asking me, "Are you sure you can carry this?" After assuring him of my strength, he put half of it in another bag anyway. Choosing to embrace the care and the good intention, I said, "Thanks." They must give the Wednesday shifts to their extra kind and patient employees. It's a good day to be gray.

I have noticed the gray turning to white around my face. I'm a bit worried about losing my hair, having scalp showing through here and there. Both Grandmother and Mom ended up with very thin hair. My voice is changing into their voices, my hair is turning into their hair. What will be next?

Thursday morning, 4 am, awake

Okay, *that* was a weird dream. All my damn snoring woke me up. At least no one hears me but you, Tina. Did I scare you? I don't remember all of the dream, but the neighbors were looking in my window with their dog, which looked more like a wolf. In the dream, I was scared. The neighbors did not look like anyone on our street. I could see the dog clearly; it was huge, dark, and scruffy. It growled when I made a noise, then stopped when I stopped. It sounded kind of like snoring to me. Dammit. Was that me? Was it because of those two glasses of wine? Seems like that is what wine does to me now. Maybe it's good Mr. Flannel doesn't sleep over after all, although maybe he snores too. The two of us together might scare that wolf off. Poor kid next door would never open his window again.

I'm still a little scared. I don't like waking up feeling scared. Too many visits from Grandfather in the middle of the night, waking me up with his nasty whiskers and stinking breath. How crazy is that, Tina? Sixty years later, I'm still scared of fucking bastard Grandfather. I hope I can go back to sleep.

9 a.m. Facebook Messenger, Hannah

Hannah: Good morning.

Charity: Good morning to you. How are you?

H: Pretty good, you?

C: Yep, pretty good. Weird sleeping. Drinking wine last night stirred up some phlegm and snoring. I'd gotten pretty cleaned out from the cleanse and have been careful since then. I overindulged. Sigh.

H: Sigh. I can hardly recall the last glass of wine I had. I don't dare. You are quite the snorer, though!

C: Not all the time. Apparently, you bring it out in me when we share a room. I'm remembering when you started your big diet changes a few years ago. It was difficult for you at first to make all those changes and get your morning routine down. That's still a problem for me. I saw the Ayurveda woman again for a consultation. Did I tell you about that?

H: No, and I've been meaning to ask. How was it?

C: Really good, and sort of overwhelming at the same time. An abundance of self-care ideas. Oil pulling, oils on the skin, steam inhalations, using a gua sha, you know that wooden tool?

H: Yeah, I have one, thought I haven't used it in a while. I did a lot of that kind of stuff when I lived in the ashram.

C: All that plus the skin brush, enemas, and all the food stuff as self-care. It's a lot. I was really thinking about it this morning lying in bed. The whole idea of self-care is so hard for me. That both breaks my heart a little and pisses me off. Almost 66 freaking years-old, and it's too challenging for me to be gentle and careful, as in full of care for myself, and gentle with myself. This is such significant work right now. It's huge! Self-care. Caring for myself. Letting myself be cared for. I'm not my mother. I'm not!

H: You really are not. From everything you've told me, you are not like her in so many ways. She was so hard on you. And on herself. And that makes me sorry. I didn't learn much about taking care of myself from my mom, either.

C: Maybe it was a generational thing. My mom always thought people of our generation were overly self-indulgent and too self-centered.

H: Some days I struggle with all the time I spend cooking, planning my food, doing those self-care things. Hours a day. It takes time away from my work. But I have to make myself important. It's not wasting time.

C: Heaven forbid we should waste time!! And thank God, I have no work from which to take time. Some days I miss it, but I'm happy to be retired.

H: I don't think I'll ever be able to retire, but I do need to work on balancing all the things I do.

C: I'm so glad you get it. Thanks for your support. The other day, I rushed my way through the treatments and didn't enjoy them the way I was hoping to. I can say I love myself, but if I'm not willing to take the time I need to take care of myself, to give myself care, then is that really love? No pleasure from that care, from that love, that's not good. Sigh.

H: It is hard. Thanks for all the support you give me.

C: Well, I'm proud of both of us, tackling this shit. Some people never do.

H: Yeah, I wish there wasn't quite so much of the shit though. Ha!

C: Well, let's just keep shoveling. I'm doing the steam stuff today again, so another chance to do it better or at least, differently.

H: Cut yourself some slack. It takes practice. I've got an appointment so have to go. Call me later if you want. Love you.

C: Love you, too.

Early afternoon self-care session: Ayurvedic treatments, steam inhalation, bath soak

Okay, third time's a charm. I'm gathering all the stuff I need, heating enough water, running hot water in the bath to get the room steamy. Then I'll drain it and run more for actual bath. That's my new idea. I wish I had a heater in here. Why isn't the tub bigger? And why don't I have a bathrobe? I've never been a robe wearer, but maybe it's time to give it a shot. I'll order one. This self-help time is all about being warm and cozy. Letting myself be comfortable. I don't really quite get why that is still so hard. Is a bathrobe really too luxurious? And where did I get that idea? It's not from Mom this time. I remember her and all of her lounging robes and gowns. She had quite a few of them at their house down in the islands. She'd put one on after swimming and just wear it for the evening. It was her way of wearing something that covered her and was comfortable. She had many pretty bathrobes which she wore almost every morning.

Do I think I don't deserve it? No, it's not that. It just doesn't enter my mind. See, that's a lack of self-care. Or maybe I shouldn't use that word, lack. Better to think of it as just not knowing enough about it. I so need to get over the idea of self-care as being foreign to me.

There's one of the reasons I love traveling with my friend Mary, who brings a robe and slippers, her pillow, and sometimes a silk sheet everywhere we go. It's all about her comfort and care for herself. I've learned a lot from watching her as we've shared rooms in Mexico, California, and Alaska. Little by little, I'm taking inspiration from her and allowing myself little pleasures.

I'm not talking big luxuries here. A bathrobe. Rubbing oils on my skin which smell fabulous. Nourishment from the oils and from the care. Taking time to love myself. Really, what's the big deal? I do have guilt about this focus, though. Um, how about all the people in the world that don't have hot water, or not even enough water to bathe in? Or, if they have water, no time for any sort of relaxation. Here is where my life as a proud liberal meets a challenge. Do I think that my *not* having a bathrobe or not spending time luxuriating in the tub will help them? That's like the old days when we were told to eat all our food because there were starving children in Armenia.

Okay, so far so good. Don't rush. I can look in the mirror or not. I want to practice watching myself, looking at my body, reminding myself of my strength, finding the beauty, finding the pleasure. I do love the facial steaming, holding my face over the hot water and breathing in the steam. It's warm and soothing under the towel. My lungs are thanking me. They work hard, they need some TLC. I don't want to huff and puff so much. I want to sing without coughing because I can't get enough air. The moisture feels good on my skin, too. I'm so grateful for my good skin. Thanks, Mom and Dad. Except for the age spots and some scars from skin cancer removal on his sweet bald head, Dad had beautiful skin. He spent a lot of time outdoors, so it did get leathery in places, but mostly it was so soft. When I was a massage therapist, he loved having me work on him. Mama had beautiful skin as well. I don't think she ever used anything else but Pond's cold cream on her skin. Do they even make that anymore? I use lotion now and then, never any soap except my armpits. And now, I'm adding in all my new Ayurveda treatments with sunflower and sesame oils. In my darkest days of feeling shitty about myself, I could always point to my skin as something I did feel good about.

Honestly, it's difficult and painful to reach some parts of my body for doing the scraping and scrubbing. I can't bend my knees very deeply and can't get to the bottoms of my feet or all the way around my ankles. That's always frustrating when I try to clip my toenails. When I'm able to do it at all, I usually butcher them. My nails are sort of fungus-y so it's not always easy to find someone to give me a pedicure.

I'm having to contort myself painfully to get to some places on the backs of my legs. It hurts, so I'll just have to skip those parts. I am embarrassed and feel shame. There are even times when it's a challenge to wipe myself after pooping. Don't go down that shame road! I'll just figure out what I can do and focus on doing that well. Now that is profound. It's a good motto and attitude. Figure out what I can do and do it well. Can't ask for more than that.

I'm finding some tender spots especially around my ankles and the insides of my knees today. Well, this, too, is something I know about myself. I might act tough but I'm actually quite tender. I've had numerous bumps and bruises along life's way. I've gotten good at hiding them. Thankfully, I don't have much experience with actual bruising; my heart has taken the brunt of abuse and neglect—including neglect from myself. That is a hard way to look at it. Would I ever talk to another person as I have myself? I have grown a lot, but I have also thought of myself as ugly and stupid. Too fat to be loved. Would I allow myself to be a witness to seeing someone else treat herself this way? I'm getting stronger about speaking up, calling out shaming, bullying. Time for some deep breathing, for forgiveness, and moving on. Lots of tears in those thoughts. *Mi pobre Corazon.* My poor heart. I apologize. I do want to take better care of you. Thank you for your good care.

I'm learning to appreciate, if not quite yet love, this beautiful wooden tool, the gua sha. It's sanded so well and fits well in my hand. The idea is to drag it over my skin to push the oils in and help them do their work. The process activates lymph and blood flow. Some days it can be painful. Today, not so much. The actual physical tenderness will shift the more I do this scraping with the wood. That makes it sound terrible—"scraping." But I know it helps. I'm taking my time. Caring is slow and thoughtful. I'm so worth the time. I'm worth the love. Being care full, full of care. Being tender. Energy spent on myself, on *myself* is precious, like these essential oils.

Like this water. Which brings up more guilt. Am I overusing water? What about my water bill? I'm thinking about all those months of water saving, during the drought. But it's medicine. *Mni Wiconi*, water is life. This is what water is for, new life. In my spiritual way, water has the power of beauty. So, help me make this treatment beauty medicine. I allow my beauty to shine. Help me believe I am beautiful. I am.

Better to pay for water now than bad health later. Right? Yes, right.

Sitting here, I'm trying to relax, but it's really impossible for me to get comfortable in this tub. It's too narrow and so my hips touch the sides. It's not deep enough, either, so I can't get enough water to cover myself. I appreciate the concept of taking a bath but never do it anymore, which is a shame. Plus, there are all these rough and scratchy non-skid stickers under me. And, in order to get out, I have to turn over and get on my hands and knees, then use the side of the tub to push myself up. I have to hope I don't lose my balance on the way.

For now, I'm trying to stay in the moment, stay in the tub a little longer, let the water do its work. Take in some more hot water and a chance to just be still for a bit. I think the only time a bathtub has felt really good was in my apartment in the Haight in San Francisco, mid 70's, the place where I did day care. After the kids left, which was usually after we all calmed down watching Mr. Rogers while we waited for their parents to come, I'd fill the tub, get a glass of wine, smoke part of a joint (or the whole thing, depending on the day), and let the stress of the day go. Those were long hard days, but in the bathtub, life was sweet. And, I had that big old clawfoot tub outside my house in the woods in Oregon. I used to have great baths there, hooking up a hose from my kitchen sink for the hot water, or just cooling off in the cold water in the summer.

This water does feel good. Nourishment. Love. Tenderness. Care. Breathing. Medicine for body and soul. Time to get up and out. That's enough for today. I'm warm and soft. I smell good. I'm well taken care of, cared for and cared about. Be honest: it wasn't that hard. Except for this getting-out-of-the-tub pain-in-the-ass nonsense!

That night, going to bed

Ancient Ones, thank you for a good day. I thank you for my lifelong challenges and my joys, for my learning, for my growing, for the struggles and the pains, for the triumphs, small and large that have made me who I am. I thank you for all the people who love me and let me love them. I am so grateful. I pray for the water. I pray for those who don't have fresh water to drink, to bathe in. Thank you again for my life.

From my writing notebook
Care

be careful
don't hurt yourself.
take care

be full of care
taking and giving

Caring and sharing and daring
Beware

Don't shed a tear
or show your fear

Pull on your big girl pants
and climb that mountain
that mountain of trust and love and hope
the great hills of tenderness
Sashay your way
through the fields of sweetness
picking flowers of care and power.
Making a magical bouquet.

In the wee hours of the night, awake

Damn, that was a good dream. Where was I? Home, I think, but not anywhere I have lived in this life. The colors were beautiful jewel tones: ruby red, amethyst purple, emerald green. I was cooking something on the stove. Of course, my kitchen was perfect. It might have been soup or something like that. In the dream, it smelled so good. Familiar. That makes me remember my personal chef days, when my clients would walk into the kitchen. "Oh my god, what smells so good?" they'd ask. Most of the time, it was the beginning of something and was simply onions and garlic sautéeing on the stove. They couldn't believe it smelled so good. Most of my clients didn't know how to cook.

So, the dream home's perfect kitchen had shiny new appliances, a six-burner stove, a commercial-sized refrigerator, wood floors, and green marble countertops. And there were children—at least a dozen sweet faces looking at me. Where were their parents? I can't remember if I was their parent or grandparent; I just knew it was my home. The children all started crying at once, so I fed them whatever was in that pot, and they were happy. The dream morphed into all of us being outside—dogs, cats, children, babies, me. The whole dream was feeling a bit like a Disney movie, all beautiful and a little too perfect. Too much to take? Hmm.

Mostly I don't have regrets, but sometimes, I regret that I didn't have children. Life is what it is. But, I would have been a good mom, and I would be a good grandma. I still wonder what if, even though I still think it's good that I didn't have that baby when I got pregnant in college. I had one night of very drunken unsatisfying sex with a guy I thought was an asshole. Honestly, looking back I have no memory of how or why we ended up in bed together—other than that it was college in 1971. We were at a party together, and I invited him back to my apartment. Alcohol and loneliness certainly played their parts. I absolutely never wanted him to know about the pregnancy. Part of my wanting an abortion was about not having *his* baby. It would not have been a baby made from love, that's for sure.

I missed a period, which had never happened before. I vaguely knew that that was a marker for being pregnant but I needed my friend to tell me I should go see a doctor. Back in those days, there were no home pregnancy tests, so off to the town clinic I went, being too embarrassed to go to the clinic at the college. After checking my pee, the nurse came in to say, "Your test came out positive."

"What does that even mean?" She pushed her glasses down her nose, looked up from her paper.

"Well it means you tested positive for pregnancy. You are pregnant." What? Oh no. I started to cry.

"Pregnant? Shit, how can that be a positive thing? That test has it backwards." I truly was confused. There was nothing positive about being pregnant that I could think of. The nurse looked as if she swallowed a lemon as she told me that the doctor would be in momentarily.

I pulled it together to ask him about abortion options and was told, "I don't give out that information." I had a French professor I really liked, so, a few days later, I gathered up my courage and asked her. She was able to give me some names and places to contact.

Abortions were especially problematic in 1971, not being legal in many states, including Wisconsin, where I was going to school. I decided I needed to keep it a secret from my family. Politically and ethically, I knew my parents supported abortion, but I didn't want to have to cope with the emotional fallout. I only told my closest girlfriends. I traveled all the way to a clinic in New York City by myself, just for the day. It was the only place I found that could take me. It was very expensive, but thank God I had the money, since I had recently inherited some from grandparents. Of course, this was not what they would have ever thought I would do with it.

That day was horrendous on so many levels. I know I didn't even feel half of the feelings that I could have felt. My two closest girlfriends drove me to the airport in Chicago for the flight, and they picked me up that same night. From Kennedy Airport, the taxi driver took me through that huge city—vast and dirty, such a strange place. I had been there before, but not on my own and only as a tourist. This was different. When he dropped me off at the women's clinic, I could tell the driver knew where we were and why I was there. I was glad he didn't say anything. With legs shaking and barely able to catch my breath, I exited the taxi. When I entered the clinic, I was overwhelmed by how crowded and noisy it was, full of women of all ages and colors. I sat in that cold waiting room with its worn out plastic furniture, feeling all the grief, sadness, despair. It was difficult to sort out my own feelings from those that seemed to live in the walls of that place. I listened to some young girl screaming down the hallway and her mother trying to comfort her. I felt so lonely and confused sitting there, waiting. Others were waiting alone too, and some were with partners, or with their mothers. Even though we hadn't been getting along, I needed my mother at that moment. And I longed for the company of my best friend who was waiting for me back at school. Was I making the right decision?

The treatment room was small and clean, but there was nothing in there to lighten the mood. The procedure was done quickly and efficiently with no tender care.

"Are you ready?" followed by some pain, then, "Okay, we're finished." Breathtakingly, horribly simple. The nurse cleaned me up and lectured me about birth control and after care, without a single word of encouragement or kindness. Then, I got dressed and was told to sit in the waiting room for an hour or so to make sure I wasn't bleeding. After that, I could go. I was cold, lonely, and feeling ashamed. In shock, I got another taxi, and back to the airport I went. Done.

I returned to my quiet basement apartment in Beloit, Wisconsin that night, body and heart aching. Pretending nothing had happened and not telling anyone, I went to class the next day, even though I felt nauseous and exhausted. I had trouble sleeping for many nights and found myself crying often. My thighs were sore and I had pain in my vagina. There was some occasional bleeding on that first day, and I had some painful cramping. Although I was taking antibiotics, I worried about infection and side effects. My girlfriends offered hugs and words of comfort but how could they understand truly what I had been through?

For so many years, I just assumed I'd get married. I assumed I'd have children. Little did I know when I had the abortion that it would be my only pregnancy, my only chance. If I had known that, would I have gone ahead and had the baby? I certainly don't think so. I had college to finish. I thought I had lots of time. Again, what if? My friends who have children remind me that motherhood is not all a bed of roses. Sometimes they find themselves wishing for something different, being slightly jealous of me and my single, child-free lifestyle—which is also not all a bed of roses. I certainly have spent my own time being envious of them. My arms and heart ache to hold a child, to hold my husband.

I know that I have tried to fill that emptiness with food, numbing myself from that heartache. All the weight I gained in my 20's (somewhere around 100 pounds) was at least in part about holding in all my secrets, covering them up, burying them deep. The weight is still there as a sort of protection and insulation. And the overeating itself creates a kind of fog that keeps reality out. I guess a part of my psyche still believes I need that armor to keep people away, softness to keep the hurt away. Sensing that the body pain I occasionally feel is that emotional pain that I held in all those years, I believe that acknowledging its presence is allowing release. Healing takes as long as it takes, apparently.

The wee hours of Saturday morning

Still not sleeping. A lot going on in my brain. Too much stirring around in my heart. Regrets. Sadness. Choices. Are regrets a waste of time or is there value in thinking about past choices? I *know* there is value in loving the young woman that I was.

11 am, Phone Call with Hannah

Hannah: Good Morning!

Charity: Good Morning. How are you today?

H: Ugh, sick. I feel terrible.

C: Oh, sorry. What can I do for you?

H: Oh nothing. I've just got to rest and try to get everything done I need to do.

C: Um, that doesn't sound like resting. Does it really all have to get done and can no one else do any of it?

H: Well, I'd like it to all get done, and no, I have to do it.

C: Okay, then. I do think you could find five minutes to stop. Rest is the topic of the day. I realized this morning that I've not been getting enough real rest. I need to stop once in a while in the day time and rest, even for a few minutes. I've been diving pretty deep into some emotions, and that's exhausting work. I've been thinking about the whole taking care thing lately too. Careful. Full of care. That talking we did the other day and
I'm still working on is this self-care stuff. I like the concept of being full of care. You need rest, my darling. Make the time for it.

H: I like the concept and theory. Reality is a different story.

C: Well, right now it is. I'm trying to rewrite that story. I need a new pen or something today, the story isn't going as well. Let's make self-care badass!

H: That's us, badass old biddies.

C: Fuckin' A, man. I can't even say it. I need badass lessons.

H: That's what I can be. A badass coach. Is your ass lacking badness? Come see me. Me, who has no visible ass.

C: I like it. Me, whose ass can be seen from afar.

H: What are you doing today to care for yourself?

C: Eating well so far. I guess, since I had the thought, I'll take a rest. I need to go outside. I'll do my skin brushing. I'll take a shower today. Good thing you can't smell me over the phone. I'm not feeling fabulous myself, so perhaps some sort of chemical reaction.

H: Ugh!

C: What will you do?

H: I'm not off to a good start. No shower yet. Drinking coffee. It seems like just getting through the day is my major goal.

C: Okay, but please don't push too hard. Stop work and think of one thing you can do just to feel good. I know what happens to you when you do push too hard. I'll ask you tomorrow how your day went. If you answer your phone, I'll know you made it. If you need help, please call me and let me know. Be kind to yourself.

H: I'm trying. You too.

C: Love you.

H: Love you too.

I really need to write up my thoughts on all this self-care stuff for this week's blog post. It's really core issue for me. Won't it be great when I can feel how far I've come and it's not such a big deal anymore?

Self Care: Learn to Love Your Self Out Loud

Lately, I've been thinking a lot—maybe too much—about self-care. I am exploring the world of Ayurvedic medicine a bit, looking at what in my diet I can change up and what I can do differently to help me feel better. I'd like to feel better physically. I've been experiencing different types of inflammation, depending on the day. Aches and pains are one obvious kind of inflammation, but how about water retention, bloating, phlegm? They certainly seem related to me. I'd like to feel better emotionally, which to me means being steadier and not having big ups and downs or feeling over-whelmed. Fatigue is both a physical symptom and an emotional one. I am experiencing deep exhaustion from my adrenal glands, and it is wearing me down in all kinds of ways. So, it's time to try some new things, open some new doors and see what's there to be learned.

I've found a wonderful Ayurvedic practitioner. With her encouragement, I am integrating quite a few new "self-care" practices which I hope will become habits. This is what I am thinking about what self-care *is*.

I see it as giving myself love, tending to my body with good food, "pampering" myself with better hygiene, and watching how I use my time. I want to be careful with myself and full of care. It's similar to tending a garden.

The thesaurus revealed some interesting word connections. A few of the listings under "care" included worry, caution, desire, love, and management. Under "careless," I found inattentive, negligent, unprepared, and indifferent. There is also a listing for "careful of"—observant. Words are so fascinating, aren't they? I really don't want to be full of worry and caution as I care for myself, but do want to feel love for myself and to manage my inner world as well as I can. I want to be attentive, to pay attention, to tend to my needs. I want to be observant.

I asked a few of my friends what self-care meant to them. They said things about nourishing themselves and treating themselves kindly. Self-care is time for ourselves. The actual activities we do as part of self-care range widely and might include surfing or getting a pedicure, time alone reading a good book, taking an exercise class, or eating good food. The activity itself is not as important as the intent behind it. I know some people who think they attend to self-care really well. I also know people who feel guilty about the time they do spend tending to themselves. And, there are those who hardly do any self-care at all. Some of them are okay with that, and some wish they did more.

In general, I eat well, get exercise, casually tend to personal care, and am careful with my feelings and needs. I am one of those who tends to feel guilty and "selfish" if I spend too much time focused on myself. I get nervous with extra attention from anyone.

My new Ayurvedic routines are asking me to spend a lot of time on *me*—potentially up to a few hours a day on self-care. I have the time, so I can. Not everyone needs to invest the same amount. Ayurveda is all about what each individual needs, and it recognizes that those needs change all the time. My new routine includes things like oil pulling (care of teeth and mouth), skin brushing (which stimulates lymph, blood, removes dead cells), self-massage using different oils and essential oils, steam inhalations, using a gua sha (a tool that scrapes the skin and moves lymph), and salt scrubs with oil and essential oils (which can stimulate different organs, move blood and lymph and work on the emotional level). There are other practices: enemas, paying more attention to food preparation, treating eating as a self-care activity, eating slowly and calmly, taking time for rest, taking time for play, taking time for creativity. Taking care of myself looks like a full-time job right now. Talya, my Ayurvedic coach, reminds me that any step forward, any *one* of all those things can be seen as a giant step—a great gift of self-care. Some days, ten minutes of self-care can feel like a few hours. Some days, ten minutes is all a person has, and it is enough. Here come those thoughts again about what is enough, about thinking *I* am not enough. Baby steps. It's not as much about keeping my expectations low as it is about appreciating every step in the self-care direction as a powerful, healing one.

As you regular readers know, my mother was not gentle with herself. She did not teach me about this. She taught me to take care of my feet and my skin, not in the sense of giving them (me) love and tenderness, but as a chore. I did not learn from her that I could find pleasure in caring for myself. I've been learning this gradually over the years, and now I find myself diving into yet another layer of the fascinating world of nurturing and nourishing myself. It's exciting, and it's at times painful. It's complicated.

I'm making progress. It is still pretty easy to put off a salt scrub or using the gua sha. Some days, I can really get into it and enjoy my skin feeling soft and being energized by the lymph movement and the aroma of the essential oils. Some days, it's too much focus on me. I'm realizing what a core issue it is for me. And after talking with people, I realize that it is so for quite a few of us. Let's work on changing our culture around taking time for our self-care, on loving ourselves out loud. Let's be a culture that prides ourselves in nurturing and nourishing ourselves and our loved ones. Who's with me?

Saturday night, dinner with Tom, a.k.a. Mr. Flannel

Here we are again. Saturday night out is a big deal. It's been a good day, and some good wine and conversation are the perfect icing on the cake. Tom and I have a love of music in common, so we talked about piano playing, reading music, and taking lessons. We have our marimba night in common and our upcoming recital for it. How fun that we saw our teacher in the restaurant tonight.

I found out Tom is younger than I thought. He's only a year older than I am. We shared stories about growing up in the Midwest. We actually lived in San Francisco around the same time. He mentioned Woodstock—neither of us went, but both of us had wanted to go. We weren't quite rebellious enough yet, I guess.

Tom and I shared stories about memorable concerts we did attend and the musicians we loved. He mentioned a Gary Burton concert, of course, since they both play vibraphone. My most memorable concert continues to be Ike and Tina Turner opening for the Rolling Stones at Oakland Coliseum. Different places on the music spectrum, that's for sure! I am a Gary Burton fan, but I'm not sure how Tom feels about the Stones and Tina. If I was looking for Tom to be my soulmate, not liking Tina Turner might be a deal breaker. After all, I named my cat, Tina, after her. God, that *was* an amazing concert. Tina and Ike, so sexy. I wouldn't have enjoyed it in the same way had I known then what a bastard he was and how he treated her. Then, the Stones. The only time I saw them. In their prime. What year was that? Oh yeah, I was at Mills College, so it must have been 1970. Just the other day.

I need some new vocabulary for this relationship with Tom. We are friends. He's not my boyfriend. Saying "special friend" sounds weird. My mom had a "special friend" for the last five-ish years of her life. She called him her "good companion," and she hated me teasing her and calling George her boyfriend. They were so good for each other, and both so afraid and uncomfortable with intimacy. They held hands occasionally, if one of them needed some help getting down the stairs or something like that. They spoke of each other and to each other so affectionately, but, God forbid they should touch. I did see some polite pecks on the cheeks. Of course, Mom was never very affectionate with anyone her whole life, so I don't know why I held out hope that with George it might be different.

Jeez, this is another way I'm like my mother. I have a man friend/gentleman caller/companion/platonic buddy who takes me places. In her case, she did the taking, the arranging, the driving. In my case? This is one of the things that makes young women crazy—worrying about becoming like their mothers. And then, one day, they wake up and it has happened.

I wonder what Mama would think about this relationship. Could we laugh about what we have in common? My whole adult life, I never remember her asking me about a boyfriend, or had I gone on a date, or would I like to bring someone home for a holiday? None of those things. As an older adult, I attempted to have conversations with her about men, romance, and love. I wanted some motherly concern over my loneliness. I wanted comforting. The only comment she really could ever make was, "Well, I keep telling you you should lose weight. Why don't you try harder?" Yeah, meaning, try harder at the losing weight, not try harder to find a relationship. And, "trying harder to find a relation-ship" wouldn't have exactly been under the heading of comforting and consoling. I often felt that she was a little jealous of my single status, my "footloose and fancy-free lifestyle." I could go where and when I wanted. No one to take care of. She let her children know throughout her life that she had given up some dreams when she got pregnant, plans she and my dad had to change. It's a challenge growing up knowing your mother would have preferred not having children.

Will there always be anger? For so long, I didn't even know I "should" or could be angry at her. I always just told myself (and still do, though with a different tone these days) that she did her best. Anger and disappointment still reside with my memories and stories.

I know I still grieve for the relationship with my mother that I never had. I saw my friends who could confide in their mothers, from whom they did not have secrets. I wanted that so badly. Now I watch my friends with their grown children and grandchildren, enjoying intimacy and honesty, and I regret.

Early morning, Sunday

Hannah wants to take me out for my birthday tomorrow. She has to be so careful with her diet, but she said she was willing to go. I'll think about where I want to eat. I love my birthday.

What was my best birthday ever? Hmm. My birthday is April 16, so there have been a few times it has fallen on Easter. I have never understood why that day moves around but no matter; as a child, it was great to have them coincide. When I was seven or eight, I had an Easter birthday. I actually got to have a big party. I didn't have many birthday parties with guests other than family, so that Easter party was quite the big deal. Our family had a large piece of property, and the weather cooperated. We hosted an outside Easter egg hunt with some friends from school, my Girl Scout troop, and some of my parents' friends. Mom made a chocolate cake which I was allowed to eat, along with some of the candy. I bet I mostly ate jelly beans, which were my favorite. My parents always hid eggs and candy on Easter morning but, as with the Halloween candy, I didn't get to keep all of mine. I could pick a few things I liked and had to give the remainder to my brothers or to Mom. Knowing those jelly beans were my favorite Easter candy, and knowing my brothers did not like the black ones, Dad always "hid" a plentiful row or two of them across the top of the black TV trays stored in their container in the corner.

That chocolate Easter cake is the only childhood birthday cake I remember. Could it really be true that it was my only one? I know there were years without any cake, but I must have had more than one. Was my mom really that thoughtless and cruel? This makes me sad for that little girl I was, watching my brothers blow out their candles and eat cake and share the leftovers with Dad for breakfast the next morning. I usually got some fruit. Maybe a bite of my Dad's piece of cake or the tiniest of the tiniest see-through slices which amounted to one or maybe two bites. For that, I was supposed to be grateful and feel rewarded for some sort of good behavior. As I grew into adulthood, I realized the cruelty of this and finally let myself really feel that pain and anger. How could parents do this to a child? I have to keep reminding myself that I was not all that fat. Chubby, sure but, there were no medical concerns—just my mother's own childhood insecurities and her pain. After she died, I began to feel how much of her pain I had carried and mixed up with mine. I still miss her terribly, but in the first years after her death, I felt relief both in my body as aches and pains faded and emotionally as my moods began to level out.

Mom did make each of us a special dinner on our birthdays—whatever we wanted. My brothers chose steak, roast beef, shrimp. I often asked for liver and onions. Yes, that's true. I still love it, but don't eat it too often. I like chicken livers more than beef now, but I'm always up for caramelized onions.

This year, my birthday falls on Easter again. I'll make myself a cake, I think. Flourless chocolate, my favorite. A grown-up version of that birthday memory. Why have cake if it's not chocolate, I say? In many shamanic cultures, chocolate is sacred, the food of the Gods. It's good medicine.

I remember the birthday parties we had in my sexual abuse therapy group in Portland. I had been in private therapy for a while and my therapist recommended I join her group. We worked together for a whole year, and each member got to celebrate a birthday. We could pick any age we wanted to have be celebrated, and were given an age-appropriate party. So many of us had either difficult birthday memories or no birthday memories at all. My party was so pretty! I decided to turn six, so the colors were little-girl-pink, turquoise, and green. And there were balloons! No one had ever given me balloons before. We shared an exquisite chocolate cake, with pink frosting with lots of frosting flowers—the kind I know I never had, from a bakery with pretty decorations. The group bought me a sweet baby doll. That doll lived on my bed for a year or two, then went to live with a favorite little girl who needed a special friend. I giggled and giggled throughout the party, just like a healthy happy six-year-old. So healing, so powerful.

My 40th birthday was awesome too. Talk about music! It was1991. My friends and I danced and danced to songs predominantly from the 60's and 70's, with some 80's thrown in there. I spent days and days making a tape of my favorite dancing music. It was an eclectic mix with lots of Motown music—Aretha, Marvin Gaye, the Beatles, the Rolling Stones, and the Grateful Dead, just to name a few. I tried to fit all my favorites into a few hours. Now, that's a funny thing to try to explain to kids. Remember taping music off of records? Or when we would try to tape it off the radio? Crazy. Anyway, we had such fun dancing and laughing. I know there was cake at that party, but I no longer remember what kind. What was really great is that most of my friends were already in their 40's and kept telling me how great it was. We all sat in a circle during a dance break, and they shared their good wishes for me. "Welcome to your 40's," they said. "You are going to love it!" And, "We've been waiting for you and are so glad you are here." And they were right, my 40's were a powerful time full of adventure and growth. That was a great party. I felt loved and respected.

Oh, and I can't forget my 49th birthday in Vegas seeing Tina Turner. What a fun weekend that was. A couple of friends treated me to the weekend. We played the slot machines, wandered down Fremont Street under the lights, and ate good food. Tina was amazing. Then my 50th, that was my first time on the island of Crete. Another fun party with singing and dancing. And delicious Greek food—*dolmades*, wild greens, roasted chicken, olive oil cake. We celebrated on and off for days, any excuse to have another dessert or sing another song.

This year is "just" 66. Not a special number, as my mom would say. No big party, because I wasn't able to gather everyone together at the same time. But there will be a bunch of small celebrations. I have friends taking me out to breakfast one day, dinner another. We'll see what else happens. Even if 66 Is not a special number, I think every year is a big deal. We all should feel special on our birthdays. Another circle around the sun is a cause to celebrate. It just might be time to have that bottle of champagne I was writing about in that last blog post.

Evening, chatting on Facebook

Interesting to hear from friends with various family dramas, some quite serious. Conversations about big family confrontations with adult children and siblings pull up my own feelings for sure. During therapy, I made an active decision to not talk with my parents about Grandfather and his abuse. I had no conscious memories of it until I was well into my 30's. Around age 32, I started having dreams about my grandfather and upon telling those dreams to my therapist, she starting realizing they were not dreams but memories. Then, the floodgates opened. I went to numerous therapy and healing sessions (bodywork, acupuncture, and rebirthings are just some of the avenues I explored) to get to the point where I was strong enough to learn more about what had happened and to cope with the emotions that accompanied it. I still don't really understand the workings of the brain and unconscious mind that would suppress those memories, nor do I understand the why, when, and how of releasing them.

Both of my grandparents were dead by the time I started remembering everything. I like to think I would have confronted them and let the family know if they had still been alive. I do remember revisiting the issue now and then both in therapy and on my own, wondering if I should tell Mom and Dad. I think I was pretty good with being clear with myself, what would be best for me.

Monday afternoon, April 16, my birthday, on my way to look for a new car

Car Buying! Oh god, I'm finally going to do it. I've had the money set aside for a while, but I realized this morning that I have been dipping into it. I need to get the car while I still have enough. It's so exciting and nerve-wracking. I'm remembering other car buying experiences such as the first one, a beige VW bug in San Francisco. I was about 25. I hardly ever talked on the phone to my parents then. Times were different, and they had that older genera-tion idea about the phone being for emergencies. Still, I had had a long conversation with Dad before buying the car. He was so worried and filled with regret that he didn't have time to come out and help me with it. He made sure I had a long list of questions to ask, what to check for and look at. The other car buying experience I'm remembering now is the one fourteen years ago, when I bought my current car, BlueBelle, little Miss Toyota Corolla. I needed a low maintenance car, and she fit the bill.

Later, driving the new car home

Okay, I didn't expect this. Happy Birthday to me! I thought I would just go look at a few cars, but here I am, on Highway 17, on my way home in a brand new car. Black Beauty—that's what I'm going to call him. He's big and strong. Handsome, black and shiny. I'm driving with my head held high. It's another VW, a wagon this time, giving me room to hold gear when I travel, more room for people and carpooling. Such a process. A plethora of paper and signatures needed. I was prepared, though. There was one car available that I wanted, and I got it. I wasn't quite ready to let go of BlueBelle today, right there on the lot. She was covered in dust, with bird poop on the windows, and she was still full of stuff, which was embarrassing. Why didn't I clear it out before I went?

It was so thought-provoking, seeing the two cars sitting next to each other. The old one, so raggedy-looking and uncomfortable, says so much about everything I've been thinking about in the realm of self-care. If it's true that you can tell a lot about a person by looking at their car, heaven help me. I'm upgrading my nourishment, my feelings about myself, and now my statement in the world.

BlueBelle still ran well, though. My parents were both sitting on my shoulder for a long time saying, "You don't need a new car yet." But I really did. I didn't even know how decrepit the seats in the old car were until I sat in the new one. The new ones have actual support and no stains. The salesman got a good chuckle out of watching me getting in and out and of the new car, listening to me giggle. I told him the seat was probably the most important consideration for me. It was at the right height to make getting in and out easy. Wide enough for me. It felt sturdy, reminding me the old ones had gotten pretty saggy. My big body can be comfortable in this car.

Who can I call? Just because I can, with my fancy new Bluetooth setup. Oh, Hannah, of course…

C: Hi, Hannah. It's me in my new car on the phone! How cool is that?

Hannah: Way cool, Happy Birthday! That's a good present.

C: Yep. I didn't think I was going to do it today. I thought I would just look, but here I am, in a new car. I got the VW. It's black and a year old with 7000 miles on it. Perfect.

H: Congratulations.

C: I'm on the highway, so I really don't want to talk long. I just called because I can. I'll talk to you tomorrow.

H: Okay, bye. Congratulations. Drive carefully.

Yay! Such a great birthday present. I am so proud of myself for finally getting myself a new car. The perfect combination of a practical present that will make my life amazingly better, *and* something indulgent. I'm so grateful I can afford it. It's easy to drive and easy to get in and out of. And now, Black Beauty makes it possible for me to do the Epic Adventure Trip I've been contemplating. And another step towards self-love and boosting the self-esteem.

Friday night, after going out to dinner with Hannah

It's a relief to go to a restaurant where the food is right in line with my thinking about what I need to eat to feel good. The name of the restaurant is "Home," so that says a lot about it there, farm-to-table and organic. At one point in my personal chef career, I had shared a commercial kitchen space with the owner, but he was not there tonight to say hello to. I could just eat without worrying or trying not to feel guilty or angry. And I love going out with Hannah because we enjoy eating the same things. We ordered a selection of appetizers and side dishes—roasted cauliflower, salad, potatoes, octopus, paté. A perfect glass of Rosé wine. No room for dessert, so that made that decision easy. Good conversation. A little gossiping. Nothing wrong with that. We chatted and laughed, moaned and groaned over the perfect spicing of the cauliflower and the unctuousness of the paté. We ate every bite of all of it. We decided one glass of wine wasn't quite enough so we shared the next one. The waiter was young, cute, and very attentive. We chuckled over deciding to give him a big tip "just because."

Now I'm home, and I'm realizing that I had not one moment of food shame or even thinking about anything other than the scrumptious tastes. I *could* have had dessert, but I didn't want it. Yay! No judging from Hannah, of course, and a sweet waiter. Those are all good birthday presents.

4 am, awake

It's Hard to Hug a Fat Person   128

What a complicated dream. I'm already only remembering bits and pieces. In one scene, I, along with several people I don't know in real life, were combination flying/driving over some rough land, doing some tricky maneuvering, like driving straight up a 90-degree cliff. We were flying over some strange-looking spots of bare dirt and areas of devastation. There were these egg-like objects—they looked like giant fried eggs, actually, and they were covered with some sort of protective film. We traveled over conspicuously large spots where they ground was compacted, where it looked as if an animal had slept. We did have a specific destination, but I don't think we got there. That's probably when I woke up. A little creepy, but not too scary. What the hell kind of birthday dream is that? I think those dreams can have a big effect on the coming year, or can foretell what the year might be like. What did this one say? Adventure, maybe. Drama, maybe. Not a romantic comedy, for sure. Seems like I might be needing that new car and a good seat belt. And some dramamine for the flying.

Later that morning, on Facebook
"Allow beauty to shatter you regularly. The loveliest people are the ones who have been burnt and broken and torn at the seams, yet still send their open hearts into the world to mend with love again and again and again. You must allow yourself to feel your life while you are in it." - Victoria Erickson

Word. Again, I am in awe of how the Universe works. That I see this quote today. This message and similar ones come across my computer over and over—about seeking out Beauty and letting it fill me, break me, heal me, strengthen me. Being willing to love again and again. To keep rising. Like that Maya Angelou quote, "And still we rise." "Nevertheless, she persisted." I need to get up and keep opening my heart. Keep loving. Keep being open to being honored and cherished. Let that in. Breathe. Feel all that there is to feel. The beautiful. The good. The bad. The ugly. The painful. The scary. The glorious. All of it. I'm getting stronger and more resilient. I've decided that "resilient" is my word for this 66th year.

Giving myself permission to step back for some breaths is not the same as going unconscious. The more I can consciously step back when I need to, the stronger can be that move forward again. Stepping back isn't quite what I'm trying to say, but it makes me think of dancing. Forward and back. Forward and back. Loving and breathing and living fully. It's not always easy, but maybe it becomes easier. There is always Hope.

From my writing notebook
Resiliency
Bouncing back
Bending
Malleable

Wait, no. I am not moldable. Is that a word? You cannot bend me to your will, make me what you desire or think I should be.
I no longer am willing to try to be someone else, someone to please someone else.
You think I should lose weight, you think I should look and act a certain way?

Step back, Jack. Hit the road.
That is so last century.

I am a crone.
I've got arms that can hold the whole world.

Sunday afternoon

The house is clean—as long as I don't open the door to the spare room! Let's see if I'll be motivated to empty out that room of its boxes and paper now that I am thoroughly disgusted by it. I'm not holding my breath. I am just a clutter-y, messy person. Some say that's a sign of creativity, although I know that's the messy people saying that. Hopefully I will always be creative, and maybe the messy part can change.

I hired a crew of housecleaners, and the house energy feels different, with no cobwebs, no dust, the corners clean. When I apologized to them for the mess, those nice young housecleaners I hired assured me that my house wasn't all that bad. I guess they've seen some pretty gnarly places. Years ago, when all the abuse memories were waiting to appear and be recognized, when food and alcohol were becoming serious problems, my house *was* one of those gnarly places. It was bad.

My little house was set in the woods five miles from Forest Grove, Oregon, about an hour from the ocean. It was my shack that I loved and then I hated. I bought it and the 2 1/2 acres it sat on in 1981, after I inherited some money from my grandparents. I did this without any advice from or consultation with my Dad, which forever upset him. I consciously did not ask him because I knew he would tell me that under no circumstances should I buy that house. It was a poorly-made piece of junk, and I didn't care. The property was at the end of a dirt road surrounded by forest owned by a timber company, with a nearby neighbor on one side, and no one else for miles on the other sides. It was fronted by an absolutely magnificent grove of cedar trees, with trillium and a carpet of moss under it all. When the realtor and I arrived, those trees spoke to me. They wanted me to live there. I decided to believe in that voice and trust. And, so, that was that. The poor realtor didn't want to sell it to me, and rightly so; the owners were not asking much for it, and his commission would be small. The man clearly thought I was crazy. Maybe I was, I don't know. As we looked around the house and he saw all that needed to be done, he asked, "Are you sure you want this place? It's really a dump! You got someone to help you? You want to live out here alone?"

I just smiled. "Yes."

The wood shingled house itself was small—one bedroom, with a wood stove and a fireplace. The construction was shoddy. Most of the windows were put in crooked, and the floors were uneven. The roof was solid and the front porch was awesome. At times, it housed a woodpile, several dogs, and a comfy chair for me to sit in and contemplate my world.

I lived there for fifteen years, part of the time loving it, driving the five miles into town five days a week for work as a teacher. It was hard work. The house had some electric heat, but the wood stove was necessary to keep it warm enough during the fall and winter. On cold nights, I'd set my alarm so I'd wake up to fill the stove. If I didn't, the animals' water froze, and the floors would be crazy cold.

I got strong from chopping that wood, stacking it, and carrying it into the house. Sometimes I loved the rhythm of that. Other times, I'd be out there in the rain desperately chopping because I had run out of dry wood, hating every minute of it, with each swing of the axe bringing me tears and frustration. I'd bring the wet wood into the house and pile it up so it would be dry enough to burn, adding a whole layer of moldy wet scent to the cat perfume.

The piles of newspapers grew in the house because I didn't have garbage or recycling service for the first eight years I lived there. One winter, that stack had gotten too close to my fireplace and some sparks caused it to catch fire. Luckily, I was right there and could just pour water on it!

I started out with a little yard in the midst of the 2 1/2 acres. I happily planted rose bushes the first year, since it had been my dream for a few years to have a little house with my own rose garden. At the time, the neighbor's goats would regularly break out of their pasture and come over to nibble on those rose bushes, which clearly had no way of fighting back. Thorns were no problem for those goats, and my pretty roses were like dessert. The goats were cute but smelly, and the billy could be quite mean when he got on my front porch. I was never able to chase him off, so I'd have to drive over to the neighbors and ask them to come over and fetch him and his lady friends.

When I first moved there, blackberries and morning glory vines grew around the edges of the property. Year by year, they got closer and closer to the house, and the "lawn" grew smaller and smaller. Every year I went to war. I chopped and chopped, and even hired workers to chop and dig. I carefully set fire to the vines a few times in attempts to keep them at bay. After the original goats moved on to different pastures, I hired a herd of goats to come and eat as much as they could. The local deer were happy to help out, but even they couldn't really make a dent. Nothing worked. Those blackberries and morning glory vines eventually took over the whole yard and worked their way into the house around the poorly-set window casements. I just got used to living in the blackberry jungle, which gradually grew from being a tasty delight to more like a prison.

Midway through living there, I decided (this time *with* help from my father) to get the house remodeled. The back wall was torn down to add two additional rooms, the bathroom was modernized, and finally, a real foundation was put under it. The man who originally built the house was the town mortician, and he had utilized broken headstones or ones upon which the names had been misspelled to prop up the corners of the house. In Oregon, in the wet winter, this was not enough of a foundation, and the parts of the house which sat in the mud had become home to many happy families of carpenter ants. During the remodel, I lived in a motor home out in the yard. One evening, I entered the job site to inspect what the day's progress had been. I was shocked to find a message spray painted in big white letters on one of the newly sheet rocked kitchen walls. It said, "Kill your cats. They stink." Whoa. Frightening to say the least! I quickly called the contractor who fired the sorry asses of the workers who had been there that day, and the work continued. The plus side of that story is that it did wake me up a bit to my cat situation. The cats were indeed using parts of my house as their litter box.

One year, there was a forest fire close by. It was not close enough for our road to evacuate, but we were on alert. We could occasionally see smoke in the distance coming from the other side of a nearby ridge. My cat population had grown by leaps and bounds to somewhere around fifteen. There were cats everywhere, some of whom slept in my bed and were quite cuddly. Others were barely tame outside cats, and some were quite feral. I knew I was going to be able to take two, maybe three, with me when we evacuated, because I only had a small car. For many days, a box of important papers, some of my clothes, and my good jewelry sat by the door ready to go, along with the available cat carriers. What a process that was, deciding what was actually precious and important. Every day, I added possessions to the pile and hoped it would all fit in my car if the time came. Fortunately, the fire never came over the ridge and we were all safe.

Throughout all this, I continued to love the trees and the surrounding forest—cedars, dogwood, fir, wild trillium and mushrooms, deer, and all the birds. I lived there for another six years after the remodel.

While living there I drove to work every week on the dusty, gravelly, mostly one-lane road. I did have work friends, but we socialized in town. Later, I came to terms with the reasons for that—the cat smells and how isolated the house was. I had the peace and solitude I needed, until one day, it became too quiet, and my solitude became isolation and loneliness. Joy had somehow become depression. My messiness brought me shame. Living there became too difficult.

I never did clean up that house. Papers stayed stacked here and there. Cats came and went but there were always too many, and the house always smelled like them. At least, garbage service finally became available. The last few years I lived there, I just sort of gave up. I became more of a recluse and more depressed. The enchantment and peace was gone. It took me a few years to figure out that I needed to get out of there, and that I was ready to go. I was finding new strength and wisdom in my spiritual explorations and I wanted to be around people. I didn't want to have to work so hard to be comfortable. I wanted to feel safer. So, I moved into a lovely 100-year-old house in town. It was sturdy, with plenty of room and a good furnace. Only semi-joking, I said that I needed to domesticate myself. The feral cats got left behind in the care of the new owners. A new chapter of taking better care of myself and my effects began. My self-esteem picked up, and my health got better. I stopped hiding. I became friends with my neighbors and socialized more. I began learning that I deserved those things. There, safe from deer, goats, and blackberries, I made a healing home with a lovely garden, and yes, there were roses.

Monday, 6 a.m.

I need time in the garden today, planting and just getting my hands in the dirt. I took care of the house, now it's the yard's turn. I've got guys coming to do some extreme weeding and to plant a new lemon tree. Ahh, Meyer lemons. That's what my blog post can be about. "When life gives you lemons…" Such a cliché but, yum. That lemon cake at the restaurant the other night was not good. What a waste of gluten and dairy for me. It wasn't bad, just not good. Such is life often, right? Just in the middle. Nothing terrible, nothing wonderful, mediocre. We need to look for the wonderful. Gotta make our own wonderful. Gotta make my own dessert! That's a metaphor for something, some sort of motto. Life is short, eat dessert first. Make sure you get just the piece you want. If you are having dessert, absolutely have exactly what you want. That is how I want my life to be, rich and spicy, just exactly what I want. Sweet.

11am, Facebook Messenger with Hannah

Charity: Hey girl. Good morning.

Hannah: Good morning.

C: I woke up so early this morning. I had to drag myself out of bed. What's new with you?

H: I'm still looking for a paddle board partner.

C: Ahh, I so wish I could go out there with you. I just can't do the getting up and down on the board part. That's a fairly crucial part, haha. In my next life, I am coming back as a surfer. I would love to interact more with the ocean. I occasionally feel pulled to open water swimming. The wetsuit is what stops me. Not the fear of the water. I just can't bring myself to do the wet suit buying, the trying on, the fitting.

H: You should! Do it. I know you love swimming. Me, not so much, but I love being out there on the water.

C: I love being at the ocean when it is wild and windy. And, I do look out there on those calm days and think how great a swim would be.

H: Only once in a while I get a little scared, but I kind of like it. It's my time to commune with Grandmother Ocean, with the spirits out there. So, what's the deal with the wetsuit? It takes a little getting used to how they feel. I don't wear one when I paddle, or I have a half one.

C: First, it's the fitting. That's not anything you ever have to think about. Well, not true. You sometimes have a hard time finding small enough things. I've looked online many different times. No one makes a women's one large enough for me. There is some sort of fashion theory that believes that if you are a size XXL you must be at least six feet tall and have arms down to your knees—and be a man. None of that applies to me as I am actually a petite woman around 5'3" with short arms, and there is not much manly about me. I remember buying some men's rain gear one time for a trip to Alaska. What a joke, and not a funny one. The crotch of the pants went down to my knees and the sleeves of the jacket were down there too.

H: Damn, I can't decide if I want to meet the man whose crotch fits in those pants or not. LOL

C: LOL, me neither. Gulp. Anyway, there are no cheap large women's wetsuits. I might even need a custom fit one, and they are ridiculously expensive. Plus, I'm just not sure how often I would actually use it. So, for now, swimming in the ocean is just a kind of dream. Maybe one day I'll get my courage up again and go try some wetsuits on. Sometimes I get triggered all over again about body issues, my size, and what I'd look like in that get up. A really juicy walrus. Then, I get pissed off and it upsets me that it's still an issue that pops up, and that I can still get sucked into feeling that way.

H: Well, someday I will kidnap you and we will just go find you one. I wonder if it would help you think that no one would recognize you in a wetsuit, especially since you probably would want a hood for swimming and goggles. It's a great disguise actually. Anyway, I get so much healing when I am out on the water. It's quiet, except for ocean noises. I've seen all kinds of fish, otters, seals, whales, dolphins or porpoises—I always forget which one is which. Is *porpie* the plural of porpoise? Which gets autocorrected to *potpie*. Mmm, potpie.

C: Silly autocorrect! Did I ever make you my potpie? Not to change the subject or anything! I have a great almond flour crust recipe with butter and egg. So rich, so good. I always have to double the crust recipe. I'll make you one sometime.

H: Don't put any peas in it. I might be a badass out on my paddle board, but I am a wussy wimp when it comes to peas.

C: You and a few other people I know. I love peas. Anyway, thanks for your thoughts and your support. I know you have your own feelings about me and my weight, and I appreciate that you can hear and hold my feelings.

H: I just want you to be happy. Just like all of us, I think sometimes you are and sometimes you are trying very hard to feel good, and then there are those times you just don't care. It's a human condition.

C: Emotions are a blessing and a curse.

H: They are messy, that's for sure. Okay, enough of that for me. LOL, I need to eat some food.

C: Oy, I'd better get busy with some errands. I love you and will see you tomorrow.

H: Love you too.

Wednesday, after exercise class

It's cool and misty out. The fog down low is wisping around the branches of the trees—enough to curl my hair but not enough to get it wet. Underneath the giant eucalyptus near the ocean, the air was fresh and smelled wonderful. Clean and reviving, soothing our lungs. Crashing waves, tall magnificent trees, and birds singing. The fog made the world mystical and magical, a blessing for my soul.

It was a medium-challenging workout. Unlike some of our class locations around town, Natural Bridges State Park has no stairs or big hills for which my legs say thank you. Plenty of work though. I feel strong. I have to say I like it that I have the strongest upper body in our class. It kind of makes up a little for my always being the slowest walker. I am generally so non-competitive that it makes me chuckle at the attention I get for this. We do all have our aches and pains and problems for sure. I appreciate that we are all so supportive of each other too. I couldn't do it, I wouldn't do it, if that were not so.

We've been together for a long time now, aging together. Something close to eight years. I'm stronger than I was then. Older and slower. A little heavier. One knee replacement. We'll see about what happens next. So far so good. My heart felt good today, lungs pretty clear. I have a good perspective on life today. I'm doing my best and that's actually pretty damn good, if I do say so. Which I do. I'll say it again. I'm doing my best and that's actually pretty damn good. I could just be bold and say it is damn good. Nothing "pretty" about it. A damn good life. I'm proud of what I've come through and who I am. I feel beautiful today.

That evening

I had a conversation this afternoon with a friend over tea and snacks that got difficult. We were talking about the challenges of loving ourselves no matter what, the challenges of being alone. Our chat sort of turned into her lecturing me a bit. Not that I had said I was looking necessarily, but she spouted on about the difficulties of loving someone else, allowing someone else to love me if I'm not loving myself. I do love myself but according to her, not enough for change to come about. I don't believe it necessary to love myself perfectly. What is "perfectly"? If I love myself a little, or some of the time, is that not enough? Most of the time, is that good enough? Are there really people who love themselves all of the time, every minute? I don't think so. I don't really think my friend does, but she didn't have much to say about that. And what about all the people who never even think about it? They either do love themselves, and so don't bother to think about it, or maybe they don't even really have that vocabulary. It's simply not part of their world. Does that mean they can't attract love into their life? No. There are people who don't feel so great about themselves, and yet they might be in a relationship that is satisfying to them. I actually am content with my life. I do get lonely and long for that intimacy, but I'm not miserable without it. I hated that when Jo and

I were talking, I felt as if being alone was all my fault, that I was wrong, doing something wrong, that only if I got my shit together, the problem would be solved. It had the potential of triggering all that old diet culture crap—"If only you lost weight, you'd be happy," etc. I got fairly defensive. She replied, "Oh gosh, I didn't mean that you are doing anything wrong. I just want you to be happy."

"Haven't you heard me say that I *am* happy?

"Well, happier anyway."

At this point, I was frustrated, wanting to cry. I asked, "How about we just change the subject? You've given me some things to think about and I hope you will look at what I said too."

I am proud of who I am. I hate that I have to keep convincing myself. Still, I really don't get why I have never had a husband or even a long-term lover. At times, I get incredibly sad—devastated even—and other times, being alone is perfectly fine. It sure isn't how I thought my life would be. And I completely believe my relationship status could change any day, any time, in the blink of an eye. Flirting a little with that guy at the concert the other night, that could have turned the tide. It didn't. At Weight Watchers, years ago I met a delightful woman in her 80's. She happily told us all one day that she had found love for the first time. "I've started liking my body more and am feeling a little sassy!" She decided to make a personals ad and thus had recently met the love of her life. They were planning their wedding. The whole room cried when she told us.

From my writing notebook
I could escape from being a disappointing daughter
(line from *Hunger*, a memoir by Roxane Gay)
For years, I had a very tenuous relationship with my family
Was it good? was it bad?
Was it love?

Under the layers of fat,
layers of love trembling beneath the shame and blame,
underneath all that disapproval and embarrassment

there   was   love

As an adult in my 20's and 30's
My rule was firm with my family.
There was to be absolutely no talking about my body

My parents were no longer allowed to worry out loud
no criticisms
no comments
Keep your judgements and opinions to yourself,
If not, I will leave
I don't think I knew what power I held with that statement

I will leave.

I can hear my father say
"Now, Mary Esther, remember what Charity asked of us"
something to that effect as he would gently touch Mom and help
her hold her thoughts.

I never did leave
Not bodily anyway
I left in my mind
I shut myself in whatever safe place inside I could find,
surrounding myself with cookies, with wine,
with what I could salvage from their cupboards
and not let their pain touch me.
I had my own.

They were afraid for me
They were embarrassed
How did this happen to them?
Why did I eat so much?
Why was I fat
even with all their efforts to help me not be so?
Why was I unhappy?
or even worse in their eyes,

why wasn't I unhappy?
Why didn't I want to change?
I didn't dare let any of those feelings in
for fear I would find my own similar questions.
If I was eating, there was no pain
If I was eating, there were no feelings at all

as a child, my father's worst punishment ever
 was being disappointed in me
"Wait until your Father gets home"
kept me in my room
dreading what he would say
Disappointment
Broken heart
I hope better for you

that disappointment was too much to bear
I could take my mother's anger
which was her way of dealing
with her own feelings which were too much to bear

As a college student I lied to my parents about a Big Thing
My Father came to see me
He was angry
oh so disappointed
How could he ever trust me again?
Utter devastation
I had survived sexual abuse
This seemed worse
He did eventually trust
He did come to be proud of me again and told me so
My mother also.
If those other words were utter devastation,
Pride was the healing balm.

Many years later,

I wish they were here.

I wish I could tell them
how I feel
how I felt then.

why I didn't want to feel anything

I'm making peace with my own disappointment
my own worries about who I let down
who I didn't or couldn't let in
Step by step
I can parent myself
I repair what I can
in the family I have left

Monday morning

I've had a lot of music in my head of late. It's always been so important to me. Music is one of those consistent threads running through my life. Mom and Dad had an odd assortment of records—classical, big band music from the 40's, some folk music, musicals. The family record album I remember most is Bing Crosby's *White Christmas Album. Mele Kalikimaka.* It was pretty worn out by the time my parents got rid of their records. And then there was that period Dad went through with all those sea shanties. He had a dozen or so reel-to-reel tapes, from some friend of his, I guess. He spent hours duplicating them, and we were forced to spend hours listening to them. A little went a long way with those.

I think I was in seventh grade when I got my first record player—one of those little portable ones that looked kind of like a suitcase. It took a lot of my allowance to buy any records, so, for the longest time, I owned a grand total of three 45's: "Help Me Rhonda" by the Beach Boys, Lorne Greene singing "Ringo," and "Glad all Over" by the Dave Clark Five. I eventually used my savings for albums which were more satisfying, and the collection slowly grew. Judy Collins. The Beatles. Leonard Cohen. My Joan

Baez album became a favorite and inspired me to ask for a guitar for Christmas. After a short, painful time trying to get my finger calluses built up, it ended up in the corner of my room until my Mom convinced me to give it away.

My classmates and I took turns bringing our record players to school so we could listen to music and dance in one of the class-rooms during our free time after lunch. We taught each other new steps we had seen on television—on American Bandstand, Hoote-nanny, and Soul Train. We dreamed of going to concerts. There were a few boys who came to our little dance parties, but mostly we girls went and imagined slow dances with the boys of our dreams.

Then, freshman year of high school, I was finally old enough to go to the school dances on Friday nights with my girlfriends. I can still see and hear so clearly the night I danced with Dave Lipp, my crush. He was a senior and on the football team. The loud-speaker announced that the next dance was "ladies' choice." Boy, is that a thing from the way back machine. It's hard to imagine that only once or twice a night was it "okay" to ask a boy to dance. The song was The Righteous Brothers singing "Ebb Tide." Could it have been more perfect? With much nudging and encouragement from my friends, and legs shaking, I crossed the gym and asked him to dance. I couldn't believe it when he said yes. Later, I overheard some boys saying it was all a joke to him and his football team. But still, that moment! With one hand holding his and the other on his shoulder, I dared to look at his dreamy blue eyes. He was lots taller than I was and a really good dancer. Even though I had slow danced with a few boys before, this was the best thing that had happened to me in my life, ever. My girlfriends were in one corner, watching and giggling with joy for me, and his posse was in another corner, also watching and doing some sort of manly version of giggling. I still love that song. It can make me shiver and feel fourteen years-old again. I wonder what ever happened to Dave?

From my writing journal
In the garden

a weed is just a plant growing where you don't want it to
somedays I'm a weed
a dandelion with lots of strength and power
to grow in all kinds of challenging conditions
but the wind plopped me down here in the middle of orchids
and roses.

a clash of color
a clash of purpose

Wouldn't I be more comfortable with the other dandelions?

the orchids are stately and elegant
the roses smell so sweet
though both are high maintenance

Me,
I hardly even wash my face.

Every day I go out to the garden and pull a few weeds
Remove the spent blossoms
Making room for the new.

That day will come when I am a spent blossom
deadheaded into the compost bin or tossed aside
The compost bin makes fertile soil.

Today the geraniums are going wild.
Orange, red, pink, white.
Mama and I fell even more in love with geraniums each time we
went to Italy.
We'd come home and dash to our nurseries for more.

It's time to start collecting the hollyhock seeds.
Beautiful purplish red.
Thousands of seeds.
I look forward to scattering some here and there

What will happen next year?
Did you ever make a hollyhock doll?
A big blossom for the skirt, another for the hat and a sweet bud for the face?
I never saw hollyhocks as a child but I sure would have welcomed those ladies to my dolls' tea table.

Hands in the dirt
Heart open to the earth
Connecting with mother
Beauty and gratitude fill my heart.

Saturday morning

Tom's coming over for supper and a movie tonight. That sounds so normal. It's what a lot of people do on a Saturday night. Maybe it's my new normal. Cool! I think of all the people I know who are married or in long-term relationships. For them, watching a movie is no big deal. But I haven't actually had many movie "dates" in the theatre or at home.

I'll clean the house a bit, make some soup for our dinner. Making soup gives me great satisfaction. It's chemistry and art at the same time—taking a bunch of odds and ends, what's in the fridge, or buying some nice vegetables, and cutting them thoughtfully. I let them stew and simmer, brew and bubble, and see what the end result is. It's usually something tasty. It never tastes quite the same, even if you use a recipe. I had some personal chef clients for whom I made soup often that got frustrated by that. "Charity, we love your carrot soup, can you make it again?" Why yes, but don't expect that it will taste exactly like today's. If it's good, you'd better relish it to its fullest, because I won't be able to recreate it. That keeps me in the moment. And, there's always the hope that the next pot will be even better. It's the mystery, the unknown. A never-ending experiment. Such is life, right?

Thankfully spring is here, and I can move away from root vegetable soup to something greener, something with stalks that energetically move up towards the sky, not down to the ground. Winter's for digging deep, finding that warmth and that nourishment that comes from below. But in the spring, we stay above ground, searching for warmth and light. Those little green shoots are pushing hard to get to the sun. They explode with the energy it takes to break out of the seed pod and burst forth. *Here comes the sun, little darling.*

That reminds me of my disc jockey days at college. A not-so-great part of that memory is my occasional use of speed to help me stay awake all night. A couple of times a year, I would decide I should be on a diet, so I would head over to our college health clinic where I would be prescribed some speed—I mean, "diet pills." These usually kept me awake and nauseous, which was maybe the reason I would lose a few pounds. Of course, I would gain them back after I could no longer stand how those pills made me feel. Every so often, one of my friends would convince me to go back to the clinic and get pills they could buy from me.

College in Wisconsin came with long hard winters, but I miss that first big flush of spring energy when finally, the world turns green. Here in California, we are green all winter. Spring does bring a big flush of color with all the flowers. Now, my garden is like heaven. It looks the best it has in a long time. So many flowers, and, as always, I want more! Flowering pink currant. I don't know the name of those purple flowers which spring everywhere. Wild spring onions with the little white bell flowers. Watsonia. Grape hyacinth. All that oxalis. Some call it a weed, but that cheery yellow makes me so happy. I'm so grateful for all our winter rain. Thank you, Grandmother.

So, spring soup for me and Mr. Flannel. A pleasant evening on the couch with a movie. Something to look forward to. I'm enjoying the simplicity, and I'm also wishing that I could make him a grand dinner and impress the hell out of him. He's not into grand dinners though. I'll save that effort for someone else.

I've done enough pondering. Now that I'm thinking about it, I want to go make some magic in the garden, then some magic in the soup pot. Too bad there won't be Mr. Flannel magic. He doesn't seem to have it in him, which is his great loss. Onward into my day.

That night, going to bed

We had trouble choosing a Netflix movie and ended up randomly with Paul Newman in *The Drowning Pool,* which was fun. Dated, but entertaining. The soup was satisfying. Tom eats simply, so sharing food with him can be a gentle reminder to me that sometimes a plain uncomplicated meal is just as pleasurable as something more elaborate. We agree that lunch is the main meal of the day, so the evening meal doesn't need to be large. I do realize that as much as eating in restaurants gives me pleasure, sometimes my belly just wants a bowl of homemade soup. I enjoyed our evening, just two friends keeping each other company and having a few laughs. I do wonder about our future together a bit. Being with him does remind me of what has been missing in my life. Tonight was completely enjoyable because I stayed in the moment.

Awake, early Monday morning

Oh, that dream. I had to wake myself up. I feel ripped out of myself! They were going to kill me, I had to stop the dream. I learned once that if you look at your hands, look at yourself in a dream, then you can make yourself awaken. That worked tonight. Such a strange dream. It seemed as if I was in San Francisco at first, because of the skyline, the waterfront. I was in a boat that was more like a basket; it was made from some sort of basket-like material. It did not look or feel waterproof. Nor did it have a motor or a sail; it was just traveling on its own somehow. By dream magic, I guess. I was sort of flying, sort of scooting over the water. I went faster and faster and left the place of the little boats, heading out further and further into the deep water. It got rough and stormy, more like the ocean with large swells. The basket boat was out of control, but I managed to head towards a little spit of land and scooted up on the beach. When I got out and walked a bit, I was unable to figure out more than that I appeared to be on a deserted island, so I had definitely dream-morphed out of the San Francisco Bay Area.

Suddenly, there were two men approaching me. They had extremely dark energy. I wasn't able to distinguish their features. I don't often feel my body in my dreams, but in this one I could. My heart was pounding, I was out of breath, and every muscle tightened. I knew this was it. They were going to kill me. I started chanting a song about life, because that was the first thing I thought of. I suppose I hoped it would be a way to get me out of the dream. I did wake up then. Damn, I was scared! I guess I still sort of am. Am I feeling out of control? Of what? The boat maybe is my support system. What else could it be? Something that isn't as sturdy as it is supposed to be? I do get afraid in my dreams more often than in real life. I guess it's not so safe to be afraid when I'm awake. More questions than answers.

Mid-morning, taking a walk by the ocean

What a beautiful morning. I can't quite get my brain to not be so busy, so I thought might as well come down here. Listening to the waves and watching the sun sparkle on the water brings me such peace. At some point, I will hear the ocean tell me to be quiet. "Listen to *me*," she will say.

I've been thinking more about this fear theme, with last night's dream. Also, I got shocked and afraid at the eye doctor the other day, when he diagnosed me with the beginnings of macular degeneration. I'm around the same age as Dad was when he got diagnosed with it. Maybe it means blindness down the line; maybe not.

Dad suffered considerably towards the end of his life, hating what was happening to his body. In addition to growing blind, he grew increasingly deaf, experienced pain from arthritis, and developed diabetes.

Well, time to not push that fear away. Also, time to be proactive. It's okay to be afraid, to think about the fear and feel it. It's not okay to let the fear rule me, let the worry take over. Time to be calm and do the work. Do the damned self-care—the blessed self-care I mean. There are Ayurveda treatments to clean, soothe, and strengthen the nerves of the eyes. Talya can do those for me. I can take more Vitamin C, do research and get myself some supplements and herbs that are good for vision. Not strain my eyes. I've learned that after spending time on the computer or phone to shift my focus, my view and look at something far away for a few minutes, preferably something living and green.

Time to embrace the chant from the dream.

Oh Great Spirit, I want to live.

Wani Wachi Alo, Wakankataya

I realized the other day that I'm scared of feeling good. That old childhood shitty self-esteem rears her ugly head. It's not okay to feel good about myself. I've been feeling strong and healthy with all the self-care and feeling my feelings.

What *is* the issue with not feeling happy? With not allowing that or allowing success? Why can't I let those good feelings move me forward in my life? Does it really still all go back to Grandfather? "You will never be anything." First Tom's, "No one will ever love you." Mom's, "If only you were thin, you'd be happy/married/have a good career/whatever." So many years of therapy work around it and still, damn it, still not fully understanding or being able to let it go. I can still feel I don't deserve happiness, that it's not for me this time around to be happy, to be full, to be my best, to have what I want, *any* of those things. To be full, that's interesting. No amount of food in the world is enough to fill that hole, that emptiness, that ache I feel sometimes in my heart or in my belly. No amount of any*thing*, no amount of food, no amount of television, of reading, of drinking, of whatever I can find can fill that dark place other than love and gratitude. Not even love from another person. It's gotta be me and all the love there is surrounding me. I know not to depend on just one person to fill me up, which sounds so sappy and New Age-y that it makes me laugh and have a Hallmark moment. But I can feel the truth of it deep in my being. The living of it, another thing. Easy to say, hard to do.

What's so alarming about happiness? It's not as if I don't have moments, big moments, of it. Being content with my life. Feeling fulfilled. I can honestly say most of the time that I love my life, that my life is fabulous. The fullness of my life really is the truth. What is there about admitting that? About saying such a positive idea, well, fact, out loud or thinking it loudly? And what's so difficult about admitting that there are also numerous days when my life sucks, when I feel *I* suck? Somedays I hate this obsessively positive attitude I feel I must have. It's time to acknowledge the elephant in the room. My life is not always great and wonderful. At times, I have a fragile hold on that peace. I get afraid that if I look back, if I acknowledge that, I'll lose it. And that once it's gone, it's gone. I've worked so hard to find peace, joy, love, all those good things. Why do I feel that it's so tenuous? That I still don't deserve it? That I'm a fraud and a fake? I don't know what brought this all up today except I must be feeling safe enough to feel it. Yes, the eye diagnosis is part of it, but surely it goes way deeper.

I feel an underlying deeper layer of darkness. Some days, I'm just barely holding it back. Staying afloat—as in the dream, skimming over that wild ocean, over the darkness. My little boat barely able to keep from going under. My little boat that is really just a basket, not a seaworthy boat.

In the dream, the darkness was right there, right under the surface. So, it is today. Just as it's okay to feel the good feels, it's absolutely important, essential to my very life, to touch the darkness. Trust my little boat will get me where I need to go.

Okay, Grandmother, here I am. I'm just going to sit and breathe and listen. Fill my lungs with this good salt air. Salt is healing. Fill my mind with your sound, your persistence, each wave like my heartbeat. Tell me a story. Help me.

A few weeks later, on the airplane, coming back from a Montana retreat with my spiritual teacher and community

I'm so uncomfortable in this airplane seat. I so need to get myself compression socks. I haven't found a pair that fit me right and that I can stand to wear. I get that they need to be tight, but most of them are too tight for me. Being too fat to find socks that fit sucks. I just have to buy fat people compression socks. I'm doing my ankle exercises and just relaxing into knowing my feet will be swollen for a day or two.

At least the tray table comes all the way down this trip. There have been so many years when it didn't, and sometimes it still doesn't. And sometimes it's still embarrassing and causes all those old shitty self-esteem messages to rise up. My belly is too big, and the tray sits on top of it at a great slant that will hold nothing. Definitely not a drink. Not that I ever have really wanted to eat airplane food, but when the table doesn't come down all the way, you have no choice but to say, "No, thank you." It might also mean not eating the food I usually bring from home. I can't write unless I hold my notebook in my hand and write "in the air."

Why is each plane different, even within the same airline? The seat belts are all different sizes and different kinds. Sometimes I need the extender, sometimes I don't. It's an extra piece of the belt with parts that attach to both pieces of the original seatbelt. Sometimes the belt the seat comes with is so close to closing. I suck in my gut and squeeze. Nope. So, I push the call button and have to ask. I'm mostly over the embarrassment of asking for one, after so many years. Frequently, the flight attendants are kind and discreet about it.

I've had a few people in the seats next to mine (usually the person in the middle, since I request an aisle seat) ask to have their seats moved. Some days, it doesn't bother me; other days it's humiliating. The most recent time I can remember was maybe five years ago. I found my aisle seat near the back of the plane next to a woman who looked to be my age, but we clearly had very different lifestyles. Her hair was sprayed into an elaborate do that wasn't going anywhere, and her red lipstick was perfect. She had on a black suit that looked uncomfortable to me. I had on a nice lavender tunic and some black leggings, and my hair was in braids. As soon as she saw me preparing to sit next to her, her mouth tightened, her eyes rolled and she hit that call button with a mighty force. The attendant was nearby and smiled at both of us when she arrived.

"She can't sit here," said my seatmate in a very shrill voice. "Find her a different seat."

"I'll be happy to move your seat," the flight attendant replied, giving me a kind look as some of the nearby passengers turned to see what was going on. It worked out well for me, as I ended up with an empty seat next to me. I used the shrill woman's tray table to hold the two drink-sized bottles of wine the flight attendant brought me free of charge and which I shared with the woman who occupied the window seat.

"That made *me* embarrassed" my seatmate told me, "What a bitch! I'm sorry that happened to you." It's hard for me not to wish that the people who ask to move end up next to someone who farts a lot, or snores, or doesn't stop talking. Karma is a bitch, and I try to keep mine good but sometimes…I know, Charity, first-world problems. I totally get how privileged I am. Just saying, it could be better if the airplane seats were bigger and there was room for anyone who wanted to fly.

My best airplane seat experience was sitting next to a giant Samoan man. Lord, he was handsome. And way over six feet tall. He was wider than me and stuck in the middle seat. His young son had the window seat, so the man could spread out in that direction, but between the two of us there was no space at all. I said something to him about our arrangement. He just smiled broadly and serenely, and said, "Don't worry, just breathe into it." He really couldn't move. He sat there with his eyes closed, smiling, for close to two hours, chatting quietly with his son. "The spirits love us, sister," he said, "even if the airplane doesn't." What a lesson. Such dignity and grace.

It's just another challenge, another time when I'm not going to let the world stop me from pursuing dreams, doing what I want and need to do in the world. I may not fit, or always feel as if I "fit in," but I do belong on this plane. It's the world that needs to change, not me.

Monday morning, writing notebook

Tiny lavender flowers in the snow fall
steady and sturdy

Baby bison hurrying to keep up
hiding behind their moms

Geese and cranes floating down the river's strong current

seeming to enjoy the race

Spring
bright energy newness
buds on the trees and a new feeling in the air
so much green, more every day!

Take a deep breath
Don't forget to look up, down, around
New life is everywhere

Don't forget to look in your heart.

What is it about Flowers?

All my life, I have loved flowers. My mom had flowerbeds all around our house growing up. We had vases with flowers in the house as well.

To me, a steady paycheck has always meant that I could afford to buy myself bouquets of flowers and pretty vases. Now, I have all sorts of choices—flowers from my own abundant gardens, luscious bouquets of organically grown blooms from the farmers' markets, flowers out of the backs of the cars and trucks people here and there sell from, and bouquets from grocery stores that offer a great variety. Plus, I'm in California—there are flowers blooming year-round! One of my loved ones who lives back east comments that she could never live in California because we don't have seasons. I laugh, and tell her, "Yes we do. We have about sixweeks in the winter when the roses aren't blooming!"

From the Mother Earth Living website, May 2008:

Flowers come in an astonishing array of colors, scents and forms— botanists estimate there are more than 240,000 types of flowering plants in the world. Although we primarily appreciate flowers for their uplifting effects on the spirit and psyche, many flowers also contain a wealth of healing compounds with measurable effects on the body and mind. The pigments that provide flowers with their bright colors, the molecules that give them their unique scents, and even the compounds that help repel predators are some of the many elements that have been identified as having healing properties.

We don't really need science to tell us these things, do we? Who hasn't stopped to smell the roses or been tempted to pick some cheerful daisies while walking by? Their color and scents draw us to them, along with our memories and associations. I have lots of geraniums in pots around my patio and front door. They bring me joy not only because of their bright colors, but also because my mother loved them, so they remind me of her.

Want to cheer someone up or share your love? You give them flowers. There is a whole language to flowers that is fun to explore on Google. In Victorian times, communication was not as easy, especially between men and women, so a whole language of flowers developed.

Whether I'm in Montana, as I was recently, in awe of the little flowers still standing in the snow, in the mountains of Crete which are covered with dozens of varieties of wildflowers in all sizes and colors, driving down the freeway and appreciating the California poppies, or hanging in my backyard with the geraniums, nasturtiums, roses, and lilies (to name a few), I love seeing flowers. Plain and simple.

Friday afternoon, after session with Talya, the Ayurvedic practitioner

Phew! Five hours. That's a bunch of talking and feeling. I'm tired. So much to process. I so appreciate her feminine and supportive process, and she can give me some tough love too. We were talking out my sabotaging myself with food and about why it is hard to sustain happiness and contentment. "I also wonder about what happens to my intentions. I start out most days with the best of them," I commented to Talya.

"That's actually pretty common," she reminded me. "All we can do is start again in the next moment. Bring your attention back to your intention again and again."

I don't think of myself as a perfectionist. However, Talya said, "Think of the 'not being able to sustain good feelings' as a kind of perfectionism. It feels to me that you like to follow the rules. That in and of itself is not bad. Rules are there for a reason, but when that rigidity comes in, it can be a challenge."

"I do tend to be a black and white thinker—all or nothing. If I mess up some part of it, why do any of it? Why not just give up?"

She gave me a comforting look and replied that the world is full of lots of beautiful shades between white and black.

Talking through the self-care stuff with Talya was difficult. It's embarrassing to talk about the difficulties of getting in and out of the bathtub and not being able to reach certain places on my body—my feet, parts of the backs of my legs. Back when I was larger, it was hard for me to clean myself on the toilet. Not able to wipe thoroughly. Consequently, I didn't always smell good. Now, some days I worry that if my arthritis develops more, I will be in that situation again. I also had to tell her that my bathtub is too small, so it's not relaxing. At least I've finally learned to say *that* instead of "I'm too big." My shower and bathtub are the same unit, so I know that perhaps one day I won't be able to get in and out just to take a shower.

It's painful to admit that I'm "that person"—the one who can't take care of herself, the one who says, "I can't do it" and, "I should be able to…" I struggle with the shame and the discomfort of being that person, and it makes me want to give up and say, "Why bother? Feeling good is obviously not for me." The voices come in with their grand chorus of, "Well, dummy, just lose some weight!" or, "Just exercise more!" or, "If you weren't so fat…" It makes me quite sad. I know how hard I have tried. If wishing made it so, I would have been thinner and fitter long ago. No matter what I did, it just didn't happen, because I wasn't kind and loving towards myself. My teacher from the Psychology of Eating program always says, "You can't hate yourself into love." Now, I want peace. I want a simple life of loving myself and living my best life as I am.

Talya had some great ideas. She used the phrase "effort without strain"—meaning, do what I can do comfortably, only challenge myself to do as much as I feel capable of handling, or a pinch more. She also is encouraging me to change my thinking from "I'm so ashamed" to, "I get to let go of." I get to let go of shame about getting in and out of the bathtub. I get to let go of feeling bad. Not only can I do this (the self-care, or whatever) but I *am* doing it. Self-sabotage is a reaction to a story that isn't true, that isn't in alignment with reality.

So, I'm working on—no, I'm not even thinking of it as work—I'm *allowing* contentment into my day. I get to be content, using Talya's words. I'm noticing when I'm being given love. I'm taking note of when I smile and laugh. Some days, that is so easy to forget.

Her bodywork suits me well. I like the warm oil and the essential oils. Her touch is loving and kind, completely non-judgmental. Because of my time as a bodyworker, I can absolutely feel when someone touches me, either professionally in a massage or in some sort of hug, and they have a strong feeling about my body—some dislike, or fear, or some kind of discomfort. Give me a firm massage with a confident kind of touch. If you are going to hug me, do it all the way! Give me a two armed, firm, good-feeling hug, and I'll give you one back. That's when I know it's a good hug, I can feel that circle close no matter where the hands and arms are. I know it's hard to hug a fat person.

Of course, Talya suggested doing another cleanse. I like the week-long gentle cleanses; there's nothing hard about them. They're just a resetting into the season. I have participated in cleanses in the past that crossed over the line into "diet" or punishment territories—such as drinking only juice for a few days, eating only cabbage soup, or doing coffee enemas daily. Sometimes I wanted that punishment; I wanted to know how hard could I be on myself. But usually, those cleanses made the purging and "clean" eating into a contest and reinforced my belief that I'm not good enough or clean enough or "fill-in-the-blank" enough. How far was I willing to go? Enough, it's enough now.

It's a good time for me to eat more cooked greens and more cooked food in general. I can do that. She also wants me to use more pungent aromatics, like onions, garlic, and ginger. I can do that. And I'm supposed to be eating blueberries for my eyes, I can do that too.

I'm really tired from that work with her, so I'm off to bed really early. Thank you for my life Ancient Ones. I'm grateful for all you give me.

From my writing notebook

We hear from Appetite again

Knock, knock!
You decent? I'm coming in.
I got my friends Hunger and Shame here with me.

  Again?
  I just ate didn't I?
  Please not now.
  I'm in such a good mood

What's with changing the locks?
Trying to keep me out, baby?
I got all the keys
I got your number.
Who's your best friend?
Where you been?
You didn't take us with you

  I was with friends at a really nice restaurant,
  Downtown, dressed up.
  Oh it was a lovely evening of laughter.
  It was crunchy and funny
  savory and sweet
  beautiful on the plate
  full of nourishment and friendship.

Um, girlfriend, about that laughing…
I think maybe they were laughing at you
I know it cracks *me* up
seeing the fat girl eat
seeing the fat girl spill her food on her shirt
You did, didn't you?
Well, the joke's on you!
They weren't having a good time with you
just a good laugh at your expense

Hey, don't cry
You know who loves you, right?
Yeah, me.
I'm the one that's always here
the one who always makes you feel better
The one who cares.

Did you know
there are still cookies in the drawer?
Your favorite kind
Yeah, I don't know how that happened either
Let's go get ice cream
in case there aren't enough
cookies to make you feel better
I got your car keys right here
The store is only a few minutes away
It's not that late
Hey, and while you're there
pick up a bottle of wine
We'll have a party
Just us.
What do you say, Shame?
   Let's do it. Late nights with alcohol are my jam. I'll even stick
around 'til morning if you want.
   I love the morning after session.
You in, Hunger?
   oh yeah, I can always eat.
   In fact, I'm tasting that ice cream now
   better get chocolate so we can stay up all night.
Man, I knew I could count on you guys
You can eat until you get sick
or drink until you're drunk
whichever comes first
We'll be right here.

I'm the one that's always here
the one who always makes you feel better

It's Hard to Hug a Fat Person   158

The one who cares
I know you better than anyone.
It's okay. Have another bite.

Saturday morning, phone Call with Hannah

Charity: Hi honey. Good morning!

Hannah: Good morning. How are you?

C: Really good. I'm off to go dancing soon, but I wondered if you were doing anything tonight and if you wanted to go out to eat?

H: Hmm, I'm not sure. Where did you want to go?

C: We can go wherever you need to go to get the food you can eat. I've been eating so many vegetables lately; I'm craving some red meat.

H: Okay, I'll think about where. How about if we meet downtown? Is 5:00 too early?

C: No, that seems to be becoming our usual time. The early bird special.

H: The early bird gets the happy hour special worms, right?

C: See you later, I gotta go dance.

H: Have fun. Bye.

C: Bye.

Yay! Red meat. Steak. I have many vegetarian friends. I deeply understand the spiritual ideas behind it and was a vegetarian in my 20's. I did not make a good vegetarian. I can eat a shitload of carbs and not be satisfied. Nutritionally, the vegetarian diet did not work for me. I also get the ethical and political connotations. Large scale factory farms are the common "enemy" of vegetarians and omnivores alike.

After Saturday morning dance

I'm thinking about how my parents loved to dance when I was a little girl. They would put on Frank Sinatra in the evening, and I'd watch them glide across the floor with their arms around each other. This was one of the few occasions I saw them be openly affectionate.

Sometimes Daddy would ask me to dance. I held onto him tightly, standing on his feet as we waltzed, rhumba-ed, and cha-cha-ed to Big Band records around our living room in the house by the lake. As I grew older and bigger, I stepped onto the floor and followed his lead as best I could. In his strong arms, I felt so safe and loved. I felt graceful. In his arms, it didn't matter that Mom thought I was too fat or that I had gotten teased at school that week. I felt like a princess. We danced together a few times during my adult years—once at one of my brother's wedding reception, doing some sort of combination of his ballroom dancing and my hippie free style. That memory brings a smile to my face.

When I was six, my friends and I got very excited when we heard a ballet school was opening in our small Ohio town. I convinced Mom to sign me up and happily went off to the first class. At the end of the lesson, which I did think was fun, my mom came to pick me up. The instructor said, "Madame Dasenbrock, please do not bring your daughter again. She is too fat to dance ballet. Here, we work hard and look for beautiful girls." I was devastated.

Later that day, from Facebook
"You are beautiful. Own it. Walk like your hips move mountains."
This is reminding me of a poem I read recently. I wonder if I can find it...yep.
These hips are mighty hips.
These hips are magic hips.
I have known them
to put a spell on a man
and spin him like a top
— Carol Shields, *Dropped Threads: What We Aren't Told*

Watching people walk fascinates me—especially confident people and sassy, powerful women who love their bodies. I love watching them work that spell.

Sometimes, I can tap into that. It's in the eyes and in the hips. Sometimes, I consciously practice swinging my hips and holding my head high and proud, being relaxed in the confidence and the sexiness, inviting notice. The hips aren't always so cooperative these days; they're not so loose anymore. I can still find that sassiness, though, and then the gait changes. I loosen up, and there they are, those mighty magic hips. I think they could still put a spell on a man. Maybe they'll have the chance one day.

I hate it when I walk like an old lady. I'm far from being one. But, from time to time, in the night when I get up to pee or first thing in the morning, I hear myself shuffling, taking little old lady steps. I say to myself, "Pick up your feet! Lengthen your stride." Occasionally, out on a walk, I make myself take giant steps. Mother, may I? Charity, please take giant steps into your old age. Walk fiercely, proudly, and mightily. No hunching, no shuffling, no bowed head. Magic in those hips, thighs, feet.

This brings to mind a few lessons from Grandmother about posture. Because my dad's parents died when I was a baby, I only knew one set of grandparents, Mom's parents. The abusive Grandfather. And yes, she was known as Grandmother. No Granny, Grammy, or Meemaw for us. She was elegant into her final years, although she did have severe arthritis in her hips and some osteoporosis that kept her from standing straight. I don't really remember her without a cane. In her later years, Grandmother had a chair she used to ride up and down the stairs. She also wore an old-fashioned corset which supported her spine. It sure was a complicated uncomfortable-looking thing. As I got older, sometimes I would help her get dressed and have to pull those laces for her, not tight like Scarlett O'Hara in the movie, but tight enough that it was hard for me to do. During the last years of her life, she had several strokes. She and Grandfather then moved into assisted living and nursing care. Only then did she stop wearing corsets. She was as fat as I am, but she was a large woman. She and my grandfather enjoyed eating and had three hearty meals a day, prepared by Chaney, the live-in cook. The food was simple but rich with sauces and butter. At their house, my food was also restricted—mainly smaller portions rather than not being allowed something. Somehow, no mention was ever made of both of them being overweight, just me.

Grandmother's presence was powerful. I can see her: always well-dressed and never in pants. She wore stockings every day, even in the summer, and she got her short hair tightly curled and styled regularly. She loved very showy cocktail rings, a few of which I inherited.

When I was in my teens and developing breasts, she would regularly say, "Charity, stand up straight, for God's sake. Hold your head up. Be proud of your bosom." She and *her* bosom were quite intimidating. She told me to imagine that I was suspended by a hook on my chest and walk forward as if I was guided by that wire that was holding my chest and breasts up. "Glide across the carpet." Sitting in her antique rose silk chair, a cup of coffee, crossword puzzle by her side, cigarette in her hand, she would watch me practice walking back and forth in front of her. "Let your bosom lead the way. Head up, shoulders back, back straight. Don't wiggle your hips."

Sometimes, this was entertaining for both of us. Sometimes, it seemed stupid to my teenage self. My grandmother and I did not have an easy relationship. She was never sure what to do with me, since she was not impressed by my academic skills nor any of my other talents. In a weird way, these practice sessions brought a needed intimacy to our relationship. As an adult, after my sexual abuse memories resurfaced, I wondered if and what she knew about her husband's activities. How could she not know about his comings and goings? I suppressed my memories; maybe she was able to do the same.

Going to bed

Dinner with Hannah was such a good idea. We laughed and laughed. I think we both needed to cut loose a bit. Steak and wine can do that to a woman, and when there are two post-menopausal old biddies, it gets better! Two old biddies—that's a phrase that has me thinking about the chickens in the factory farm again. It's such a derogatory term, one for a useless bird, past her prime, producing no more eggs. Those are the chickens that get made into soup. It's kind of the same for post-menopausal women. We don't get eaten, we just become invisible and not so valued. But let's not forget how nourishing and healing that chicken soup can be, good for body and soul. I'd like to reclaim that term.

Ancients Ones, I thank you for this wonderful, full day. My life is rich. I do give thanks for all the experiences in my life—the good the bad, the ugly, the painful. I also give thanks that now there is much more of the good. I'm thankful for my family, for the joys and difficulties.

Tuesday, after marimba class

I had fun teasing Tom before class. He was arranging a time to get together with one of his fellow students to practice, and he was telling her how to get to his house. "Ooh, should I be jealous that she gets to go to your house and I haven't been there yet?" I asked. I had my arm around him as I was talking.

Blushing, he put his arm around me and squeezed me a few times, as he fumbled around with saying, "No."

I laughed, "I'm just teasing." He is so often serious, I find myself wanting to stir him up a little. We're doing something this weekend. There are a few possibilities to be discussed later.

Later that day

I've been thinking about my eyes, of course. I haven't really cried about the portent of macular degeneration yet. But, I'm sure I'll start crying soon—at a movie or during reading, triggered by some sappy thing. I appreciate that I'm being calm, and I don't think it means I have pushed it aside and am denying my fears. Well, maybe a little. I don't want to go blind. I have spoken with a few people who've told me they have the same diagnosis, and it's not quite the dreaded disease it used to be. Doctors have options that weren't around when Dad was coping with his degeneration.

He was declared legally blind after some years of having the disease. I wasn't around often during that time, so I, for the most part, got Mom's version of how he dealt with his process. My mother had no patience for any kind of infirmity, physical or otherwise, whether it was her husband's blindness, my fatness, or her friends' various complaints. She viewed illness as a character defect. "If only you were a better person, you wouldn't have diabetes, or arthritis, or be fat, or have polio," was her thinking. She never actually said the words, but everyone around her felt them. I know she loved Dad, with all that she could, but she did view him as weak. I'm still amazed she managed giving him the care he needed for as long as she did without help. I can hear her saying to Dad about his hearing loss, "Henry, just listen to me for Christ's sake!"

George, the man with whom Mama had a relationship after Dad died, was so good about her views of illness as weakness. He was a charming, well-spoken gentleman from Hungary, who escaped during wartime. I liked him a lot, though he could get a little pompous now and then. Once, when I was visiting her, he asked to have a meeting with Mama and me. He came to her apartment where we sat in the living room with glasses of wine. He sat quite close to me. After cleaning his very thick glasses with his handkerchief, he spoke quite seriously to Mom about his concerns about her beliefs about illness. He had been a pediatrician and was a very compassionate man. George was older than she was, so he fully expected that he would require some care and tenderness from her as he continued to age. He said, "Mary Esther, I need you to promise me that you won't think less of me if I get seriously ill. I'll need you to be kind and to help me."

She looked astonished at his comment and sort of stuttered, "Well, of course I will." Listening to him and watching her process this was quite satisfying to me.

Then, he shocked both of us when he turned to me. He so kindly said, "Charity, I know how you have struggled to meet your mother's expectations of you. I know how hard you work to make her proud of you." He told me it was time to let it go, to embrace my body and be content. Turning to Mama, he told her that it was also time for her to let her expectations go and let me be who I was. That was a powerful little meeting. I was around 60 years-old when this happened, and it was the first time that someone other than my father stood up for me like that.

As it turned out, Mom got cancer soon after that and needed his care and support first. He handled her compassionately and lovingly. I'm glad they had each other for the years that they did.

Friday morning, phone Call with Hannah

Charity: Good morning!

Hannah: Good morning. Thanks again for dinner last weekend. I almost cancelled, and I'm so glad I didn't.

C: Me, too. We both needed to laugh. Yesterday was a bit rough for me, thinking about my eyes, thinking about getting blind, going deaf, and becoming decrepit. Hopefully, we will be around for each other for years to come and can grow old together or separately together. You know what I mean.

H: I do know what you mean. We've talked about it before, how we will manage those years if things get difficult. Sometimes I'm not sure I want to live to be in that state. I want to grow old if life is full and good, but if I just fall apart and need lots of care, I'm not sure.

C: Oy, we all dream of living life to its fullest to the very end and then just going to sleep and never waking up. That probably doesn't happen to that many people. I was reading an interesting article the other day about our right to end life law, how people are having a hard time finding doctors to help them. The law requires two doctors to sign off on people's wishes. Sometimes the process takes so long that it's too late for the people trying to get the okay. They pass the point of being competent to make that decision and end up dying painful or prolonged deaths. Sorry, what a way to start the day.

H: Well, we never know when it'll be time to go. I did call with a cheerier subject. I've got a bunch of extra perennials and some annuals one of my neighbors gave me. Would you like some? I'm not even sure anymore what they are. I forgot to tell you the other day and they're not labelled. You want any surprise plants?

C: Sure, I would take some. I've got room. I've let go of wanting my flower beds to have a color theme. When I first moved here, I had it all planned out. Red and purple in one bed. Orange and purple in another. Pinks in another. The birds and the wind took care of some of that for me. Those darn orange nasturtiums popped up in my purple and red bed!

H: The nerve. I've never been that formal with my gardens.

C: That was my one and only attempt.

H: I have to come into town later today. I could drop them by.

C: Great. I think I'll be here, but if I'm not, just leave them by the side of the house. Thanks so much.

H: Okay, hope I see you later. Bye.

C: Bye.

Awesome, I always want flowers! You can never have too many, nor too many colors!

Saturday morning, after dance at the Santa Cruz River Festival

I'm loving this sundress I'm wearing. It's green and blue, which are the colors of the festival. I've got on my trusty bright blue leggings, which really are too warm for this hot day but the dress is too short for dancing. It thrills me that I'm comfortable wearing a sleeveless thing. Just last year, I wrote about that being a challenge for me. I guess it's not so much now. My arms are still fat and flappy. Some of my friends have said they think their upper arms look better covered up. I have said and thought that, too, but why, really? Our arms are the same size whether covered or not. They jiggle the same amount unless you are wearing a wetsuit or something really tight. I am shocked by the number of women who are sensitive about their triceps area, ashamed of the jiggling. It is what it is. It is really hot today and feels good to have bare arms. Having a loose arm hole is good too. My bra shows a little, but I don't care about that either. I think people know I am wearing a bra. And if I didn't have one on, they would know that too. I'm glad that raising my arms isn't a big deal for me these days either. I have no idea when the last time was that I shaved my underarms. I've never been very hairy, but as I get older, my hair is leaving its usual spots and traveling upward, ending up on my chin.

I've always been casual about that sort of self-care—beauty treatments, make up, shaving, all that. I'm part of the last generation that had to wear girdles. We couldn't wear pants to school. Briefly, in junior high, I wanted to wear makeup, but my parents wouldn't let me. When I was finally old enough to try it out, I quickly decided makeup was more trouble than it was worth.

High school fashion was a paradox. I wore preppy matching skirts and sweaters, which is what many of the girls wore, and I had to keep dieting so those would keep fitting me. My sophomore year, my Mom made a deal with me. If I lost fifteen pounds by a certain date, she would buy me a new set. I managed to do it, and I cherished my maroon-and-white plaid wool skirt with matching Fair Isle knit wool sweater. Another side of me liked wearing odd-looking clothes that I made myself. Being on my high school's costume committee, I had access to the school sewing machine and fabric stash. My favorite of those was a dress made out of ugly curtain material—white cabbage roses on a dirty sort of pink background. It had giant belled sleeves. All the grownups hated the dress, which, of course, made me love it more.

Currently, I enjoy wearing colorful clothes. Larger-sized clothes are more readily available these days. I've said goodbye to the clothes of my younger days—matching sweater and skirt sets, ugly job interview polyester denim pants suits, and blue jeans that I have to lie down to zip up.

From my writing notebook

oh the times I used to cry buying clothes

shapeless
black or brown polyester
or the flower prints
giant tropical blooms, colors not found in nature
or tiny pioneer prints like your great grandmother's quilts

What a surprise in junior high school when my mother decided to make some of my clothes.

Dusting off the sewing machine
gritting her teeth and cursing up a storm
We had some good days
looking at patterns and material
dreaming of looking beautiful

She sent me to 4-H, taught me how the machine worked, and off I
went
I fell in love with color, with patterns, with creativity

princess seams
zippers
button holes

As a senior in boarding school, I stole a sheet
My friends and I turned it into a formal dance dress
complete with an empire waist, short sleeves
long and quite white
decorated with magic markers
red yellow green blue
peace signs, good wishes,
hearts and flowers
I got in trouble for the missing sheet
but my boyfriend loved the dress.

Going to bed

Great Spirit, thanks for another day. Thank you for all the
blessings in my life, for my health, for all the abundance, for all
that I've gone through to get to this place of health and contentment in my life. Help my legs be strong, my lungs be clear, my
eyes. Help me welcome love and laughter into my life.

Come on Tina, time to sleep. I hope I can. I'm a little wired
from some caffeine. You never have a problem sleeping. You are
there already. That's not fair.

Sunday morning

Okay, things are not going so well so far. I woke up way too early. I have a headache and a neck ache from sleeping wrong. There are no lemons for my morning drink. Do I dare have black tea? I had some chocolate yesterday, which is what kept me awake. Damn, I'm doing it. I might be sorry, but that will be later and I'd like some black tea right now. I wish I had some cream. What's with all this wishing?

Now the crossword puzzle is too hard. Of course. That goes into the recycling right away.

Next, my plans to see my friend Mary have gone down the tube. Jeez, what else. Uh oh, don't ask. No jinxing the day even more. I guess I'll do some laundry. Yeah, that will cheer me up.

Whining. Bitching. I don't actually get this way too often. I do like the find the bright side to everything, and I eventually will today, but I'm gonna grump around a bit longer.

Going to bed

Well, the "what else would happen" was going out and getting three big slices of pepperoni-veggie pizza and eating all three of them. I started thinking about what I wanted to eat. Pizza snuck in there, and I couldn't stop the cravings, or rather, I decided that I didn't want to stop them. What is it about pizza that sucks me in? One answer is the "forbidden food factor." I had so many years of denying myself even a slice because it's so fattening. Another answer is that I just plain like it, which is hard for me to admit. I like pizza. I do. Sadly, there is nothing in it that is good for me. Even if it's gluten-free, the crust is not so good for my belly, with all that flour. I remember someone telling me to think of paste when I think of flour. In elementary school, we made paste out of flour and water. It worked really well. And, I remember plenty of us nibbling on it to see how it tasted. Now I think about that in my gut. None of the other ingredients are all that good for me, although today's pizza, though not organic, was at least pretty high quality. There was not much sauce or cheese. A few vegetables. I put some salad greens on my pizza at least. I savored it, took my time, and drank some tasty wine with it. I got pleasure from the experience. I guess now I'm trying to give myself a hard time about it but not quite giving it my all. The only "real" problem is that it was a lot of food, and my belly did hurt in the night. I have post-cheese phlegm this morning. But, have I forgotten how to beat myself up overeating? "Really, Charity, is that all you've got?" It's not working. I'm not going to punish myself. It's not happening today.

Who was I talking with about pizza the other day? We were remembering the first time we had it. I know I never had any kind of real pizza growing up. The closest thing we had was Chef Boyardee in the box, which consisted of a little bag of crust mix, a can of tomato paste, a tiny pouch of grated cheese, and tiny bits of dried up pepperoni. It probably tasted as bad as it sounds. But still, it was our special treat for special occasions such as New Year's Eve and was usually accompanied by our equally infrequent bottle of soda pop.

Okay enough analyzing and reminiscing, let's hope I don't get acid reflux.

3 am, waking from a dream
Jeez. No acid reflux, but what a dream!

I was bushwhacking through the jungle, on what started out like a narrow deer trail. I chopped my way through some tropical flowers of vivid purples and oranges, and bushes which got denser and closer. The surroundings became thornier, darker, hotter. I had my walking stick, and since it was the kind that had a knife blade on the end of it, I used it to cut some of the plants down. It didn't work all that well. I'm not sure if I was alone or not. As I contin-ued, the leaves got even larger, and the thorns got sharper. I could sense something gigantic flying overhead, and I was frightened because I couldn't see it. The trail eventually disappeared, and I could go no further. I couldn't move. I couldn't turn around to go back, and I couldn't sit. I had a moment of wondering if I would die. Was this how everything would end? Would I be stuck in this place forever?

Then, I got the urge to pee, and I woke up. Pee saves the day. But, again, what did I miss? Was there some important lesson about to be dropped on me, like giant bird shit? Oh well. So, it was beautiful, and then it wasn't beautiful. I had a tool but it stopped being effective. I got literally overwhelmed by the leaves, plants, etc. I have been feeling overwhelmed. I need some bigger tools I guess. I'll ponder that later when I'm more awake.

5 am

I'm awake, but I'm not going to get up yet. That dream is still with me. I'm thinking about the overwhelm, thinking about my eyes, about letting myself feel the grief. I'm always the positive thinker, the "moving forward" person, which is good, but now I think I need to let myself feel it all. Right now, I'm overwhelmed and sad, and I don't want to feel any of it. Maybe that was the dream, maybe it was the blindness flying overhead. What I felt was huge, which potential blindness is. I couldn't see it. Not much subtlety there. I could go blind. Oh, that makes me get cold. I need to pull the covers up more, tuck myself in. Where are you, Tina? Dammit, now I am going to cry. So much for not feeling the emotions. Let them in. I could lose a significant amount of vision. I could go blind. It's hard to say those words.

There's so much beauty in the world. What if I never get to see the faces of the people I love again? I can feel Dad hugging me and touching my cheek, in those days when I knew he couldn't see me anymore. To him, I was a shadow with a few details around the edge. What would it be like to never see a sunrise or sunset again? Or my flowers, the apple tree, the lemons. My new pomegranate tree. They're all so beautiful and precious. I've been to gardens that are all about the smells; I could plant more things that smell good. I don't have to stop having a garden, working and playing in the garden. My piano! Oh, that's heartbreaking. I love it so.

Back to the dream, there's the trail getting smaller. My vision could get smaller, and right now that feels as if life's pleasures would get smaller. I need to keep room for healing, for something different to happen, for miracles. I do believe in them. I need to keep clearing the trail, to get a bigger knife, a machete, more tools, and to keep whacking at those bushes. Prayer is a good tool. Writing is a good tool. More tools will come to me.

And then there were the thorns in the dream—so many of them. Maybe they are my emotions? Oh God—I wouldn't be able to drive. I'd become dependent—needing help to get around, to do the tasks of daily life. It hurts to think about it all.

No wonder I feel overwhelmed. Bless his heart, I loved Dad so much, I'm glad I have him before me as an example of both what to do and what not to do. Being more of an extrovert, my people skills are better than his ever were. I'm not going to end up all alone. I'm not. He didn't. He had Mom and her tenacity. Without her, I'm not sure what would have happened. I won't be alone, but who will help me? Who? What if I can't live alone anymore?

Later

I'm surprised I slept a little more. I feel calmer now. I guess it's all just going to keep coming and going. And I just need to ride those waves and feel the feelings. I have a regime of supplements, healing and self-care treatments. I have people who are helping me, people I can trust with my feelings. It might be good to talk with the ophthalmologist again. He did say it wasn't a "done deal," and there are treatments. Shots into the eyeball—but that is better than the alternative.

I think this potential challenge is helping me stay in the present and be aware of all I have in my life—the abundance, the beauty, the love. If my seeing time is limited, I don't want to forfeit it. I don't want to live in the past or be afraid of the future; I want to enjoy today. I long to be content, to feel full and fulfilled. I will choose to see the beauty in the world, to drink it in. I want to embrace the sweetness of my loved ones. I'll need strength for these changes. It's so time to get over myself and shine, shine my way into whatever comes. And remember, we don't know what will happen. This is how to live a good life, diseases and ailments looming or not, right?

I see my pattern here, always trying to find the sunny side, the bright side, the good, maybe even a lesson that could be learned. I'm learning how to let in the dark and scary, let in the fear, the anger, whatever those emotions are. I hate to cry but I've got to let the tears flow when and where they will. And keep finding the sunny side of the street.

Monday morning, driving home from coffee shop work session

Ahh, I feel accomplished. I needed that change of scenery, and, thankfully, there was a parking spot by the busy coffee place today. It's across town from my house but it's big with plenty of tables and good kinds of tea. I need solitude and quiet, but I also need to balance that with the buzz of people being busy and productive, of others having a good time with friends or enjoying their drink and their book. I read and deleted a bunch of emails; it's always satisfying to see that inbox number get smaller. I also read a few articles which had been waiting for me. Plus, I finished a blog post.

Must be Jelly cuz Jam don't shake like that!

It was sunny and in the 90's last weekend. Today, that's a fond memory, as the sun isn't out yet this morning, and it's a bit chilly, a typical weather pattern for Central Coastal California at this time of year. "June Gloom," we call it. Last Saturday, I went dancing and then to an outdoor music and art celebration of our local river. The sun was beating down, and I was happy to be in a green sleeveless dress with a wild pattern of palm trees—which also happen to look like marijuana plants. I always get interesting comments when I wear it. I wore some bright blue capri leggings underneath, since the dress is a bit short for my comfort. The festival's theme was blue and green, so my fashion choice was right on point.

In past years, in hot weather, I have been too self-conscious to wear something sleeveless, choosing to hide my arms or even not going out in public at all. I've been afraid of that we all have come to call the "underarm jiggle." Out of curiosity, I looked that lovely term up on Google, and here's what I found:

Flabby   underarm   exercises
How to tighten underarm flab
Exercises for flabby arms and bat wings
Flabby arms before and after
Exercise for flabby arms without weights
Exercise for flabby arms with weights
How to get rid of arm flab after losing weight
How to get rid of arm flab in two weeks

Do you see anything that says anything positive? Or how to accept the jiggle? No, and isn't that a shame?

Two years ago, I did a video series, *Body Positivity A - Z*. I chose "Jiggle" as my J word. You can find that and the rest of the series on my Vimeo Account.

As is often the case, I went to my Facebook pals for research, asking them how they feel about baring their bodies in the summertime. I got the full range of replies from people of all ages and body sizes. I was happy to see how many of them said things like, "Fuck it, I wear what I want and if someone doesn't like it, they shouldn't look." Several of my friends live where it gets really hot, and they regularly bare their arms and legs—some more joyfully than others. It seems that the arms are a common area of discomfort, and many choose to keep them covered. Some friends are uncomfortable showing their knees. Only a few sounded truly comfortable with themselves.

We are not taught to be comfortable in our skin, to be comfortable in our clothes, to be carefree. I get reminded of this at times such as in these Facebook conversations. Women in their 40's, 50's, and 60's are still uncomfortable in their bodies. There is something so wrong with that.

I would be remiss if I didn't report the answer from the two men who responded with such love and respect for women, and with an undertone of righteous anger. They wish women would just wear what makes them feel good, whether hot or cold, young or old, thin or fat. Shave if you want, they said. Don't shave if you don't want. Be comfortable. Have fun. Wise words.

I understand the hesitation and the shame. I've been ridiculed and harassed about my body for most of my life. I've had open sores and rashes from my thighs rubbing together. I've been told, "No one wants to see that!" when I've been wearing something even somewhat revealing. Thankfully, I also have known the joy of wearing something I love and feeling beautiful. I have been told by thin people that they like my bathing suit, that they wish they had one like it. I enjoyed dancing the other day in the hot sun and the freedom I had in my loose fitting, cool sundress. I love colors and patterns, and I can rock a pair of leopard print leggings just like Rod Stewart in his disco era. We're all works in progress.

I challenge you and me both to push the envelope just a little. See what happens. I'm thinking about getting a two-piece bathing suit and at least wearing it in my backyard. When it's hot and sunny, I'm going to keep wearing a sleeveless sundress.

It's Hard to Hug a Fat Person   174

That afternoon, snoozing in the backyard sun

Here's my Tina. Come enjoy the sun too, girl. Got your legs up in the air, freshen up your lady parts. Mine could use some freshness too, but not today.

I'm so not interested in sex these days. This isn't new. It's really not ever been a big part of my life. Our culture fills us with so much about no one wanting a fat woman, which is so untrue. After so many years of hearing such powerful negative comments about my body, I took that attitude in and made it mine. Intellectually, I've been able to call that bullshit for many years, yet I still got hooked by it, and have spent years believing no one will ever want me. And sex with Grandfather, that will reinforce it. Getting raped—that will too. Twice! both "date rapes." A weird expression. Situations that I willingly entered, situations that then got out of hand (another extremely weird expression!)

I spent the summer after my freshman year at Mills College, where I went out on a date with the guy I met over the phone. Perilous, and I was lucky to survive.

The second time, I had moved back to San Francisco after college, in 1973. I got off the streetcar near my house along with a nice-looking black man with long hair. I was sneezing and coughing, and he invited me to his place for some tea. I was tired and feeling a bit sorry for myself, so tea sounded good, as did making a friend. We sat on his saggy brown couch, and we did have tea. He decided that rubbing my feet would also make me feel better. Indeed, it did. So far, so good. Despite having been raped four years earlier and having had a boyfriend in college, I was still pretty naive. The foot rub led to kissing, and to taking some clothes off. He and the situation were moving fast—too fast for me. Suddenly, I got really scared, and I was not able to get enough breath. "Stop! Wait!" I yelled.

Ignoring my panic, he just laughed. "Hey, let me make you feel better, girl." I continued to scream, kicking at him with my legs. He was a small man but quite strong, and I couldn't push him off of me. He laughed again and said, "Shush now, we don't want the neighbors getting bothered." After a few more minutes of pleading and struggling, he did stop. He jumped up. "Now are you happy?

Such a fuss. I thought you were having a good time." I got my clothes on as quickly as possible, ran out the door, and hurried the few blocks home to my apartment.

I haven't learned experientially about the glorious power of sexual pleasure, of sharing intimacy with a loving partner. After that experience, I shut down for a while. At some point, I did learn about self-pleasuring. With help from books and some specific kinds of bodywork, I learned about my body's needs and desires, but I never have been able to have an orgasm with a partner. I've had a handful of brief encounters here and there, but not for more than thirty years now. I've pushed those desires away for so long that I'm not sure they are retrievable, nor am I always sure I am interesting in looking for them.

Tuesday evening, after dinner with Tom

Out to dinner with Tom tonight, although it was a little crazy in the part of town we picked. Tourists. Parking. Fortunately, all of it just made us laugh. Well, okay, we grumbled a bit first as we looked for a parking spot. We didn't have to walk too far to a seafood cafe right on the beach where we could sit outside. We managed to hold hands for about a block. A delightful sunny evening accompanied by a spectacular sunset full of reds and pinks over the sparkling ocean, excellent company and conversation, a glass of wine, satisfying fried fish, right on the beach. What more did we need? Well, dessert, apparently. "What do you think about having some dessert?" he asked.

I said, "Let's do it." We got in his old beater blue Toyota (a vehicle we had in common before I got my birthday car) and drove a mile to a popular bakery-cafe and shared a piece of lemon raspberry cake. I don't think he had any idea how significant a thing that was. No hubbub, no discussion of whether it was good for us or not, no discussion about sugar equals bad. No guilt. Just two forks and making yummy noises. Hurray for normalcy. Hurray for it being casual. Hurray for deliciousness.

We put our arms around each other briefly a few times this evening. I'm still not sure what makes us let go like that, but I do like the moments of intimacy. I need that feeling of closeness. It's not about wanting sex. Those feelings seem to come and go. Right now, I need the warmth, not necessarily the heat. Warm is good. Solid affection, loving touch, human bumping up against human.

We also had a goodnight kiss. Again, no heat, but sweet warmth. Lips touching lips. In this case briefly, but touching is touching.

During dinner, the ocean was really calm and it made me want to be out on it. I asked Tom if he'd ever want to go whale watching. I got a "maybe." I'm going to Alaska next week and will see plenty of whales, I hope, as they swim the Inland Passage. I've been there before. It's one of the places the spiritual community I belong to goes each year for a retreat. We stay at a beautiful lodge where the water is deep and whales often come in close to shore. We can hear them blowing water out of their air holes all day and throughout the night.

The land and sea is still so wild there—whales, eagles, ravens, bears, salmon. Being there is a chance to be away from houses and people. There will be almost endless light as we approach the Summer Solstice.

From my writing notebook
I go days sometimes without being touched
not even simply brushing up against a body
or a handshake

I get that it's hard to hug a fat person.
You might not like the squishiness
or the feel of my breasts and belly.
Your arms don't fit all the way around
I get that you might feel uncomfortable with that
I want to feel those arms enclosing me, enveloping me
Let the energy close the circle
I'm sorry if it feels awkward for you.
I can sense that awkwardness you know
Sometimes it hurts
Sometimes it's just life
Hold me tight anyway

Put your all into however much you've got.
Touch that means acceptance and love
That means hope

Made my Mama squirm
those hugs that were too tight and too long
Let me go, that's enough already!
Nope, mama, I'm not done. I'm not going to see you for a while
and this has to hold me until then.
She would surrender for a few more seconds then worm her way
out
with a sigh of relief

I used to take walks with a friend and she would hold my hand
Firmly, confidently, lovingly
Sharing energy
I miss that

Massage school days
so many of us wounded by touch or lack of touch
healing ourselves through that gift we gave others

What a powerful force touch is
With not enough, we wither away, we dry up
Violent touch, we die or at least our spirit does

Let's hold each other tightly
Let go at the same time

Monday morning, cooking
     Doing a little batch cooking today while I'm in the mood. I'm
starting with quinoa, since I'm adding a bit more grains into my
diet to see how that goes. So far, not great. It seems like they tend
to make me sleepy. I'm going to make a salad of cooked stuff, but
I'll eat it at room temperature now that the weather's warmed up.

Sautéing up some leeks, fennel, carrots. I'll add some raw celery, grate some beets. Such a pretty color combination. I'm using those good Ayurvedic spices and herbs—cumin, fennel seed, turmeric. Salt and pepper. Lemon juice, olive oil. I'll be able to add protein to the salad or not. It'll make a good breakfast with a fried egg. Oh yeah, I'm also roasting part of a leg of lamb, rubbed with garlic, salt and pepper, rosemary. It's a couple of pounds, so it will feed me for quite a while, and I'll have to freeze some. I'm roasting some purple potatoes too, which somehow don't seem to be in the nightshade family. And, duh, purple! What's not to love about that? I'm making peace with food, using all my senses, bringing in the love.

From Facebook

"Imagine if we obsessed about the things we love about ourselves." —meme from a friend's post.

Whoa, right on. I often think about the endless time and energy I put into feeling bad or worrying. I know how to obsess! I can really obsess about how difficult some task or project might be for me to do. Am I going to be physically up to it? How will I perform? Will I hurt or embarrass myself? I can also get obsessed with asking myself questions. Obsessing keeps me out of the present, out of my body, not paying attention to what is happening. I miss a lot because of this, I think. How much time I devote to wishing I was doing this or that instead of literally doing the activity. What would happen if I put that energy into love, into what I like about myself, what makes me happy? The sky's the limit. Or better, there is no limit.

Ten days later, on the plane, returning from a retreat with my spiritual teacher in Juneau, Alaska

Sadly, there have been no magical airplane renovations since the last time I flew. Oh well. I am so filled with contentment from my time in Alaska that I'm managing the discomfort. There was such peace and quiet there. The air was so rich and clean that I thought I could taste the nutrients. I feel purified from that good breathing, from the soft rain. I can smell the evergreen trees and the new spring buds, the wetness of the forest. I'm holding all those healing shades of green in my heart. Listening to the eagles and seeing whales filled me. The first time I went to Alaska many years ago, I was blown away by hearing the eagles singing in the trees, like chanting. I didn't know they did that. I wish we had seen more whales. Some call them the shamans of the sea; so much history and power they have, singing those beautiful songs. They pass them along, one to another, and so the songs travel through all the oceans.

We sit in a circle outside when my shamanic community is together and when the weather cooperates. Listening to the shaman chant, we drum and rattle to call in the spirits. These ancient songs have been sung for millennia. We feel the presence of our ances-tors. We celebrate the season, we celebrate our lives. We ask for help and healing. Sometimes those whales show up, and it seems to us as if they are listening and participating.

My body hurt more than I thought it would. There were plenty of stairs to climb in and around the lodge. One day we walked on our own through the rainforest with its fallen decaying trees and giant ferns to a grand beach where the eagles come to rest. I truly was okay with stopping and sitting on the bench by the trail and not getting to the beach. I sat and looked, listening to hear if the wildflowers had anything to say. There were little brown wild orchids and native purple iris. Angelica everywhere, with its big lacy white flowers. Pale pink astilbe. So many shades of green. Ferns everywhere. Appropriately named "devil's club" with its fierce thorns. Everything smelled so clean, fresh, and alive. I just kept breathing in the beauty and the healing. I tried to just shut my mind off from wondering about their herbal properties and wishing I had my camera. Working on staying present is such a good practice for me.

I did enjoy having a quiet moment by myself. I spend many hours by myself. Alone is not the same as lonely. I do get lonely now and then, though. Feeling sorry for myself is an ancient emotion. It's a fine line between alone and lonely. But now, I'm remembering all that beauty and how my life is filled with it. I'm remembering the Ancient Ones love me. This is why I am healing. This keeps me growing and moving forward.

From my writing journal
Everyday alone
do this by myself
do that
Somedays
with so much comfort and grace

It's a fine line between alone and lonely
all you need to do is change a few letters

I'm not lonely every day
I have freedom
I have choice

The voices call out
reminding
"No one will ever love you"
"You will always be nothing"

There are 20,000-30,000 species of solitary bees in the world
They live alone, fly around alone
The female is said to have a feeble sting
She lays one egg, seals it up.
then flies away.

Afternoon the next day, phone call with Tom
    Tom: Hi, Charity. It's Tom.
    Charity: Thanks for calling me. How are you?
    T: Well, today is okay. I've been really tired. I'm not sleeping up to par. But enough about me, how was your trip? Did you have a good time?

C: I'm sorry you've got troubles. If you need to share them, I'm here. I had a wonderful time. Fresh air, eagles, whales, rain, good time with my friends. I'd love to see you soon. Want to do something this weekend?

T: I certainly do. I wonder if you'd like to join me for a hot tub. It's in a gym so it's bathing suits. I usually go on Thursday evenings. Is 7 o'clock too late for you?

C: Oh, that sounds delightful and healthy. I could use a good soak. Seven is perfect. I'm pretty sure I can go. Let me check back in with you tomorrow, okay?

T: Sure. We can talk then about some ideas I have for concerts to go to.

C: Great. We've been to some really good ones, haven't we?

T: We sure have.

Oh boy. Bathing suit date. Hmm. This will be interesting. A good body positivity test. It's not as if my body shape is a surprise to him, and it's not as if he cares, really. I certainly don't care about his body shape, which also isn't a surprise. I like that he's a bit soft and cuddly. Too bad he doesn't enjoy cuddling, but that's another story. I'm still good with our friendship-relationship, though sometimes when we talk I find my mind wandering. When I travel, I don't really miss him. Something is changing for me in our friendship, but I don't know what. I'll just roll with it for a while.

After a session with Talya

Talya's workspace is in her tiny home, and it completely reflects her personality— full of color and positive affirmations about life. I feel protected and nourished every time I visit, both from the environment and from her loving yet fierce way of reminding me of my own wisdom and strength. I'm so glad I got to this space with her. When I first met her, I was eager to learn from her and was somewhat intimidated by her petiteness, her beauty and her grace. I felt so big and graceless. She has so much compassion and approaches all our conversations and treatments from a place of total love and acceptance. It's a good reminder of how to be in the world—when we are met and received with love, it's easier to feel that love for oneself and then easier to send it out into the world, meeting others with that love.

I appreciated our conversation today about fire and water. It's gratifying to connect my shamanism and my time in Alaska to what's going on in my body. There are four elements: Earth, Air, Fire, and Water. We have all of these in our bodies. Shamanism would say we *are* all of these. Water and Earth are my dominant elements. I am damp and muddy, with mud gunking up the flow of my juices and dampness keeping the fires in my body low or even out. That fire is needed for energy, to keep our digestive system efficiently processing everything, to give us passion and purpose in life. Shamanism says that Fire's power is wisdom. During our last session and in today's, she wondered where my fire was. Today I asked, "How can I relight or help that fire burn brighter?"

She loved that question and suggested that I can build it by making more hydrochloric acid in my stomach, by drinking apple cider vinegar before I eat. She also explained that spices like ginger and cayenne will get the saliva flowing before I eat. I already am cooking with warming spices such as cumin and coriander and liberally sprinkling black pepper on my meals. Since it's summer, I don't need a lot of heat, just warmth.

"Don't drink anything cold or eat too much raw food." Talya adds. I'm learning to see all of this digestive information as my fanning and feeding the flames of Grandfather Fire, the part of him that lives in me. I do see him and know him as my ancestor, the original Shaman, full of wisdom, who needs tending and care. He needs fuel as any fire does. I think that holding this image and this way of feeling Him in my body will deepen the connection.

Talya and I also talked about water. Our bodies have about the same percentage of water as the Earth has. In Shamanism, the Earth is our mother and her power is love. I have excess fluid—or, at least, it's not where it's supposed to be and is not flowing freely. Talya reminds me that this is where my body treatments come in. Using the *gua sha* will help me to push the extra fluid out. If it's a hard day for me to do that painful practice, I'll visualize caring for Grandmother Ocean whose waters we all carry within us. Mine need balancing and cleaning, so pushing out the old and allowing the new to flow and move the gunk is crucial. In my shamanic practice, Water's power is Beauty, so this is another opportunity to embrace my own beauty and recognize all the beauty in the world. So, I'm building the fire and cleaning the ocean.

I feel as if my tool kit is a bit fuller today. I'm recalling that dream I had a while ago about the trail that got impossible to follow and not having a big enough tool to clear the obstacles. That has turned out to be a really important dream, and it is helping me add to my tool kit so I'm prepared to get out of the thick, to keep moving in the right direction.

Thursday night, after hot tubbing with Tom

Okay, that was a big deal, just hanging out in my bathing suit with a man. The warm water kept me calm and protected. Thank God there were no chemicals, so I could really stay in and enjoy myself. Tom was already in the outdoor tub at his gym when I got there. We managed a hug, wet and warm, skin to skin. I haven't had a bare-chested man's arms around me in about five years, I think. I had a little flash of longing, both sexual and emotional. Neither of us felt the need for conversation, and we quietly took in the healing of the warm water. I'm just so relieved that I felt relaxed and comfortable in my bathing suit. Tom didn't care. He has been around me enough; he knows I'm fat! It's not a secret. My tattoos aren't a secret anymore either. My leopard tattoo is high on my hip. When Tom saw her tail peeking out from my bathing suit, his eyebrows lifted and he said, "Whoa! What is that?" so I pulled up my suit a bit and showed him the whole thing. "I had no idea you had a tattoo."

I winked at him and replied, "A woman needs a few secrets." I giggled and showed him my deer tattoo on my other leg.

I do wish my bathing suit fit me better. It has bra cups inside, and they are way too small. It looks all right to the outside viewer, but it is uncomfortable. The suit is a pretty blue paisley, with a nice neckline that covers what I like to have covered. I'll keep searching for a good suit, but this one will do for now. Ugh, bathing suit shopping. I know no one who enjoys it. I've had better luck finding ones on the internet that fit, but then there's more risk of the suit not fitting. The hassle of the return and trying something else can be too much. Another example of societal pressure for women. We must look cute and sassy if not sexy in our bathing suits. Sizes are not universal nor do they stay the same year to year. People are getting bigger, so companies changed sizing so what used to be an XL is now a size 14 or 16 instead of an 18. This is supposed to make us more comfortable. Please, just make suits for all sizes, women's and men's, that are comfortable and made for swimming.

So, the hot tub "date" was a first. Here's another one—on Wednesday night at dinner with some friends, Tom called. I was expecting his call to confirm our hot tub time, so I answered and went outside. My friends were so surprised, and so was I. Never in my life have I answered my phone at a restaurant and gone outside to take the call. It made me giggle when I came back in. It felt good to make a little show and brag a bit.

Going to bed

Ancient Ones, I thank you for this great day. the beautiful weather, the sun, the warmth. I thank you for my growing comfort in my body. I'm grateful for Tom's acceptance and attitude. Thank you for my health, my good luck.

Friday evening

I wore shorts all day today. I recently bought some black and white knee-length ones—sort of like bike shorts, but softer and looser. So comfortable. I had been wearing them around the house and just kept them on and went out for a hamburger and a glass of wine at my local bistro. There was no earthquake. The fire alarms did not go off. No one had a heart attack. As far as I know, no one paid one single bit of attention. Yahoo! So proud of myself. Body Positivity rocks. Wear what you want, girl. Practice what you preach.

Sunday morning, phone call with Hannah

Charity: Hi, girlfriend. What are you up to today?

H: This and that. Working. Working on the house some more. Always.

C: Yes. I vaguely remember my dad warning me about the countless hours of work a house is when I bought my first one in the Oregon woods. It really was a shack, and he came and worked on it for me. He truly wasn't happy that I bought it without his advice and he never really did feel okay about me living there. I didn't ask him for any because I knew he would tell me not to buy it. But he kept a set of work clothes there for years and managed to come every other year with a list and without my mom. After picking him up at the airport, our first stop would be the hardware store for supplies, the first of many trips there. I loved that house for most of the time I lived there, just at the end, it became a burden.

H: This place feels like a bit of a burden right now, but I can't go anywhere, so I'm rolling up my sleeves. What else is new with you?

C: I had a hot tub date with Tom the other day. That was so healing. Not just the hot water but the fact that I was quite relaxed with him. Being in my bathing suit wasn't an issue for me at all. Yay!

H: Yay! Your new bathing suit is cute.

C: Thanks. I'm not in love with how it fits, but I managed to relax. I've been feeling more on an even keel with good energy lately, as if the Ayurvedic diet and the self-care is making a difference. My toenails are clearing up, and the skin on my feet is stronger. I don't feel as fragile, which is really good. Of course, now you and I and our Shamanic community are getting ready to go to Shasta, which will be a whole different story, but I believe we each are stronger internally to handle the challenge better. Don't you think so?

H: Today, I agree with you, but for me, it seems life can change day-to-day pretty quickly still.

C: Well, I will have my eye on you and will help you out when needed.

H: Thanks. Thanks for all your support and love.

C: You are stuck with me.

H: Life could be worse. Haha! Sorry to run but I've got to go. Love you.

C: Backatcha.

After a trip to the farmers' market

It's been too long since I went to the market. I always enjoy my shopping there. So lively, with the colorful organic produce and flower displays from our numerous small farms. Central Coastal California is a hotbed of successful sustainable agriculture and ranching. There are so many people dedicated to good food, to taking care of themselves and the planet. I appreciate chatting with the farmers and their families. Today, the music was not that great, but still it's fun to listen to live music and watch the people around enjoy it. I got several bunches of greens, tiny new carrots, beets with their greens still attached, sausages and bacon from pasture-raised animals, and some gorgeous flowers. And I got seduced by pie at the bakery booth. There was one piece of gorgeous strawberry rhubarb pie left, a rich pinky red sparkling with a bit of sugar on the top crust. It was mine. I don't often moan over many things, especially desserts, and especially out in public. But, today, I sat down at one of the old wooden picnic tables in the middle of the market and ate that whole piece of pie. I moaned a few times while licking my lips and fingers, catching the bits of crust that threatened to fall to the ground and become bird food. Oh. That was the best damn piece of pie I have had in ages. It was not gluten-free. It was not sugar-free. Yet, it was perfect. Look at me, the gray-haired fat woman thoroughly enjoying and appreciating my pie, out in public, no less.

Wednesday evening

Here I am, not having written a blog post in a while. Maybe I should do something about bathing suits, sparked by my time with Tom, my time in Alaska, and my wanting to get back into the swimming pool. Okay, let's see what I've got…

Does my Bathing Suit Make you feel Fat?

I got an interesting and amazing compliment from a man recently during a conversation about bathing suits. He told me that

I, "always look good in my bathing suit." What? I was not only shocked to hear that from him in particular, but also just plain shocked to hear it at all. Someone thinks that? Whoa!

This last week, a male friend (not the one above) invited me to join him in a hot tub. We had not seen each other in bathing suits before, and I found myself getting a bit anxious. Not so anxious that I didn't want to do it, but I did wonder how it was going to go. And, it actually turned out great. I was completely comfortable, and so was he. We even managed to hug each other goodbye while in our suits. While it seemed we were both being careful, it was still a warm, comforting hug between friends. It had been a long time since I had a man's bare arms around me and that much skin-to-skin contact.

Plus-size bathing suits have come a long way, baby. I am comfortable in my one-piece suit, but I love that there is now a fabulous attitude of "wear what you want" for all women (which some followers call "fattitude"), and there are now two-piece bathing suits, tankinis, and bikinis in all sizes and shapes. How great is that?

This is an area in which I feel I have made a lot of progress. I might buy a two-piece suit, but mostly I'm about comfort, and a one-piece suits me (pun intended) well. I just want to be able to swim laps, frolic on the beach, sit and have a beach-y kind of cocktail, or hang out with my housemate in the backyard—whatever's on the agenda. Why not?

So, today, I have immense gratitude to the men who gave me gifts of acceptance this week. I have gratitude for the wonderful healing powers of water and sun.

Please enjoy your summer, and don't let your fears and shame about your body keep you inside on a beautiful day.

From my writing notebook
that piece of pie

why
oh why am I thinking of pie?
sugar
that stuff that wants you to die

the yeast calls out to be fed
the cancer cells want you dead

have you ever smelled a beet sugar mill?

that's where they go in for the kill
GMOs, pesticides, chemicals galore
Listen to Big Ag screaming MORE

but oh that pie
dark oozy blackberries
perfect looking crust
 just a little extra sugar sprinkled on top

Calling my name as I walk by
Pssst,
hey, look at me
Listen
Yesssss, you
look over here
see the glisten
Ssssssatisfy that ssssssweet tooth

the forbidden
the foreboding
the dark and delicious

I bet you can't eat just one piece
come on buy the whole thing
Step right up
Life is a carnival

You know you want me

I swear by all the Diet and Weight Loss Gods
I won't eat it
I will never eat pie again
I promise
I'm sorry
Please forgive me for being weak
I do know better
I'll try harder

I'll keep trying
No sugar
No carbs
No gluten
No white flour
I promise

but oh that piece of pie
Come on over here and see what I've got, little girl
Just for you
The first one's free

A few days go by
I still think of the pie
It wasn't the pie who was dissing me
It wasn't the pie who was pissing me off
It was those voices in my head
They make me cry about pie
They haunt me with their hunger and their pain
Insane

Farmers market
organic pie
just a little sugar
fresh local berries
Made with love by the people who sell it

I make a plan
Ask my friend over
She says she can
We make tea and eat that pie
Sigh.
One lovely piece of warm blackberry pie
shared with love
eaten with the attitude of gratitude
Each bite savored
Our delight never wavered

that piece of pie shared with a friend
came to a very happy end
And that's what pie is for!

Friday evening

I had a frustrating shopping day today. I've had such good body positive experiences lately—wearing bathing suits and shorts, feeling comfortable in my body. Today, I finally ventured out to buy some desperately needed bras and underpants, a process which can be just as challenging as shopping for bathing suits. I've worn the same kind of bras from Lane Bryant for years. I know they fit comfortably and come in all colors and patterns. I went online to double check that the store was still in the shopping mall I wanted to go to. The website was up, and it told me the store was open today. Um, wrong. It closed a few months ago. I went across the way to a different women's clothing store. There was not *one* bra anywhere near my size. So frustrating. I had a kind saleswoman, although her eyes kind of bugged out when I told her what size I needed. Then, she announced it over the microphone to the store.

"Can I get some help please? This lady needs a size 46D bra. Do we have any?" No, they did not.

Since I was already there, I went in search of their plus-size department. Some stores, including other Macy's, have integrated their larger and petite sizes in with the other women's clothes. Not this one. This one is still living in the dark ages, and the plus-size department is down in the basement. Really, the basement—with god-awful bright fluorescent lights, as if they might make us feel like we were upstairs with the thin people. I can remember in the past having to ask random sales people where the larger clothes were. Often there weren't any, and if there was a plus-size department, I was told in a stage whisper to go downstairs. In case I wasn't already embarrassed to be asking, the salespeople, usually women, seemed to be embarrassed to tell me. Their inability to make eye contact with me gave them away.

Times really are changing, although slowly. I have read that the average American woman is now a size 14, which in some places is considered plus-size.

So, bra shopping has been put off for another day. Hopefully, my saggy, losing-their-hooks, ancient, why-the-hell-haven't-I-replaced-them-yet old ones will hold me up a little longer.

Going to bed

Thank you for a busy, full day, Ancient Ones. A drive along the ocean. I pray for you, Grandmother Sea, that you can stay healthy and fill yourself with your own power of beauty. I'm so blessed to live here. Help me have the energy I need to get all the things done and live a good life. Don't let me get overwhelmed. Help me keep my heart open and take good care of myself.

Saturday afternoon

Time for a gin and tonic. Mmm. It was a busy day, and it got a bit stressful. I wasn't able to maintain that relaxation I found stretching and moving this morning. I'm ready to wind down and sit down with my book and my drink.

Such a funny history I have with this drink. Mama was a gin drinker. I grew up with my parents having cocktails almost every night when my dad got home from work. My mother, having grown up with her parents having cocktails every night, continued the tradition. Once in a while, we children could join in cocktail hour with some kind of little special drink. Dad drank Scotch and water and had his nightly plate of cheese and crackers. Poor Dad had to give up both habits when he was diagnosed with diabetes in his 60's. My mom never gave up her gin, though. As time went by, her cocktail glasses got bigger, and the drinks got stronger, and, after my dad died, she drank more. It was hard for me to watch. I would make a comment now and then and occasionally try to have a serious conversation letting her know I was worried about the amount of alcohol she was drinking. She usually just shrugged it off.

I did go through a phase of drinking hard liquor in my 20's. Sometimes I drank a lot, usually in order to get drunk. I guess I was lucky that it didn't take a great deal of alcohol to get me there. I never drank gin, though. That was my mom's drink, and during that phase of my life, I didn't want to see my mother often. I was so angry at her. Half of the time I didn't even know why. Some days, all I could hear in my head was her voice being disappointed in me. "Just lose some weight, Charity. It's not that hard. Just don't eat so much." "You could find yourself a _____ (fill in the blank with good teaching job, boyfriend, husband, a better apartment) if you lost some weight." "I just don't understand you." Well, Mom, in those days, I didn't understand why I was so angry or unhappy or fat either. Nor did I understand you at all.

I hated the way gin smelled. After Mom died, I began to realize how many of *my* friends enjoyed gin drinks. One evening, out with friends, I ordered a cocktail of some fancy local artisanal gin and fresh grapefruit juice. My mother would not have approved, as she always turned up her nose at expensive alcohol. Artisanal gin? Give her good old-fashioned English-style gin any day. Back to my drink—what do you know? It was good.

Not long after that, I bought some of that fancy artisanal gin full of lots of good herbs and spices. Gin does have some medicinal properties. There are a couple of California varieties that are quite "forest-y" in their aromas and flavors. And, of course, I buy fancy artisanal tonic water and organic lime juice. Oh Lord, my mom is turning over in her grave right now. She would be thrilled that I have discovered the joys of the G and T, but so horrified at my version of it.

For some reason, Mama's death gave me permission to enjoy "her" drink. I toast her still whenever I have one. In many Shamanic cultures, on the fifth anniversary of a loved one's death, a plate of that person's favorite food is left out with a candle. I set out a gin and tonic with a little bite of chocolate for Mama on her day, and a Scotch on the rocks beside a plate of cheese and crackers for Dad on his.

I had my first experience with alcohol when I was fourteen. Our family lived out in the country and mowed about two acres of the eight that we had. There were no riding mowers for us; it was my brothers' and my job during the summer to push the mowers around. We had two of them, and the three of us, with occasional help from Mom, traded off fifteen-minute sessions. On one brutally hot and humid Ohio day, I was completely soaked with sweat and had itchy grass sticking to my legs. When I came into the house for my break from mowing, I decided to have one of my dad's beers. I had seen him do the same many times after working outside in the heat. Well, fifteen minutes is a pretty short amount of time in which to drink your first full beer. I finished it, hid the empty bottle, and went outside for my next turn. It went by quickly and I felt pretty good! On my next turn inside, I decided to do it again. Upon my return outside the next time, things didn't go quite so well. I had trouble—trouble mowing a straight line, trouble seeing where I was. We had a small pond full of tadpoles and fish which we mowed around. My dad liked us to mow as close to the water line as possible so it looked neat and tidy. While mowing one of those tidying rows, I pushed the mower right into the pond! I found myself standing up to my knees in the mud, holding onto the mower for dear life, laughing my head off, and trying not to fall down. As you can imagine, my mom, who had seen me go into the pond, was able to figure out what was going on. As I remember, the natural consequence of getting sick was punishment enough.

Thinking about my history, I'm so lucky that I'm not an alcoholic or an addict. Some might say I have a food addiction. This is a tricky area. Food is a necessary part of life, for one. I think the chemical imbalances that are created by overeating and by eating unhealthy food can be corrected. By what? By food. I parted ways with the twelve-step program for overeating when I decided that I did not want to identify myself as an overeater for the rest of my life.

I started to travel down a pretty rocky road of bad choices with alcohol when younger, but I truly believe that the Gods intervened and sent me friends and teachers at the right time so I could change the direction of my life. I met my spiritual teacher and community around age thirty. Part of our studying Shamanic ways is going on Vision Quest. I had finished a four-day fast on Mt. Shasta not long before I had that first dream about my grandfather; four days of praying, four days of no food and no water. When telling my teacher about memories of abuse returning, he told me, "You have done four days vision questing on Mt. Shasta, you can handle anything now." I was strong enough to face those memories and not have to work so hard to keep all those buried feelings at bay anymore. That strength has continued to grow and has provided me with a strong faith in myself and what the Gods arrange for me in my life.

That night, going to bed

It got chilly this evening, since the clouds came back in. It feels good to cozy up with you, Tina. You were sort of restless today. Did you pick up on me getting ready to leave again? I'm just going on my usual summer camping trip to Mt. Shasta, and I'll be gone for two weeks. I'll be with my spiritual family, and you'll be at the vet's for part of the time, getting those nails trimmed and getting a break from the cats who've moved into the garage. I think we're keeping them. I see you getting used to them, so that is good. You don't have to like them, but I don't want them bothering you too much. You are and will always be Queen around here.

Ancient Ones, Grandmothers and Grandfathers, I thank you for my life. I thank you that I am able to know you and feel your presence in my life. My life would be so different if not for this. I know you have always been guiding and supporting me. Thank you for helping me make good decisions when I did, and for standing by me when I didn't. I'm trying to be as open as I can, to trust in you and to continue to have that faith.

Coming home from camping

Ahh, I'm happy to be on my way home. I'm hot, dry, tired. Looking forward to my bed. I do sleep on a cot in my very big tent, so it's sort of luxurious camping. I'm also looking forward to listening to music and reading. I read a lot, and I guess I take it for granted sometimes. My whole family still loves to read. Growing up, sometimes after dinner, you would find all five of us, parents and children, each in our own corner of the living room or in our bedroom, tucked in with a book.

Reading gives me immense pleasure. I read actual books from the library, though I am also fond of my e-reader and no longer have a serious desire to have walls full of books. I'm so grateful we grew up reading and appreciating reading, appreciating quiet, entertaining ourselves with great escapes into those grand adventures on the pages.

Our family visited our Michigan grandparents, Mom's family, a few times a year. They had an amazing library, and we were in that room often. Books covered two walls. The two large easy chairs and the sofa were old and comfortable. It was often dark in there, but there were several good reading lamps. Both my grand-parents smoked, as did my mom for the first twelve or so years of my life, so cigarette smoke permeated the room.

The family had cocktails in the library every evening before dinner, except in the summer, when we were out in their screened porch. The library was Grandmother's domain. She sat in there for most of the day, reading, doing crossword puzzles, and playing Scrabble against herself. I'm sure it's also where the family's serious discussions were held. I loved sitting in there and reading, when I wasn't upstairs in the room I always used. I realize now it was a place of refuge and respite from Grandfather's sexual abuse. In there, I was safe.

I recently learned from my younger brother that Grandmother would hand him a book, send him off to read it, then quiz him on it when he was finished. She did love sharing her books, though I don't remember getting quizzed. The library was full of all kinds of books from her childhood. I learned to love fairy tales there— *The Green, Red, Yellow Fairy* books, *The Secret Garden*, *The Live Doll* books. Grandmother introduced me to Nancy Drew and the Hardy boys. She had all the *Wizard of Oz* books, and she gave me her copy of the first story, the one they made the movie from. When I was older, Grandmother introduced me to mysteries and detective stories. Learning from her about classic authors such as

Agatha Christie, Rex Stout, and Dorothy Sayers instilled in me a lifelong love of that genre.

Later

I'm aching from the uneven ground we camped on. My feet and ankles are a mess, swollen from the heat and walking. My belly hurts from not eating enough food that's good for me and too much food that's not. This is just part of how I feel. In spite of all of this, I am happy.

I've gone to Mt. Shasta every summer, and sometimes in between, for more years than I can keep track of. My spiritual teacher, his students from the east coast, and the group I am in from the west coast gather for ten days. Our days are filled with praying, hiking, finding rivers and waterfalls to visit, singing, making ceremony, and spending time together.

As always, this year was so powerful and precious. Being on Mt. Shasta, being outside for two weeks is amazing. Yes, there are challenges for this big body of mine. We are very active and I have to really push myself. We walk many miles a day, just getting around the campground. I used my car for some of it this time. Somehow, so far, it continues to be totally worth it. Surrounded by the beauty of the forests, the glaciers on the mountain, hawks, osprey and eagles flying overhead, the possibilities of bear sightings. I'm working on not letting the aches and pains overpower the love.

I'm looking forward to times when travel is primarily about where I am, what I see, why I'm there, not about the challenges and difficulties. What I loved about being there. This time, at Mt. Shasta, it was about the stars. Our tents are scattered about several small meadows and overhead is a wide, wide view of the sky. The campground is fairly isolated so it gets quite dark. I see more stars there than I ever have anywhere, anytime. The whole Milky Way. Almost every night, I just stood looking up in total awe. Listening to that deep silence of the night. It's profound to feel so small surrounded by something so grand as the forests and the stars.

Home

Hey, Miss Tina. Here I am. I'm so glad to see you. I know you had a hard time, I'm sorry. I'll do my best to make it up to you. It didn't seem to work out to get you to the vet. I'll have to make an appointment for your nail trim. That will make you feel better. And we'll get you a flea treatment. You don't know about my big trip yet. I'm going to be gone for two months. I'm still not sure I can be away from you that long. Come sit with me on the couch. I know I need a Tina snuggle.

Later, going to bed

Bed! A real bed. I like having you in it with me, Tina. I was expecting it to be cooler at home. It's not. It's almost too hot to sleep. That's not right.

I am grateful to have a bed, to have a place to live that I love.

Friday afternoon

I just had a lovely splurge—cheese! It's one of my favorite foods, but I just can't eat it all that often. Let's just say "phlegm" and leave it at that. Today I had some nibbles—okay, bigger pieces than nibbles, but who's counting or looking? Remember that, Charity. Who's counting or looking? You see anyone else here? I had a couple different kinds of goat cheese and some really good crackers, plus a delectable glass of Rosé. I felt sophisticated and decadent.

What is it about cheese? My dad loved it, and growing up, we always had plenty in the refrigerator, from what my mom called "rat trap cheese"—the plain orange cheddar—to fancier kinds, when they were available in our little town's grocery store. Dad traveled to Europe for his work and developed a love for more sophisticated varieties. One of my strongest cheese memories revolves around Limburger cheese.

One day, after my parents had hosted a cocktail party— and I have to say, who but my mother would serve Limburger cheese at a party?—my mother sent me to Junior High with my usual "diet" lunch consisting of a piece of cheese and an apple. Yep, the cheese was Limburger. The paper bag went into my locker for the morning. Pee-eew! By the time I retrieved it, the whole hallway smelled like old rotten farts and the bag was completely saturated with grease. I carefully took it into the lunchroom where I couldn't even open the bag. No way was I going to eat the cheese or the apple, which I was sure had been totally contaminated by the stink. My opinion was confirmed by all my classmates who were either fake gagging, fake puking, or having real breathing difficulties. The whole lunchroom was, really, it being a small school with a small lunch room. The poor lunch ladies unhappily accepted the bag and threw it away with their garbage. I didn't have any lunch money, but my friends were kind enough to scrounge together enough for me to buy one of the school lunches. We all laughed about it for days once the trauma was past. Mama, what were you thinking, sending that with me?

And, what were you thinking when you thought that a small piece of cheese and an apple was an appropriate lunch for me to take to school at age thirteen? How was that sufficient nutrition for the day? Did you even think about people making fun of me? And did I have any say in the matter? I did eventually rebel and refused to continue with the apple and cheese lunch. From there, I think we moved onto the hardboiled egg and grapefruit diet. It was not as smelly but, still not all that appealing to a fourteen-year-old. There were many days when I stole money from Mom's wallet to buy one of the hamburgers which the school offered as an alternative or addition to the lunch. That wasn't enough for me either, but at least it didn't get me teased or bullied. By ninth grade, Mom gave in and let me buy lunch at school.

In my twenties, I became a vegetarian and consumed giant cheese sandwich after giant cheese sandwich. It didn't really matter what kind of bread. I would slather on mayonnaise and add a big thick slice of cheese from a block, maybe Swiss or sharp Cheddar, washing them down with diet Coke or maybe beer. I hardly chewed or tasted beyond that first combination of the cheese and the tang of mayo. How my belly handled all that food, I don't know, but even after eating as many sandwiches as I could, I felt empty. Eating a whole pizza loaded with cheese or a whole pot of pasta and cheese sauce didn't do it either.

During this time learning how to be on my own as an adult, I had a strong element of, "Fuck You, I'm not on a diet and will eat whatever I want whenever I want!" when choosing foods to eat—and, honestly, I still go there once in a while. It took years to get to the place of making positive food choices. In fact, it's taken a great deal of therapy to even acknowledge that I actually have choices about food and eating. Only fairly recently have I been able to recognize true hunger or accept when I am not hungry and say no to eating. I've worked on forgiveness for those choices, eating and otherwise, that didn't turn out so well. I still pray a lot about it.

What I do know and feel deeply is that my sensitivities to both gluten and dairy are directly related to this rebellion period. On the scientific side, there is evidence that we crave what we are allergic or sensitive to. Sensitivity to certain food develops with overconsumption of that food. I believe just as firmly in the esoteric side of things—that there are still unsaid words and feelings in the phlegm that cheese produces that cause me to gag. Decades-old exhaustion comes over me when I overeat wheat or any kind of bread. There is still unreleased shame in a sandwich or a slice of pizza, which often causes me to eat it way too quickly and without a moment of pleasure. I went from overconsumption of those foods during the rebellion phase to a period of fierce prohibition. I denied myself dairy and wheat for many years for nutritional reasons, yes, but more importantly out of fear. Fear of bingeing, fear of history repeating itself.

Recently, I have started occasionally eating sandwiches again. They're such a simple food to many people, but to me they're "treats." I try to use high quality ingredients when making them or purchase them at a healthy deli or restaurant, and I always try to eat them slowly and thoughtfully. I'm working on the idea of nothing being "forbidden," which, interestingly, some people equate with eating whatever I want, whenever I want, and as much as I want. I do not see it that way. I see this as a step towards being thoughtful and loving. I'd also like to get away from that word "treat." It reminds me too frequently of the old diet days, with all the talk of "cheating." Food is not a moral issue.

I am repeatedly astonished at the power of food. It gives me life, and it has the power to help me grow and heal. It also has the power to knock me on my ass again and again. It's my choice.

Phone call with Mr. Flannel

Charity: Hi Tom, I'm home from my trip.

Tom: Oh great, it's so good to hear your voice. How was it?

C: Good to talk with you, too. It was wonderful and powerful. And tiring and hot. I'm happy to be home. How are you?

T: Oh, okay. I've got some doctor things going on. I'll tell you about them some other time.

C: Okay, but you feel all right?

T: Yes, the usual.

C: I'm wondering if you'd like to have supper together this weekend. Saturday or Sunday?

T: That sounds good. Let me think a minute. I have a meeting on Sunday, so Saturday is open. How about that?

C: Wonderful! How about 5? Come pick me up and we will figure out where to go.

T: Wonderful indeed. See you tomorrow.

I'll be happy to see him. But what's with this not telling me about his health? Some sort of secret? I have to remember I'm just a "buddy." Sigh. It continues to crack me up how formal he is and how I pick up on that when we have a conversation.

Saturday, going to bed

Tom and I had dinner tonight. It was okay. I can tell I'm getting frustrated with him. Not that I want more from him in terms of a deeper relationship, romance or sex, but I'd like him to be more open. My more cynical women friends say men can't do that, but thanks to some men I dearly love, I know that that is not true. I'm not sure how long I'll be interested in spending time with Tom.

Tuesday afternoon

Bodywork two days in a row. Now *that* is juicy self-care. Getting touched. For sure, I do not get touched enough. Today the touching and care went deep into my muscles, calming and relaxing the ones that felt overworked. The touch also went deep into my heart and helped me feel loved.

This morning I had another Ayurveda session with Talya. She did an eye treatment that involved gently pouring warm, melted ghee onto my eyes. It soothed and rejuvenated me by having some specific action on the ocular nerve, which, along with the main nerve from the nose, goes directly into the brain. Talya's soft voice encouraging me to "receive the ghee" struck a beautiful chord with me and helped me open. Receiving is one of my challenges. I consciously made myself quiet and refrained from talking with her as I often do. I focused on just receiving the ghee and receiving the loving care, the quiet and peace. It was marvelous to be able to calm my mind.

I naturally give. One of my strong qualities is my generosity, so I have had to learn a lot about the boundaries related to giving and receiving as I have gotten older. You can say "no" and still be generous. Sometimes that is a better gift. Knowing when, what, and how to give is valuable. As is knowing the same about receiving. I had a heartfelt conversation once with a friend who let me know how deeply it hurt her when I wouldn't receive her time, her love, and her self.

I shared with Talya the ways in which I feel my body has changed and is changing since I started working with her. The skin on my toes is stronger and not peeling so much. I'm not as affected by bug bites. My food choices and appetite are changing as I learn to better discern my hunger level. I'm more aware of my energy level, and I notice what conditions affect it.

We also talked about plans for my big trip. I finally decided to go after wavering for about a year. I'm getting excited, scared, and anxious, all at once. It will be two months on the road, driving all around the US visiting friends, National Parks, and bodies of water—going where the wind takes me. An Epic Adventure! Am I crazy? That's a really long time. Can I do it? I feel so called to go. I must. My biggest concern is Tina. How will she be without me for that long? How will I be without her? She is used to me traveling, but I don't know what kind of sense of time cats have. Does two months feel longer than two weeks to her? It must. She will have a really good caretaker, this I know. Regardless of all of my concerns, I have to give this thing a try. I've given myself full permission to turn around at any point and come straight home. No shame.

I'm so excited to see friends on this trip. How blessed I feel to have so many and so many people opening their homes. "Sure, come stay!" they have all said—old friends, newer friends. And there is so much to see! Despite my painful thoughts about the politics of our country, America is still incredibly diverse and beautiful, with oceans, mountains, plains, cities, farms, and forests—breathtaking places to see either for the first time or again. I see myself driving across the Great Plains of Montana, the Badlands of North Dakota. I'm eager to see the Great Lakes, which were such a part of my childhood, again. I can't wait to do some exploring. Niagara Falls. New England. Then the cities: Boston, New York, Philadelphia, Baltimore, D.C. Down the southern coast. The Outer Banks of North Carolina. I've read so many novels which took place there. The Deep South. I've never been to Alabama or Mississippi, though I've known how to spell both words since I was a child. All the way across Texas to Big Bend National Park. The Southwest. I'll have some fun in southern California and then head home.

I plan to take photos and write the whole time, all while staying open to the synchronicity of the Universe.

Friday afternoon, resting

What a productive and satisfying day so far! First exercise class, then I got a lot of chores and errands done. I had more energy today than I have had in a long time. Perhaps my eye treatment the other day cleared some negative energy. I needed hearing aid adjustments and cleaning—done. I ordered new purple glasses. Ooh-la-la, I cannot wait for those. I hope they come before I leave.

There is still a great deal of preparation to be done for this trip. I've got a week! I hope I will be totally ready, both on the physical plane of having what I need and on the emotional plane of being ready to spread my wings and being able to charge myself up with the beauty of the Earth and the love of my friends.

Going to bed

Oh, I give thanks for my life. I pray for my loved ones who are seeking help and healing, those who are sick and have challenges. Thank you for my good luck, the abundance in my life. I'm so grateful to be loved and have people to love.

Saturday morning

Dang, I feel too creaky to go dancing, and I haven't been pulled to go in quite a while. Just letting that be. Maybe I'll find dancing on my trip, maybe not. Perhaps I'll be anxious to get back to it when I get home. I'm making choices with no guilt.

I have plenty to do around here before then, that's for sure. I want to spend time in the garden today. I need to get my hands in the earth, pull some weeds, tidy it up out there a bit, water. I need to feel grounded. Somehow doing those chores in the garden facilitates the tidying and weeding of my mind and emotions, as well as the watering of those internal seeds that have been planted. I will need to be ready to surrender to whatever care the garden gets while I'm gone. I think I'll miss being out there.

Plenty of people want to talk to me about my Epic Adventure. Many women friends are impressed by my bravery and my independence. "Aren't you worried about all that driving?" Hmm, not really. "Aren't you scared?" Well, sort of. But, I must do what scares me now and then. I don't mean that I want to put my life in danger, but I do need to be out in the world. This quote has traveled the world, "A ship is safe in harbor, but that's not what a ship is for." I need to take risks, face fear, and do the thing anyway.

For me, the hard part of the trip is not driving or facing the unknown. The hard part is the leaving. There's a world of difference between going and leaving. Going is what's ahead, and I'm excited about that. What will I see? What will I do? Leaving has to do with what's behind. Leaving Tina and the coziness and comfort of her sleeping next to me. Leaving my community, my loved ones, the singing and praying together, the walking and talking together. I've had many an exercise teacher who has said that the hardest part of working out is putting on your shoes and getting out the door. Same with this.

I think I will also feel some relief in leaving my house. I get to leave the damn oak moth caterpillars that fill the tree in the front. I get to leave my disorganization, which is driving me crazy. When I come home, I'll be ready to face it. My friend who is helping me out with things while I am gone will take better care of my garden than I have been. He already asked me if he could do some reorganizing in my kitchen. Who knows what I will come home to? It could be awesome. I can take some time and figure out if Tom and I have a future.

Later that day

Oh my God, I finally talked with Aurora! My sweet girl of my heart. We texted a few times and set a time for chatting. And we did. I have been waiting for this communication for years, for her to find me and reach out to me. We haven't seen each other since her Dad's funeral twelve years ago, and I think only talked to her once or twice after that. It's a sweet miracle. And, what is even more synchronistic is that I could tell her I'll be in Portland next week and can see her. How amazing is that? I am thrilled beyond measure. She wants to talk with me about California, since she's thinking about moving here. It was a little awkward on the phone, we both acknowledged. There's a lot of time and distance to cover. Or maybe it doesn't need to be covered. We will see. I'm so excited. After not hearing from her and losing track of her, I had to put away my disappointment and just have faith we would come back together.

Now it's hard to stop thinking about her and remembering all of our interactions and activities when I lived in Oregon. We played a lot. Basketball, sometimes; just running around visiting playgrounds other times. I introduced her to bowling and miniature golf. She was so competitive! We started out with "Go Fish" and

"Chutes and Ladders" when she was five, moving on to more and more complicated card and board games. Singing and dancing. She "forced" me to be notably more energetic than I usually was, which was so good for me. We both loved clothes shopping. Oy, bathing suit shopping. I think she was ten when she wanted a two-piece, which was okay with me. The ones she picked out were more like bikinis, though, which, even though they are common now, I still think are inappropriate for young girls. She particularly wanted a gold lamé one. I do have a tacky side which can appreciate gold lamé, but not for a girl that age who actually needed a suit for energetic swimming. I want to remember to remind her of that whole incident. She was so pissed at me for not letting her get it.

She traveled with me often. Always so curious, asking questions about everything. Of course, we had the occasional struggles with bed times and getting homework done when our travels together required taking her out of school. Her dad and I had many differences, but he was supportive of all that Aurora and I did together.

Sunday evening, on Facebook
"No is a complete sentence."
It looks like a good article, but I have to pay to read it. I don't think so. But, I can think about it anyway. There's so much power in that word. Throughout my life, I've had to really work on being able to say it. I finally could say "No!" to my Grandfather and stop his abuse. I've been able to say No in situations where people were hurting and insulting me. I've learned to say No to going on damaging eating binges. Now I'm working on saying "Yes" to love and care for myself. My Epic Adventure is about saying Yes. Two tiny words. Little words with big power.

From my writing notebook
Is it yes or no?

Knowing when to say which
when to say what
why and where and how

Yes means yes
and No means no

I say No to you telling me how I should feel about my body
What you think of me is
none of my business

I don't need to explain
No is a complete sentence.
No
that is all you need

I say No thank you
I have compassion and can see your pain
but no thank you
it is not mine.
You may keep it and
shine it up and show it if you want.
but, No
not mine
not this time

No
no more
no less
Enough

Monday morning

Well, I'm as ready as I'm ever going to be. Black Beauty is up-to-date on service, and he got washed, vacuumed, and packed up. I hope my VW stallion lives up to his heritage and takes me on the journey of my life! I am learning to treat my car with the same care I'm working on applying to myself. Black Beauty, my trusty steed—he's gonna get a lot of miles added on. Good thing he is a station wagon.

I didn't get a chance to see everyone I wanted to see before going, but I saw most of them. I got a little teary saying goodbye to folks. It's a final kind of word. I tried to say "See you later," which feels more open-ended. Whether you're going on a trip or not, you never know when you'll see another person again, or if you will at all. It's good to not leave anything unsaid.

I'll be shedding some skin on this trip. I'm not entirely sure what that means, but it feels true. Changing habits. Having new experiences. A chance to work on all kinds of stuff, including being more comfortable with my extrovert side, finding strength, and welcoming love and kindness. I am so freaking excited! Let's get this show on the road.

I've been calling my trip "Charity's Epic Adventure," but truly, that's what life is, so this is just another chapter.

Calling Hannah

Hannah: Hi! Are you ready to go?

Charity: Hi. I think so. I'm finally nervous about it all. I really haven't felt it until now. Funny, right? There have been so damn many details. I did make lists but that doesn't guarantee that everything was on the list. I hope I've surrendered and will do no more list making.

H: I'm still not quite believing you are actually going.

C: Me neither. I'll believe it when I leave the driveway.

H: I'm excited for you and proud of you. And, I'll miss you so much.

C: I feel the same way. I'll be so glad I have that fancy phone system in my car so at least we can talk whenever we want. Well, as long as there is reception.

H: What are you most excited about? Looking forward to?

C: That's hard to narrow down. Seeing friends is an obvious answer. Aurora! Our plans are still tentative but I'm getting together with her. That thrills me.

H: I can't wait to hear about that and how she is doing. I hope you call me that day.

C: Okay, I will. This will make you laugh because of your own experiences, but I'm really excited about seeing Lake Superior and the other Great Lakes.

H: That year I spent there was enough for a lifetime.

C: I'll send you photos. That's another thing I'm so looking forward to—photography. Stopping wherever and whenever to take pictures. I hope I have fun with that.

H: I'm a little jealous of that part.

C: Well, honey, this is it. Off I go early tomorrow morning. I'll be in touch.

From my writing notebook
shedding my skin

metamorphosis
morphing
this life dwarfing me
shedding
dreading
what lies beneath
will it frighten me?
enlighten me and brighten me?
all of the above is the correct answer

when in doubt, choose d) as your answer
says a young friend trying to study for his SATs
You can't study for that test, I say
It's the sum of what you've learned
all these long years

You can't prepare for what's underneath that skin either
are you ready?
Hold it steady
It might be incredible
Is the skin edible?
Can we eat our past and expect to forget it?
express it

shit it out
No consequences
no regard to the environment where you leave it?

It's all too much to keep carrying around
all those layers upon layers

I once made a 13-layer cake
1/4 inch thin layers
vanilla cake
caramel icing
whipped cream
how do you eat something like that?
Why do I think of this now?

shedding layers
shredding papers
the past slipping and sliding through

What lies underneath
is it pretty or tasty like the caramel?
slimy like an onion
what's inside?
They say
the ubiquitous they
the self-righteous they
they who have not shed their skin
they say
that inside each fat person is someone thin
trying to get out

Is this what lies underneath the shedding skin?
What if a fat person is trying to get in?
let me in
let me out
let me shed this skin of doubt

Like the snake, I crawl across the rough spots
urging the skin to loosen
to dry
to go
the jagged edges of life cut and help it break away
the hot sun dries it
the wild wind blows it every which way

The new skin grows thicker
Quicker now it forms
a new life for what's underneath
What was underneath is now gone
Does it matter anymore what it was
that lay there?

Tuesday morning, bright and early

Well, Tina. This is it. This is the hardest part—leaving you. We'll be all right, no matter what. You are pretty healthy, but you are old, so who knows what might happen? What if I never did anything because I was afraid? What if I stayed home because I was afraid of what might happen or not happen if I go? What if I never answered the phone because it might be bad news? I know it's not your thing, but I have to hug you for a while, so just put up with me for a bit. You have awesome caretakers coming, and you will be treated like the queen that you are. I have awesome things awaiting me, and I will treat myself like the queen I am.

Great Spirit, thank you for my life. Thank you for this great opportunity. Let me use it in the best way. Please protect my loved ones, my house while I'm gone. Please protect me and guide me.

The first night, Weed, California

And I'm on my way. I know the drive I did today by heart, having gone back and forth between Oregon and California for the last thirty years, visiting friends in California when I lived in Oregon and now driving up to Oregon frequently to stay with family. I stopped and took a little walk on Mt. Shasta, one of the places on the Earth that truly has my heart. I left prayers of grati-tude and for a safe journey.

Loads and legions and oodles of feelings today. Relief that I'm finally doing it. Some freaking out that I'm actually doing it! Excitement. Anticipation. Hope that I'll have a good time. All of the above.

Portland, Oregon, going to bed at my brother and sister-in-law's house

I met with Aurora! I got to see my girl again, my daughter of my heart. I was so excited and anxious all morning, waiting and trying not to have too many expectations. I wondered what to talk about, knowing we had a time limit of about an hour and a half. Would we need to talk about why we drifted apart? I've had so many emotions after so many years—sadness about not seeing her for so long, sweet memories of our time together, anger at her dad, hope for our future.

I got to the café after she did. We rushed to each other and gave each other great big hugs. Both of us had grins almost too big for our faces. It was a bit startling to see her, after thirteen years, as a grown woman, though I could still see that little girl and the teenager inside her. She has beautiful dark brown eyes, a quirky smile that's a bit lopsided, and those very expressive eyebrows. She wore makeup, but not a lot. Her hair is darker, almost black.

The line in the café was long but we both ordered chai and kept our arms around each other while we waited. A table opened up and we eagerly sat down. I could hardly take my eyes off her. It was a bit awkward at first and challenging to know where to dive in. Once we began, we managed perfectly, our words just rolling off our tongues as we laughed and remembered. I got a little weepy. We shared stories about our present lives—about my retiring, about her waitressing and going to school. She asked, "Any men in your life these days?"

"Not really." I told her about Tom, Mr. Flannel. "You?"

"No," she said firmly. "I'm taking a break."

We shared a few fond memories. I was so happy to hear how important her Aunt Charity still is to her. She sees me as someone steady from her childhood, a woman who was present and available for her. Aurora told me, "As a kid, I knew I needed good women in her life, and that I still do." She knew she could count on me. I'm so glad. It fills my heart.

I got to say, "Having you in my life was so important to me too. You gave me so much just by loving me, becoming the daughter I never had, the daughter of my heart."

"Awww, I still love you," she replied. I loved helping her and spending time with her, giving her presents and stuff she needed, but way beyond that, we helped each others' hearts heal. Growing up, I often felt unprotected and unloved. By standing with her and being her advocate and loving auntie, it felt as if I were taking care of my own inner child self.

"I still love you, too. I'm so sorry that we drifted apart. In retrospect, I wish I would have made more of an effort to find you again."

She shrugged her shoulders and smiled, saying, "I always knew we would see each other again, that we would get back together when the time was right."

Aurora went with me to many of my Shamanic community gatherings. She remembered the camping trips at Mt. Shasta—the thousands of stars, the freezing cold water in the creek, the hot sun in the meadow, and our friends. Some of her memories were definitely those of a child—all the walking, so many adults telling her what to do, getting bored sometimes, and the times she was the only young girl. "I remember singing at someone's wedding in Hawaii and some of the parties we had when I got to sing. I remember you making me do my homework on the airplane coming home from a bunch of our trips."

"I loved our singing together. We used to do it a lot in the car. Sometimes we'd get really loud and sometimes we just sang because we loved the songs." That little girl could make a great big beautiful noise!

"I don't really sing anymore," Aurora told me.

We laughed about all the Disney movies we saw over and over. We both thought it was funny that the movie we saw together she remembers the most was *Twister*—tornadoes and tragedy! It was her choice to go see it. I didn't want to see it and didn't think it was a good choice, but see it we did.

She still has her great sense of humor. Oh gosh, how we could laugh and laugh, Making stupid jokes, telling silly stories, just being goofy. She taught me a lot about loosening up. Then, as she got older, we could blend the silliness and the seriousness and have some really great conversations. I look forward to having those with her again.

Aurora feels really connected to the ocean and is thinking of moving, maybe to California. She's ready to explore her options and wants to visit soon to check them out. We will see.

There were more big hugs and grins as we said goodbye. I had a hard time saying it. It was just so moving to finally hold her. I didn't want to let go. But she had to get to work. Work! My girl going off to work in her white blouse and black pants, with an apron in her purse. My girl, who is now thirty. I had to remind myself and her that I met her twenty-five years ago!

After we parted, I sat in my car and cried. They were happy tears, shed as the memories continued to flood in. We both texted each other before driving off, saying how great it had been. My morning worries came to naught. We had plenty to say. We didn't talk about her dad, and that was perfect.

This is just the first week of my trip and already something so amazing has happened! A piece of my heart has returned. Thank you, Creator, for this.

Eastern Washington, at a highway rest stop
Seems weird to have wifi here, but yay! I've been taking some great photos so far. The Japanese Gardens in Portland. Chihuly glass in Seattle. All the golden grain fields, windmills, and rolling hills here. I've had fun posting photos on Facebook and my friends are really enjoying seeing them and being able to be in touch with me this way. I was wishing I had some company today, and I guess I need to remember my virtual connection is strong. I've got a big community of friends vicariously traveling with me.

Montana

First a stop with a high school friend whom I hadn't seen in fifty years. Beth and her husband of almost that long welcomed me with open arms. We talked and walked and reminisced. Beth had traveled with my family on our Epic European tour of 1968, which definitely had a lot of ups and downs, bumps in the road. My parents and four teenagers.

Next to see Tim and Maureen, folks from my spiritual community who own an art gallery. I got to hang out at the gallery and soak in that artist vibe. Tim made us his special oat and nut waffles to send me on my way after several days. I didn't make any art while I was there, but I could feel my creativity getting sparked and making plans for projects when I get home.

North Dakota

"Family and friendship" is the theme of the trip so far, having stayed with family in Portland and both new friends and dear long-time companions in both Seattle and Montana. Next was my best friend from college.

Sherry and I spent a few days out at her family cabin on the shores of a little lake then a night at her house in town with her husband and three enormous ragdoll cats. We reminisced for hours, catching up on years of news and gossip. I was relieved to find we still had no end of topics to talk about. She and her sister who was also visiting stitched away on their quilts, and I brought out a crochet project as the three of us chatted and laughed.

Sherry and I loved our college days—our close friends, folk dancing out on the quad after dinner, playing our recorders, watching "Star Trek," then the news, then "Hogan's Heroes." We actually were both good students—she a sociology major, me a psychology major—having met and bonded as transfer students our sophomore year. We packed in a lot of adventures— afternoon drinking breaks and a few hitchhiking excursions. And we both loved crazy socks. After graduation, she, another classmate named Laura, and I went on the original Epic Adventure all around the country to celebrate. Seven thousand miles in six weeks! It was fun to see what she and I both remembered, such as our disastrous time at the Grand Canyon. We (though, really, I was the one responsible) had left the poles for her family's huge canvas army tent behind at our previous stop, so a miserable night was had by all. Of course, it rained. Sherry and Laura attempted to make a sort of gigantic but ineffective sleeping bag out of the tent and got sopping wet and cold. Since the car was mine, I slept in the back seat, which was drier but not any kind of comfortable. In the morning, we went for a brief walk, barely able to look at each other or the beauty of the canyon. We drove about an hour (which was all we could stand), checked into a motel, and slept all day. They eventually forgave me.

We spent a glorious sunny day armed with cameras, water, and snacks in the Teddy Roosevelt Badlands National Park for a day of photography and adventure. Herds of wild horses and bison abounded, along with fascinating rock formations. The prairie dogs made me laugh. We created new memories with our mutual love of taking photographs. Thanks to her, I now lust after her higher-tech camera.

Watching the wild horses in the park did give me a thrill, seeing their freedom and appreciating that there are still places where they can run wild. Sherry's passion and enthusiasm was contagious, and I got caught up in photographing them. The day fed that creative part of me as well as nourished my heart spending time with an old friend. Sherry is one of my friends who drove me to the airport the day I flew to New York for an abortion. She is one of the few people I told about being raped. I owe her a great deal for holding secrets for me for so many years.

Take a Breath

I am two weeks into my two-month journey around the country. Most of my trip has been smoky so far, due to the multitude of forest fires throughout California, the Pacific Northwest, and Montana. It has gotten me thinking a lot about breathing. Some days, it has been a bit hard. I have a history of lung challenges and an allergy or sensitivity to smoke, so I have been wondering how I would do. These lungs have gotten considerable healing this last year from herbal tinctures, focused breathing exercises, steam inhalations, and essential oils and I can see it has paid off. Phew!

I lived in the woods in Oregon for many years. My cabin was only five miles from the small town of Forest Grove, but it felt farther. Those of us who lived on our road lived with the fact that it might take the fire department too long to get to a fire. The house next to mine, which was about 1/4 mile away, had totally burned to the ground some 20 years before I moved in, and teenagers had set a fire in the rock quarry nearby which burned for quite a while before anyone knew.

How often do you think about your breath? It's calming and reviving to pause and take some deep ones, isn't it? It's seemingly such a simple thing. It's involuntary. Our body does it for us— except when the body breaks down and can't, or when there are obstacles, such as smoke. Being in this environment is a good reminder to me to not to take breathing for granted. Each breath is life, is a new change to keep living.

In shamanic cultures, eagles and hawks represent the element of air. In Montana, one of my friends and I happened upon a hawk sitting on the fence one smoky morning. He reminded me of how sacred breath is, how sacred air is. How I have to try to remember that with each breath.

So, how about stopping right now? Take some deep breaths. How often do you do that? Try alternate nostril breathing. With your thumb and third finger of one hand on each side of your nose, hold your nostril closed under your thumb. Breathe in deeply through the open side. Hold for a second, then hold closed that nostril through which you breathed in while breathing out through the other. Breathe in through that same nostril. Hold for a second, then release your breath through the other nostril. Alternate back and forth for several minutes. No need to do it quickly. Focus and take full breaths. This is called alternate nostril breathing, or "Nadi Shodahana," and it is good for focusing and sharpening your concentration. (And good for long car drives!)

Another breath-related action is to notice is whether your in breath or out breath has more energy. Are you taking life in fully or are you pushing it out and away? Maybe you are in balance, in and out are about the same. Curious, huh?

Just Breathe....

Upper Peninsula, Michigan

I'm having a few solo days here. It's good to be quiet.

Being on my own and exploring is getting me out of my comfort zone a bit and helping me find my adventuresome spirit. I'm excited to be somewhere I've never been. Yesterday I drove from North Dakota into Wisconsin through an absolutely breathtaking part of Minnesota. Green. Quiet. Lots of water. I got a little lost and a little worried. In that moment, I thought, "Oh, this is why my friends are a little scared about this trip." I was out of GPS and cell phone range for most of the day. I did have a paper map. I could see where I was and where I wanted to go, but not how to get there. I was truly "off the grid." The navigation frustration gave me a headache. But, my good nature ruled the day, which proved to be full of really great photo opportunities. I just kept driving, knowing I would show up somewhere relatively soon, which I did. I stopped at a National Wildlife Refuge and witnessed scores of flying and floating birds. Where is my bird identification book? Oh yes, I don't have one. I so wanted to see a moose, but that was not to be this time around. I sat beside a little lake and just watched all the activity, feeling my body relax and frustration fade away. I truly am comfortable being by myself. I have confidence in my driving abilities, I don't mind peeing in the bushes, and with luck, I won't get really panicky about anything.

In Wisconsin, I veered off the highway and discovered a picturesque little state park. Quite a few picnickers and tourists there were enjoying the river and the rapids, wildflowers, and squirrels. I had a great time wandering around, taking photos, and getting mesmerized by the water eddying around the rocks.

I continued on into Michigan and the Great Lakes. They are huge and powerful, and they feel a little like the ocean to me. Our family went to a Quaker family camp each summer in the late 50's through early 60's up in the interior of Ontario, Canada. I had such a good time at that camp. I remember swimming and attending Quaker meetings on the banks of the small frigid lake, surrounded by dense forest. Driving from Ohio, we passed through the Upper Peninsula of Michigan and saw Lake Michigan, Lake Superior, and Lake Ontario. Crossing the big bridge at Mackinac, then a brand new kind of bridge, was always a scary thrill. This time, though, I was the one who had to cope with sweaty hands and remembering to breathe while driving in the midst of the semi trucks. I wanted everyone to slow down so I could look around. I wanted to stop somewhere to take a picture of the bridge, but there was too much traffic to try to figure that out.

From my writing notebook
How often are we alone?

Here at this Minnesota lake, I am completely alone
no one for miles
In this refuge for wildlife, I find refuge from the road

Here I sit
resting
watching and listening

praying for protection
praying for freedom
finding the Sacred in this stillness

Here in this place the birds can live as they wish
They are free, flying high and calling out their songs
Eating bugs and frogs as they float on the water with the cattails
and lilies.
Wildflowers swaying in the breeze, providing sanctuary for the
Butterflies
Weeping willows provide
shade for the fish seeking dark quiet

Here I sit on the earth
my feet in the water

Not too long ago, I was frightened and
not sure where I was
Intuition said, keep going
Finally I found this place

Refuge
I sit and breathe
Freedom
I listen

I grow strong in the silence
It must be absolutely frightening to be a refugee

Boston, at my friend Leslee's, a friend I know through my personal chef work and the professional organization we both belonged to

It was a quiet morning. Leslee and I were chatting in the kitchen, while she was waiting for her mom, whom she takes care of, to wake up. She was having her morning coffee, while I drank my Dandy Blend coffee substitute that I brought with me. Her spacious kitchen is home to a magic European coffee machine built into the wall, programmed for Leslee's perfect cup and for her husband's as well. The machine knows exactly how she likes it, how strong, how long to brew, how much to put in the cup, what temperature for the milk and the coffee. It probably also knows what her favorite color is and where she was born! Leslee left for a moment, and I accidentally (really) picked up her cup instead of mine. Now, I haven't had coffee in many years, For the last year or so, I have been dreaming of coffee. I smell it, and then I want it; I imagine how it will taste and wonder how it will affect me. Could I start drinking it again? Will it still taste good? Will it still make my heart palpitate or give me jitters? So far, I have resisted, giving my body more time to heal from those ill effects which led me to quit. I continue to live vicariously through my coffee-loving friends.

I took a sip. Whoa—I heard the angels sing! That wasn't my Dandy Blend. Must be heaven. Perfection. I took another sip. Yep, still hearing angels. Yeah, this is coffee.

Leslee came back and I told her. Picking up my own cup of my usually tasty drink, I sensed that I really didn't want to go back to drinking what began to seem like a sad little drink.

"Leslee, please oh please, make me a little cup of coffee just like yours." Giggling at me, she and the magic machine answered my plea within minutes. I was on my Epic Adventure. I could be wild and do what I want, right?

O.M.G., the best! Savoring the moment, I drank it ever so slowly, relishing every drop down to the last swallow. I got quite giddy. I wanted more! Sadly, I also got a little too jittery, which ended the coffee exploration for now. Of course, immediately, I was totally spoiled. If I did decide to try coffee drinking again, where would I be able to find such pleasure, or hear the angels sing again? I'd have to come back to Boston, obviously.

Phone call with Tom, off the New Jersey Turnpike

Charity: Hey Tom, I'm calling you while I'm calming down from my scary whirlwind drive through the edges of New York City.

Tom: Hi. Whoa, I've never driven there in my life. Better you than me. How are you? We haven't spoken in a while.

C: I've started the portion of my trip staying with friends in New Hampshire, Boston, and Connecticut and not driving every day. It's a great change of pace. I've been well taken care of. What's new with you?

T: Oh, nothing really. Still doing my maintenance and yard work job. I enjoy the people and my coworkers, but even a few hours a day makes me tired.

C: Have you not been feeling well?

T: No, not really. What did you do in Boston? Eat some lobster? See the sights?

C: I did eat lobster. My friends live out in the suburbs but we went to the city one day for some shopping and visited the Holocaust Memorial which was quite moving.

T: I'm sure it was. I have to go. I look forward to hearing from you again and seeing you when you get home. Another month, I think.

C: Yes, around that. Be well.

Well, that was short. I have to say I don't miss him all that much. I know much of that is because I am busy. But I'm coming to terms with the fact he really is a bit boring. Absence makes the heart find the truth, maybe.

Outside of Philadelphia, Pennsylvania, at Jessica's house, my cooking friend with whom I will travel through the South for two weeks

I have truly enjoyed traveling alone these past weeks, and now I'm looking forward to having Jess join me in North Carolina. We will travel together to Houston, Texas. The friends we will see along this part of the journey are all colleagues from our personal chef days and the association we all belonged to. Jess is smart and funny and, while she doesn't love to drive, she will be an excellent researcher and navigator.

I'm staying only about thirty minutes away from where my parents used to live and about the same distance from where their ashes are buried. I'm feeling a bit guilty about not checking in on Mom's friends who might still be around. Before she died, she asked me to keep her address file and keep in touch with her closest friends. The Chinese-looking cloth-covered address box is sitting on my desk at home. She had that box for years, faithfully recording from whom she got Christmas cards so she would remember to send them one back. In the days following Mama's death, I spent hours sitting at her desk, using her seemingly endless supply of pretty notecards to let people know of her passing. Sorry, Mama. I'm sorry I didn't even think of bringing the box with me. I'm sorry I didn't keep in touch with your friends. Is it terrible that I want to use my time instead to go explore a local garden and take photos? Is it terrible that I want more time with my friends and not hers?

Regrets really are a useless waste of time and energy, yet family history can be fraught with them. What *do* I wish I had told Mom or Dad? About Grandfather and the abuse? No regrets there. I made conscious, thought-out decisions in therapy several different times not to. I used to wish I had told them about having an abortion. I'm pretty sure they would have been supportive. I never thought about telling them about the rape that summer in San Francisco. So many secrets. Dad died about twelve years ago and Mom, six. There is no one I need protect or not tell anymore. I'm still feeling the energy shifts as I get used to a life without that need to protect and keep those secrets. Right after Mom's death, I felt a big weight lift from my shoulders.

I don't feel any deep connection to the particular Quaker meeting house on the grounds where their ashes are buried, and I don't need to go to meeting to remember them. Dad put immeasurable time, energy, and money into that 300-plus-year-old gray fieldstone building. All that time and money took its toll on Mom, who thought his time and money would be more useful elsewhere.

Those old meeting houses have a lovely peaceful energy to them, though. This area is well populated with them. When I enter one, I feel the energy of all those years of prayers and good thoughts. It feels deeply embedded in the wood of the benches, in the stone of the walls and floor, and in the quiet whispers as people come in and find a seat.

In addition to the Quaker meeting we had at home with the family, we attended Sunday School at our local Presbyterian church. My parents had met the minister of that church and liked him. I attended Quaker boarding school from the tenth to the twelfth grades, and I helped organize a Quaker meeting on the nearby Beloit College campus. Nothing particular sparked my feelings, but by the time I graduated from college, I had grown dissatisfied with any kind of organized religion and did not want to set foot inside any meeting house. I began to explore other spiritual paths. As time went on, I would join my parents on First Day morning (Sunday). I came back to appreciating the peacefulness and quiet time spent there with them. I guess there still is a bit of Quaker-ness inside me.

North Carolina

I'm taking a day to slow down, but not for too long, since I'm on the Outer Banks and a storm with hurricane force winds is predicted. I'll need to go tomorrow. This is one of the places I've so been looking forward to visiting. I've never been here before, and I am both enchanted by the old weathered homes and quite discouraged at how built up this tiny island is, with neighborhoods of houses all looking alike, box store after box store, and garish tourist trap amusement parks. But, the coastline is still magnificent.

The beach I visited was pristine. and the dunes were somewhat protected, with wild grasses growing abundantly and a myriad of bird tracks in the sand. Because of the impending storm, I'm not able to go take the wildlife and wild horse tour I was hoping to do. But spending a few hours watching the crashing waves and photographing the grasses and birds has filled my soul. I wanted to jump in the water and have a dunk, but the waves were tall and strong, so I just got my toes wet. I found myself a delicious fish dinner served by probably the best waitress I have ever encountered. She was friendly and very solicitous.

"Hon, you do know there are hurricane warnings out? I truly hope y'all are leaving tomorrow." I assured her I was. I was the only single diner there, and she made me feel at ease with her suggestions both about the menu and the island. The restaurant was closing the next day and all were heading to the mainland to escape the hurricane. Tourist season was almost over for the year, anyway.

I feel filled with the power and beauty of the sea. I have immersed myself in nature on this trip as frequently as possible. The vast Northern Plains, the last of the prairies, golden grasses as far as the eye can see. The many lakes and streams in Northern Minnesota, Wisconsin amidst the forests and farmlands. The Great Lakes! Magnificent and powerful. I did go in the water. Brrr! New England, too early for the fall leaves, but charming villages, early American architecture, lobster! Then down the Atlantic Seaboard through the big cities. I survived my speedy drive carried along by traffic on the outskirts of New York City. Not so much natural beauty, that part being more focused on the beauty of friendship. I'm looking forward to the white sands of the Gulf Coast, all that there is in Texas, from dry desert to big cities to the hill country.

For so many political reasons, I am ashamed to be an American. However, there is no denying we live in an absolutely beautiful country. We are blessed with such a variety of scenery. We still have wide open spaces. Yes, the future of those places is in great jeopardy. I am forever filled with the big blue skies, the forests as far as the eye can see, clean lakes, rushing rivers. Majestic mountains. The grasslands that remain. Oceans and beaches.

Thank you, Ancient Ones, for this magnificent land and sea, for all that lives here, all that grows here. For the trees and the mountains. For all the water, fresh and salty, as well as the glaciers, rivers, streams, and lakes. And for the power of Beauty. Let me remember to fill myself daily with that beauty. To find it in all things. To find it in myself. To find it in others.

Phone call with Hannah

Charity: Hi honey.

Hannah: Hey, where are you?

C: North Carolina, the Outer Banks. The landscape is gorgeous here. Sand dunes, interesting grasses. Too many houses, though. Apparently, a big storm is brewing so I'm leaving a day early.

H: Oh jeez, good. We worry enough about you as it is.

C: Really, you are worried?

H: Sort of, and sometimes. I'm always glad when I get these phone calls. Too bad about the storm though. I saw that in the news, the hurricane winds.

C: Maybe; they are not really sure. My schedule getting messed up once again. I don't know where the time is going! I skipped a few planned stops in Michigan and Long Island, and somehow, I'm behind where I thought I would be. So, according to that, it's good I'm moving on, but I did kind of need another quiet day. Oh well.

H: You can be quiet when you get home, whenever that is.

C: True! I miss you. I'm having the best time and am so glad I am here, but I miss you. I'll try to call more often, but tomorrow I'm meeting up with my friend who'll be traveling with me for a few weeks. Happy about that.

H: I'm happy about it too. Less worrying for us.

C: I guess there is some comfort in being worried about. That sounds weird. I don't want you to worry or need you to worry, but I sort of like it that you are. It's a form of love.

H: Yep.

Montgomery, Alabama

A new state for me. The deep south. Jess and I were a bit nervous driving today. Occasionally humming "Dueling Banjos" from the movie *Deliverance* and hoping we didn't have car trouble, we drove without stopping from Atlanta to Montgomery. We were both pleasantly surpassed by the charm of Montgomery and greatly moved by the honor paid to Martin Luther King.

From my writing notebook, after visiting the Southern Poverty Law Center Memorial

"Until Justice rolls down like water and righteousness like a mighty stream"
- Martin Luther King

I see your names etched in the black marble, being washed by the water
rolling down, streaming, spilling over,
baptized and blessed again and again,
your souls are clean.
That water is for all of us
We need the water to bathe our souls and hearts
soothe the pain
cool our anguish
My spiritual way teaches me that the sound of water carries away our problems,
Let them go.

I see your names, the dates of your deaths
your sacrifice for the people
Inside, I see your photos,
Inside, I sit and watch a video
I hear your names and see your faces,
I hear your stories
I sit in the dark and I weep
I sit in silence and feel the anguish and pain in my belly

Stark black and white photos

images of lives long gone

She was shot in the head
Their throats were cut
He was shot while helping people vote
Killed making the world better
Ministers shot while living their promise to God
Black women, white women
Young men, black and white, come down from the North
Stabbed
Dumped in the river
5 children bombed in church
Innocent bystanders gone

We know we are not really black or white or brown or yellow or
red
so many beautiful shades of skin
As I traveled east on my journey, the palette of diverse shades
grew
and as I moved South, the palette grew darker and wider still
Such beauty

As a preschool teacher many years ago, I yearned for more than
one "flesh" colored crayon in the box. There still aren't enough
crayons nor boxes large enough to contain all this array of shades.
There aren't enough names for all the colors.

I've had people question my journey through the South
Why?
Why would you go there?
This.
This is why.
To remember and mourn.
To promise to work harder in my life for justice and equality. to
feel hope and peace.
To let that water baptize and bless me.

Katy, Texas, trying to get to sleep

I look forward to the almost daily heart-opening Facebook updates from my friend, Leslee, about her mother, Miss Josie, and posts from my friend Sharon about her "Mommie." They both have been their mothers' caregivers for many years now. I know them from my professional personal chef group, and we are avid friends on Facebook. So many of us have learned a great deal from these families and their sharing of their stories.

Miss Josie has vascular dementia, Alzheimer's, and CPOD. She's bedridden and on hospice care. Still, she continually surprises her family, her medical team, and everyone else with what she does remember and can still do. Her first language is French, and she can still speak it. She adores men, is a big flirt, and makes hysterical jokes. Her daughter takes amazing care of her, feeds her really well, and tends to all her needs.

Miss Josie also loves stuffed animals and dolls. Her favorite is a doll representation of Woody, the Pixar movie character. He is in her arms, snuggled to her bosom, or tucked under the covers for his nap for most of each day. Leslee posts regular photos and videos of her mom, sharing her still quite alive sense of humor and her stuffed "friends." Miss Josie gets sent animals from all over the country from her Facebook fans and her daughter's friends. I brought her a penguin when I visited them in Boston a few weeks ago. I named him Pierre and told her that he spoke French and some English, so soon they were conversing a bit in French.

I was so moved watching Leslee interact with her mother. She pours profuse attention and healing into everything she does from giving her sponge baths, to cooking and pureeing her food, helping her take her pills to posting her photos and videos on Facebook, and just sitting and being quiet with her.

Mommie, Sharon's mom, is on Facebook as well, so, almost daily, I see her upbeat and uplifting posts, as well as Sharon's posts about her devotion and love for her Mother. I see photos of them out on a walk with Truffles, their dog. I hear about their restaurant meals and what movies they have watched. They are each others' greatest cheerleaders. Mommie needs kidney dialysis on a regular basis and is in a wheelchair a lot of the time. It makes me miss my own mom and feel a little jealous of their relationship, although I also know their relationship has not always been like this. They both have learned to treasure this time they have now.

I have stayed with them before, but I only had time this trip to meet them for lunch and a quick visit. We ate *campechana*—a Tex-Mex specialty of seafood, avocado, and salsa which I've had every time I have visited these friends in Texas—drank some wine, laughed, and got caught up on our lives.

Is this process "caretaking" or "caregiving?" Those two words sometimes get used. Interchangeably. Are they really the same? Giving and taking are certainly not the same. Maybe it's a sort of historical linguistics thing. Maybe it's just that it's hard to separate giving from taking, and vice versa. When I give care, the receiver takes it, and in turn gives me something back by taking my care.

In Shamanism, we say that the Great Spirit created the world with love. Christians say it in similar ways. My childhood Bible, if I let it open where it willed, would open to the page in Corinthians all about Charity, a page which I turned to often. "There abideth these three things, Faith, Hope, and Charity, and the greatest of these is Charity" (I Corinthians, 13:13). Of course, I always knew that this passage wasn't about me, but I loved to pretend that it was. And, of course, the Beatles said, "All you need is love." In any religion, in any language, love is the greatest power, and it is the key to a good life.

Caretaking a loved one is not easy. It takes a lot of strength, both physical and emotional. It takes courage. It takes endless love. After my time spent with these two families, I'm reminded that it gives the giver those qualities as well.

Santa Barbara

It's the last night before I head home. I'm splurging for a room in the charming Hotel Milo. It's like a rabbit warren, several buildings with rooms in all directions, typical early California architecture. It's right on the waterfront so I'll have some fun in the morning, wandering around. In general, I've been lucky to find places to stay. Only a few nights did I end up in dumpy places. Some of that was my fault, because I waited too long to stop or passed by too many nicer-looking places, not allowing myself to the treat of an extra nice place. Some days I did actually need to save money. And some nights, it was perfectly okay to not have a great room. I was just there for sleeping. Of course, I have great memories of staying in a few fabulous hotels, mostly thanks to Jess, my travel partner through the South who both wanted ease and comfort and enjoyed pushing me out of my cheap motel comfort zone. My body remembers all the different beds and all the varying degrees of comfort. My own bed will be cozy and welcoming tomorrow night.

This is not my best dinner tonight. A sandwich and some wine in my room. I'm also looking forward to this part of getting home—getting back to eating my own food. Simple things like the kinds of coconut yoghurt, chocolate, or kombucha that seem to only be available in California. I can picture myself in the middle of the farmers' market, just breathing in all the scents of the herbs and ripe fruit. Honestly, I feel pretty good about how I've eaten overall. I might have gained a few pounds from so much sitting in the car and yeah, too many glasses of wine. But look at what else I've gained. I'm not going to worry about it. I'll be happy to cook again. No one except Leslee let me cook.

Tomorrow, Tina! All my reports on her health have been good. I'm so glad. Tomorrow, I will see my garden. It's been well taken care of while I've been gone too. I'm sure there are still tomatoes. I wonder what else? And of course, I'm excited to see my local family. I'm looking forward to catching up with Hannah and Tom. I need my Karla and my exercise class buddies.

Late November, 2017, sitting on the beach in Santa Cruz and watching the sunset

My trip was so full and busy, I just never took enough time to sit on the beach in Wisconsin by Lake Superior, Lake George in New York, or those glorious dunes on the Outer Banks of the Atlantic Ocean and ponder life. I didn't really slow down enough during that whole big circle around the United States, more than 12,000 miles of driving. It's hard now to believe the trip actually happened, and that now I am on the beach in Santa Cruz, just a few miles from my house. Even though it's winter, the sand is warm and the sun is out.

I received so many gifts—from actual presents of jams in Texas, soaps and tea in Seattle, pedicures in Portland and Boston, restaurant meals, home-cooked meals, and botanical garden excursions in Pennsylvania and North Carolina to really getting to know my friends on a more profound level. I mended some old wounds of loneliness and of feeling unworthy and underappreciated. Some gifts I'm still "unwrapping"—gifts of love, joy, awe, and bravery, just to name a few. Writing some emails about my Epic Adventure today brought smiles and chuckles, good stories I now have with those friends, remembrances of being awestruck by our country's beauty, and some longing to return.

I went to five National Parks, as many public gardens as I could, the Presidential Libraries of Jimmy Carter and Lyndon Johnson. I added two more states to my list of those I had spent the night in—Alabama and Mississippi, leaving only Oklahoma and Arkansas (which leaves me wondering why I didn't just add a few more days onto my journey and go to those places).

What did I learn? I remembered I am brave and confident. I had been becoming more introverted than I wanted to be, and this definitely was a time of coming out of that shell. I invited myself to the houses of close friends and to some I hardly knew. We had great conversations about all kinds of things and there was no end to our common ground. I laughed a lot which, while not new, brought me such relief. Laughter is indeed good medicine.

I'm still pondering that cup of coffee I had in Boston. I'm celebrating all the satisfying food I ate, all the deliciousness my friends cooked for me, all the fabulous restaurants I went to, solo and with companions. My meal in a simple family-style restaurant in small town, New York State was delicious and memorable. I had a perfectly cooked steak, medium rare, and the waiter made sure I knew it came from a local ranch with ethical practices. I asked for extra vegetables and got a large serving of stir fried squash and carrots that was delightful. I ate perched on a stool at the big wooden bar because the waitress didn't want me to be alone at a table. I sat between two charming gentlemen, one my age, the other much younger, and the three of us had an entertaining conversation covering traveling and vacations, places we had lived, with a few political comments thrown in here and there. They each bought me a glass of wine. I had my book with me and never opened it.

I stayed the night in New Hampshire with Elizabeth, a woman I met years ago online in our Personal Chef Facebook group but had never met in person. She took me on a tour of her little town of Amherst, and we had lunch in a hole-in-the-wall restaurant. I fell immediately in love with the chef/owner, an older dark-skinned man from Peru. Elizabeth and I shared a delightful bowl of curry cooked by a Peruvian in New Hampshire! Then we went to the farm where she is a CSA member and later together made a mouthwatering meal from our purchases of pork, greens, and fresh herbs. When in Charlotte, North Carolina, our hostess put together an amazing Low Country Boil—shrimp, clams, corn, potatoes. It all gets plopped right on the table and everyone digs in. A large napkin was required. Another night that makes me smile is the quick stop in Lafayette, LA for dinner with Winona and her husband. I've known her online for over ten years. This meal was also pork (which I don't usually eat that often)—pork belly tacos. Trendy and delicious! Throughout the whole trip, I was essentially able to stay relaxed about eating, kind to myself, and non-judgmental.

I felt cared for and respected. Sometimes in my day-to-day life I don't feel smart enough, fit enough, or "just" not enough. I know I hadn't been feeling *unloved*, but perhaps underappreciated and underacknowledged. As I traveled from place to place, I honestly was surprised at how happy my friends were to be with me. They see me as funny, as intelligent, sometimes even amazing. Will I carry some of that childhood poor self-esteem always? I *am* loved. I am cherished. People want me to come back and visit again. I feel full, blessed, and forever changed by that love. As I traveled, my heart opened. I didn't have a big "aha" moment, just a gradual warming and knowing. Giving and receiving: a person needs both. I feel secure, steadier now.

This is hard to say, but one of the other important gifts is feeling proud of myself. It's been drilled into me my whole life to be humble, to not to brag about myself. There is a fine line between that old shitty self-esteem and humility, and I haven't always been clear which one is showing her face. It shows up as, "It's not okay to feel good about myself, to be out loud about it." Obviously, that's so not true. Once in a while, we need a good parade and a chance to toot our own horns. Let's celebrate being brave and leaving home for two months. Let's celebrate being brave enough to invite myself for visits.

Being gone for so long, driving such distances by myself, and looking for adventure all took me a sizable distance out of my comfort zone. I only got apprehensive a few times. One night, on my way through western Texas, I got a little nervous in my motel outside of Big Bend National Park. It was a dive, a little more rundown and grimier than I first noticed. It definitely needed a top-to-bottom paint job. However, the price was right, and since there was a huge highway construction project going on in town, there were not really any other choices. My room was on the back side of the motel, and there were only two other cars and a truck in the parking lot. The faded red pickup belonged to a man who was going in and out of the room next to mine. He caught me off-guard and spiked my adrenalin. Was he a nice guy, and was my own history just messing with me? I was essentially alone with him. With all these empty rooms, why was he right there next to me? He was young, wore dirty work clothes, and needed a shave. He let the door bang closed every time he went in or out of the room. On one of those trips from his car, he brought a six-pack of beer with him. Was he going to drink it all? I couldn't be too judgmental there, because I had a bottle of wine and a bottle of bourbon stashed in my car. After some thought of changing rooms, I decided I was too tired to cope with the hassle. Eventually, I didn't hear him moving around, his TV quieted, and I forgot about him. I looked at Facebook and caught up on emails while eating the Caesar salad I had found in a grocery store along my afternoon route. My sleep was restful, and my neighbor and I exchanged greetings as we each packed up our cars the next day. He had on clean clothes then, and he had shaved. He drove off with a smile on his face, and so did I.

With the sky full of delightful and ever-changing cloud formations, I spent the next morning touring and photographing Big Bend National Park, followed by an exhausting full afternoon of driving. Mile after mile of an alien-looking landscape—arid open spaces dotted with large buttes and mesas. No houses; just a camper, small trailer, or shack every few miles. No cars coming the other direction and no one passing me; no inhabitants that I could see at all. Definitely no cell service or wifi. *This* is what my friends had been worried about. What if something happened to the car or to me? Happily, nothing did happen. I had filled my gas tank that morning and knew eventually I would get to the freeway that would take me into New Mexico.

Some of the going out of my comfort zone was had to do with meeting a bunch of new people and receiving so much attention from them. I found friendly people everywhere. One event that had the potential to be a big problem but actually ended up being a highlight of my trip took place in Minnesota, where I crossed near the headwaters of the Mississippi River. There was a lovely rest area where I stopped to pee and take some photos. At this spot, the river is still young and small and rushing around rocks. The banks are lined with more rocks, along with gorgeous deciduous trees and wildflowers. I found myself in the company of about thirty middle-aged and older men in campers and pick-up trucks—some old and battered, some brand-spanking-new—hauling boats of all sizes. They were hanging out in the parking lot and at the picnic tables, drinking beer, talking, and laughing. I had to pass through all of them on my way to the restroom. As I came back out, my nervousness waned as many of them smiled and said hello. I took my photos of the river and walked towards my car. A couple of the men called out to me. Apparently, they had been chatting about me after having seen my California license plates. "What are you doing? Where are you going?" Their mouths dropped open and eyes widened as I told them about my trip, that I was on my way to Boston and beyond, and that, in a month or so, I would be crossing the Mississippi River down south and going the other direction.

Boy, did that impress them! I guess they weren't used to women being adventurous on their own. The men, mostly father and son duos, were on their annual fishing trip without their wives. They jokingly invited me to come with them, especially after I told I hadn't been fishing in a really long time. It was a fun conversation that's given me a great story to tell as well as a big confidence boost.

The most heartwarming part of the entire trip was seeing Aurora again. We've texted each other now and then since. Since she was excited about my trip, I spoke to her and sent her photos from various spots along the way. I do feel as if a part of me has returned. I recognized that I held considerable grief about our growing apart, but ,over the years, I had done pretty well covering it up, putting it aside. Of course, one meeting doesn't heal everything right away. We are talking. I will see her when next I go to Portland. She'd like to come here. We do have a future together. A second chance. A chance for a different sort of relationship for the little girl who desperately needed a mother, and me, who desperately at times needed a daughter. A grown-up relationship.

Now, I need to get a handle on the clutter in my house—my too many possessions. I traveled for two months in my car, living out of suitcases and boxes. I did get tired of wearing the same clothes, but I honestly had what I needed. Some of my "things" I missed and longed for, but not as much as I thought. Conversely, a bit of what I did pack remained unopened or unused.

I traveled from friend to friend, where I stayed in their homes and saw how they took care of them, how they dealt or didn't deal with "stuff." I appreciated seeing a really broad spectrum—from people who were truly comfortable in their spaces ("what you see is what you get, no apologies") to lots of apologies for the mess and the clutter. All the same emotions I have were present in them, from shame to comfort to pride and joy. I truly think that how others take care of their own homes is their business and not mine, and I find it fascinating how house cleaning, clutter, and possessions are universal issues.

One of the realizations I've had since coming home is that I plainly have too many possessions. This has bothered me for years.

I'm deciding now to cut way down. If I got rid of half of my books, how would I feel? Can I let go of half of my clothes?

My garage! It is full of boxes and God-knows-what. I have started the process of going through it all and purging what is not needed. Boxes and bags of paper—bills mostly, bills I paid over the phone, or bills I paid after I got several notices. Some important papers need to be organized and filed, but most of it can be recycled or shredded. Then there are the jars and kitchen equipment, craft supplies, stuff. Do I need this many suitcases? I've hired a helper named Chrissy, and we are tackling the whole house, box by box, drawer by drawer.

I'll be honest. It is really hard. Not only are the boxes and drawers full of what might be junk, they are also full of shame, guilt, disappointment, and embarrassment. I feel ashamed that I can't seem to get a handle on the mess. I'm embarrassed about the bills that pile up and the masses of paper. All this must be examined, brought into the light.

I am aware of how this all weighs on me. Yes, weight. It's a heavy burden. There seems to be a common connection between clutter and weight that is beginning to be more talked about. Addictions. Weight isn't just about pounds and calories. It's about emotions, memories, history. Holding on is holding on or maybe holding in, I guess. The clutter weighs on my lungs, I'm noticing. I came home and looked at all my stuff and found it hard to get a deep breath. More grist for the mill—what am I holding on to? I'm hoping to find some answers by letting go.

From my writing notebook
Piles of shame
I open the door and look at the piles
paper
boxes
clothes
piles of garbage and shame,
dust and disgust.

How did this happen?

I could just once again close the door
no need to go in
Forget it
no need to look or touch or feel
but…

I step in
one foot, the other foot

Under that bag of papers, look
Sweep away the cobwebs, look
open the box,
and carefully look.
oh
Look!

laugh at the memories, cry about the forgotten
Under that pile lies a precious feeling that's been lost for years

As each pile disappears
breath emerges
as the embarrassment disappears,
I find strength and calm
Peace
I've done enough today

Saturday evening, after a full day of cleaning the garage
    Good god, I am exhausted. I feel sick from the dust and mold. I have a headache from the pressure I feel. So much. Too much. I feel guilty about having an over-abundance of stuff. Definitely a first-world problem. It feels good to donate what I don't want anymore. There are people who don't have a second set of clothes, let alone three shirts of the same color. Leaving the guilt behind is difficult, but it's an important part of the process. Sorting and feeling, feeling and sorting. Taking breaks for fresh air and processing.

What feels different from other times of purging and organizing is I am more determined than usual. The voice of my mother pops in and reminds me she has heard that before way too many times. I'm trying to ignore her. I have feelings of shame and embarrassment but less than I imagined I would—or maybe I can just let them go more easily. Chrissy is great—encouraging and without judgements. She is eager to help and happy to make order out of chaos. I work to allow myself to feel some of that satisfaction she feels as well. She helps me find hope that I can change. And to recognize that, in fact, I have changed.

Ancient Ones, thank you for my life. Thank you for my home and the privilege of living here near the ocean and the mountains, with all the Earth's bounty. Thanks for the people who love me and let me love them. Thank you for the energy I have to change my life, and help me make it better, simpler, cleaner. Help me remember I have enough. Thank you for meeting my needs.

Wednesday morning

I'm feeling overwhelmed by my cleaning project and my inability to multitask. I am neglecting my piano, my garden, cooking, and yes, my self-care. What is this about? And is it a bad thing?

Boy Howdy, could I multitask when I had my personal chef business. Some weeks it felt like I was making Thanksgiving dinner three days in a row. On any given day, the chicken enchiladas in the oven would be smelling like Mexico. Decadent chocolate brownies were waiting on the counter for their oven visit. Timers were set. Notes and reminders were out. My apron would be totally stained, and I would have just licked the brownie batter bowl. There'd be three pots on the stove: coconut milk shrimp soup for which I forgot the lemongrass, a key ingredient; broccoli steaming on the small burner; and a skillet set to sauté some ground beef for make-your-own tacos. I would gulp down some cold water, wipe the sweat from my face, and then tackle the sink full of my dirty pots and pans just to make room for more. I was good at it, and I carried home great satisfaction at the end of the day. But that was then, and this is now.

I need a plan. I'm hoping that this project will flow into other areas of my life. I can see and feel how everything is connected—the clothes, the clutter, the food, the work, the social life. I want to look at it all and be excited, not overwhelmed. When space opens up in the house, then what will there be room for?

I know a clean and organized fridge can lead to organized eating and using the food I have instead of randomly buying more. Organized clothes could do the same.

I'm thinking about that word "belongings," now that I am sorting through all of mine. How is it connected to the idea of belonging? One is a noun, the other a verb. One is static, one active. The verb is one of my lifelong issues, thanks to being a member of an all-black-sheep kind of family. I was the last one picked for teams at school as well as being near the bottom of the popularity totem pole in junior high, struggling in high school, and then finally having a solid group of friends my senior year. Even now, I struggle with feeling left out. The other day, I went with a group of friends to a restaurant. They all piled in a car together, but there wasn't enough room for me, so I drove by myself. Someone skinny could have squeezed in, but that's not me. Somehow, my old triggers made it a big deal. Another time at Mt. Shasta, there were matching tee-shirts announcing my spiritual community's thirtieth annual summer camping trip. My size wasn't available, so again, I was left out. I remind myself of the gift of belonging that I received on my Epic Adventure—the love of my nationwide community. I need to remember to do reality checks: who is doing the leaving out, really? Am I actually physically left out or am I not fully participating? Am I afraid to look at that? I need to tell my friends when I feel left out.

From my writing journal
Overwhelm
Underwhelm
What is a whelm?
I am whelmed by the depth of your vocabulary?

overwhelmed
to be buried
defeated completely
to have given too much to someone
to overcome completely as with force or emotion
If you are overwhelmed, perhaps you can learn to say no
I am correct in saying I am overwhelmed by my garage project
buried in clutter, debris, chaos
I had a friend I overwhelmed with my helpfulness

underwhelmed
disappointed
failed to make a positive impact
failed to astonish
You failed to astonish me with your declaration of gratitude
My mother was continually underwhelmed by me.
I was underwhelmed by that concert the other day.

Whelm is actually a word
archaic, not in use anymore but perhaps it should be.
to submerge, engulf
take over
I am sometimes whelmed in the use of the Dictionary and the
Thesaurus
My thoughts of clutter have whelmed me!

These are whelming times.

9 am, phone call with Hannah
    Charity: Good morning!
    Hannah: Good morning to you. I was just thinking about you
and all those fun conversations we had while you were on the road.
I still kind of miss you calling me from God-knows-where.
    C: I know, me too. Lord, was I glad I have phone abilities in
my car. That saved me many times on that trip. And talking to you

was always such a blessing, keeping me grounded and guided towards home. Maybe I should just get in my car every morning and call you!

H: Good idea. How are you? How's the house cleaning?

C: Oh boy. In some ways, it's really hard. I am so ready to have less stuff and to change some things around. Reclaim my space. Often, I'd like to just take a bulldozer and shovel it all out of the house.

H: I know that feeling, and I have much less than you do.

C: Years ago, I lived in a little rental trailer and had a storage shed that was absolutely crammed. When I moved into the bigger trailer next door, I got a wild hair and just tossed a bunch of the boxes that I hadn't opened in my year of living there. I didn't even open them; I just tossed them! I ended up throwing away a few important things. Oops.

H: Oops, indeed. Are you finding important things in your garage?

C: I'm having to sort through all the paper just in case there are important pieces. In some of the boxes, I'm finding treasures. Exquisite art crafts from Mexico that got packed away and forgotten. Photos. A collection of my mom's belongings—silver pieces, old jewelry, mementos. A whole box of personal chef menus and recipes. Some items have made me chuckle. Why on earth did I save those particular pieces of jewelry? What's with all the unfinished art craft projects? And other finds have made me ashamed, like bags of trash and unopened mail. So much to look at and feel.

H: I'm so proud of you.

C: Thanks, I so hope I will stick with it. This is not my first cleaning and purging rodeo, nor my first attempt to fit my car in the garage. This time, though, I really need to get through it all and set up systems so I won't get back to this place. Do you think you have good systems?

H: For the most part. I deal with paper pretty well because I just don't have room for it, and my computer skills are more solid than yours are. Renting rooms in my house has helped me pare down quite a bit too. But, far from perfect. I just don't seem to find the time to deal with it. Maybe one day.

That afternoon, phone call with Tom

Tom: Hello, my friend

Charity: Hi, Tom. Good to hear from you. What's new?

T: Honestly, I haven't been well.

C: Oh, gosh. Anything I can do?

T: No, I'm doing okay.

C: I know how private you are but please, let me know if I can do something for you, help you in some way.

T: I appreciate that. Not to worry.

C: I think that is what friends do. Well, what I do for my friends anyway. I've been meaning to call you to let you know that I've decided to quit marimba. It just isn't fun anymore. It's made me cry a few times lately and it's definitely not worth that.

T: No, it's not. At our age, we don't have to do things that make us cry. Not that I've been crying about it, but I've been thinking of dropping it also.

C: Oops, someone is coming to the door. I'll call you later.

T: Okay, bye.

I lied about the door. I'm finding it more annoying and discouraging that Tom is so private. Telling me he isn't well, then telling me he is fine doesn't work for me. I definitely can respect that need for privacy but I need more intimacy in my relationships. Of any kind. I don't really know him well, or even enough. I think we are nearing the end of things, if we are not already there.

Ten days later, feeling helpless on the couch

I feel so miserable and sick. The doctor says it's not flu or pneumonia; in fact, he actually called it "the Crud." Massive numbers of people have been hit by it, apparently. We all had to wear masks in the very full waiting room. I haven't felt this ghastly since I had pneumonia. I'm starting to hate my couch. But sadly, it makes sense that I'm sick. I've been through a lot over the last few months. And with this house purging, the coping with dust and mold, the coping with the emotions that are emerging, it's not surprising. Breath is life, and a lot of that shit in the garage and the closets feels more like death, or at least stagnation.

Right now, I need to go out into the real world and find some soup. I'm wondering how dressed I have to get. Should I take a shower? I am *not* putting on a bra. I guess that is the sunny side that I always like to find. I have been braless and shoeless for days.

I'm sure not hungry, which is always odd because it doesn't happen too often. Even when I'm sick, I can find a way to eat most of the time. Today, I just want soup.

I am glad so much of the house organization is done. Chrissy is sick too, so Project Purge is on hold. It's funny to be anxious to get back to it.

From my writing notebook

Purging my possessions
  empty spaces in my house
  empty drawers and cupboards
Clean out the dust and debris
I need room
to breathe,
fresh air

Heaps of dust and dirt from the paper and unused things

I am learning to appreciate the empty spaces in my garage, in my drawers
Can I now learn to appreciate the empty spaces in my belly?

God I've been so sick.
It's been hard to eat for days
How strange is that?
For me to lose my appetite is ever so interesting.
I'm trying to feel it out, to converse with it, to learn from it.
I'm a little afraid.
I don't want to eat.

I'm looking at the hole,
nothing filling it up,
keeping it busy, keeping it occupied.
Hello in there…

remembering being hungry as a child.
Not hungry because we were poor and didn't have food to eat
but hungry because
"more"
was forbidden to me.
Remembering being punished for eating on my own.
When I was finally truly on my own,
filling myself, and filling myself,
never feeling full, never allowing emptiness.
Alternating comfort and punishment.
I went years without ever being hungry, at the same times always
hungering.

Moving today from fear into kind of liking the hunger.

I can feel a different kind of power.
Freedom.
Being sick, I need to rest. Being empty, my belly can rest. can
settle.
Being empty, my belly can heal and can feel.
A gut full of memories and emotions down there packed in tight.
Loosening them up, jostling them around frees them up to move
on.

Maybe the emptiness will trigger all my old diet stuff.
the teeth clenching, the headaches,
the anger, the shame.
If you are hungry just brush your teeth, or chew some gum.
If you are hungry, go to bed.
Hungry? Forget about it.
Fill up with celery, cucumbers, lettuce.

Maybe I will start to want to feel this way.
Empty.
Perhaps Ready is a better different word.

Appetite coming back as I feel better.
Will I jump back to just filling my belly up?
Is my garage just going to fill back up with boxes?
That junk drawer get overflowing again? I don't know what to do.

I don't know what to do.

That is not true. My new rules are that when a box comes in the house, it gets emptied, things put away, and the box goes out to the recycling bin.
Done.
The laundry gets done and gets put away before it ends up on the floor.
I try to be gentle with these thoughts.
I have a history of breaking the rules.

General de cluttering experts now say if it isn't beautiful or doesn't give you joy, don't keep it. If it's not useful, don't keep it.
My belly says same goes down here.
I am gentle with what I put in my empty healing belly.
Kind food, kind thoughts.
Nourishing food, nourishing thoughts.
Thoughtful.

Monday morning, late December, on Facebook, sitting outside on the patio in the warm sun

"None of us are getting out of here alive, so please stop treating yourself like an afterthought ... Say the truth that you are carrying in your heart like hidden treasure. Be silly. Be kind. Be weird. There's no time for anything else." - No author listed

What does the "hidden treasure" make me think of? That *I* am the treasure. Hidden in plain sight. When I was cleaning out my garage, I found so many prizes and surprises—sparkly necklaces, beaded boxes. I had hidden those parts of myself, pieces of my past like photos, CDs from my massage career, and books I used to love. I found a box from my parents with pottery my dad had made and some of Mom's old jewelry. I'm still working on integrating the past into who I am now. How do I hold all these pieces of my mother—the cherished gifts and the sadistic diets? And Dad's pottery that he couldn't see since he was actually blind at that late point in his life. He was so frustrated that it wasn't perfect. My mother hated the pieces and sent many of them to me over the years. I see how beautiful they are. This is what life is, that reconciling. I will carry my stories my whole life. I've opened that chest and let my hands sift through the sparkly things. I can drink in the scents, give myself permission to feel pride and strength. I'm loving the sparkle and shine.

I *can* put myself first, and that doesn't mean there isn't room for anyone else's needs. Putting myself first might be something simple such as not always having to let someone get in line in front of me, to letting people know they need to speak more clearly, to making sure there is room for me at a shared table in a restaurant. I don't want to be like my mother, who didn't even have herself on her list, who never allowed her needs to be important and kept those needs buried. I won't let myself be an "afterthought" and am so proud to be "weird."

With this quote, I also resonate with the feeling of "if not now, when?" When I was asked why I was going on my Epic Adventure, I mostly just said, "I have to go." I didn't feel an impending sense of doom, but why wait? What am I waiting for? Who? Why? Nothing, no one, because.

Another unattributed quote I have heard is this one: "Stay close to people who make you feel like sunshine." I'm thinking of my sunshiny loved ones. I need their love and warmth to fill my immune system. I've been feeling healthy enough to sit outside and soak up the actual sun.

I'm looking at my garden now, with its fabulous aroma of roses and honeysuckle. There's kale to harvest and onions to pull. Back inside the house, my eyes are drawn to the paintings of the Balinese dancers on my office wall. My favorite photo of my parents stands next to a beautiful carved wooden heart on top of the bookcase. Snuggling with Miss Tina, I feel so blessed here. I'm acknowledging the change and growth and assuring myself it will continue.

I felt much freedom on my adventure—freedom to turn up the volume of my life a bit, freedom to love myself enough to truly let others in and let them love me. And, my friends who don't allow me to feel negative about myself create an opening for me to actually feel more love. It's about opening the door.

I renewed old friendships, made some new ones, and cherished my phone calls with my friends back in Santa Cruz. Somedays, I couldn't wait to talk with Hannah or one of my other friends, not because I was lonely, but out of the sheer joy of friendship. My phone calls and texting with the friends I saw along my epic route carried that same joy.

I am clearer about who I am and who my true friends are. I want to keep them close. I know more about what I want and need in life, being more able to accept myself, embrace and respect myself. My self-esteem has a new shine to it.

From my writing notebook
Am I only my wounds?
In Japan they practice an art called Kintsugi
sometimes translated as the golden rejoining
Taking cracked
 or broken pottery and
mending it with gold
healing the wound

Kintsugi moves us
from the impossible to the possible
Can I see myself as beautifully and perfectly imperfectly whole?
Can you see yourself?

We won't give up.
Nothing need stay broken
Beauty makes it whole.
Out of mending, art.

the scars become precious

lines of gold run deep through my life
signs of mending and patching
burnished with time

Brilliance
Resilience

Love runs deep through my veins
my veins of gold

the end… but not really!

Made in the USA
Middletown, DE
16 January 2020

83300373R00149